AF703150

Conversation Analysis and Psychotherapy

Edited by

Anssi Peräkylä, Charles Antaki, Sanna Vehviläinen, and Ivan Leudar

CAMBRIDGE
UNIVERSITY PRESS

CAMBRIDGE UNIVERSITY PRESS
Cambridge, New York, Melbourne, Madrid, Cape Town, Singapore,
São Paulo, Delhi, Dubai, Tokyo, Mexico City

Cambridge University Press
The Edinburgh Building, Cambridge CB2 8RU, UK

Published in the United States of America by Cambridge University Press, New York

www.cambridge.org
Information on this title: www.cambridge.org/9780521871907

© Cambridge University Press 2008

This publication is in copyright. Subject to statutory exception
and to the provisions of relevant collective licensing agreements,
no reproduction of any part may take place without the written
permission of Cambridge University Press.

First published 2008

A catalogue record for this publication is available from the British Library

ISBN 978-0-521-87190-7 Hardback

Cambridge University Press has no responsibility for the persistence or
accuracy of URLs for external or third-party internet websites referred to in
this publication, and does not guarantee that any content on such websites is,
or will remain, accurate or appropriate. Information regarding prices, travel
timetables, and other factual information given in this work is correct at
the time of first printing but Cambridge University Press does not guarantee
the accuracy of such information thereafter.

Contents

The data extracts that are presented in Chapters 3, 6, 7 and 8 are translated into English from Italian and Finnish. Original language transcripts, with word-by-word translations, are available at the Cambridge University Press catalogue page of this Volume at http://www.cambridge.org/9780521871907

List of illustrations

Figures

Tables

Contributors

Charles Antaki
Dept of Social Sciences
Loughborough University

Fabrizio Bercelli
Dipartimento di Discipline della Comunicazione
Università di Bologna

Kevin Booth
Birmingham Trust for Psychoanalytic Psychotherapy
Queen's College

Tommaso Colombino
Work Practice Technology Group
Xerox Research Centre Europe

Mia Halonen
Research Institute for the Languages of Finland
Helsinki, Finland

Jacqueline Hayes
School of Psychological Sciences
University of Manchester

Ivan Leudar
School of Psychological Sciences
University of Manchester

Clare MacMartin
Department of Family Relations and Applied Nutrition
University of Guelph

Anssi Peräkylä
Department of Sociology
University of Helsinki

John Rae
Centre for Research into Cognition, Emotion and Interaction
School of Human and Life Sciences
Roehampton University

Federico Rossano
Max Planck Institute for Psycholinguistics
Nijmegen

Wes Sharrock
School of Social Sciences
University of Manchester

Ulrich Streeck
Psychotherapy and Psychosomatic Medicine
Goettingen

Shirley Truckle
Birmingham Trust for Psychoanalytic Psychotherapy
Queen's College

Sanna Vehviläinen
Centre for Research and Development of Higher Education
University of Helsinki

Maurizio Viaro
Dipartimento di Discipline della Comunicazione
Università di Bologna

Foreword. Filling the gaps

Willam B. Stiles

Conversational analysis (CA) has long promised to fill the gaps in psychotherapy theory by conceptualizing and describing the moment-by-moment exchange between therapist and client. *Conversation Analysis and Psychotherapy* makes a large payment in fulfilment of this ambitious promise. The authors build on continuities with normal conversation to examine therapy's distinctive features.

Though devoutly grounded in observation and sometimes professing to be atheoretical, CA has accumulated a wealth of interlinked theoretical concepts, well illustrated in Chapter 1 in the editors' introductory overview. Each chapter proposes further theoretical categories and distinctions that elaborate the abstractions of therapy theories and the coding categories of psychotherapy process researchers (e.g. Stiles, 1992). The authors place conversational actions in sequences and detail ways that they serve therapists' and clients' purposes. CA's comfort with the complexity and responsiveness of therapeutic conversation often makes psychotherapy theories seem blunt and vague by contrast.

But CA complements rather than competes with psychotherapeutic approaches, such as psychoanalysis, solution-focused therapy, child therapy, or the Minnesota 12-step model. As Streeck (Chapter 10) points out, CA does not attempt an explanation of psychological change or prescriptions for interventions. Instead, CA elaborates therapists' abstractions. Many therapists would agree that each word and inflection is there for a reason; CA actually studies the reasons in relation to the therapeutic approach. Toward this end, for example, Vehviläinen (Chapter 7) fills gaps in psychoanalytic theory regarding what counts as resistance and how resistance is managed. Halonen (Chapter 8) shows how facilitators using the Minnesota 12-step model rephrase participants' zero-person references (a peculiarly Finnish linguistic resource for diffusing or evading responsibility) to place agency on the client. MacMartin (Chapter 5) unpacks therapists' attempts to impose an optimistic framework via questions – and clients' ways of evading the imposition – in narrative and solution-focused therapies.

The task undertaken is linking CA's rich descriptive language of possibilities to therapy theory and practice. Such an integration demands sensitivity to the complexly different meanings of terms in different theories (Leiman & Stiles, 2002); CA concepts cannot be inserted unchanged into gaps in therapy theory. Therapists and conversation analysts must learn each other's theories and make adjustments if the product is to be mutually useful. As Leudar *et al.* (Chapter 9, explain) therapy theories and terms frequently uncover crucial events that clients and lay observers (and even therapists who use other approaches) fail to recognize or appreciate. Likewise, CA points to regularities that therapists often overlook, even when they enact them every day.

For me, as a person-centred therapist, a good example is the concept of *frame of reference*. As expounded by Carl Rogers (e.g. 1951), frame of reference is roughly understood as *viewpoint* or *perspective* (i.e., therapist's or client's; speaker's or other's). In person-centred therapy, therapists try to understand and intervene within the client's frame of reference. The characteristic therapist intervention is a reflection – a statement that discloses empathy, expressing the client's experience as the client views it, that is, in the client's frame of reference. Rogers (1951) used this concept to distinguish reflections from interpretations (including psychoanalytic interpretations) – statements that place the client's experience in the therapist's frame of reference or one supplied by a theory.

The frame of reference concept and the distinction between reflection and interpretation resonates with many of this book's concepts and distinctions. Kindred ideas include Antaki's (Chapter 2) proposed cooperative–combative continuum, Bercelli *et al.*'s distinction in Chapter 3 between *formulations* (something meant by the client, at least implicitly) and *reinterpretations* (something the client has said expressed from the therapist's perspective), and Peräkylä *et al.*'s characterization, "In and through the unfolding of a collaborative description, the minds of the participants remain together for a short while" (Chapter 1, p. 6). Vehviläinen shows how, by focusing on the client's actions in the here-and-now (client's experience), the analyst can initiate interactional trajectories towards a psychoanalytic interpretation (therapist's frame of reference). The additional suggestion that such focusing on the client's prior action maintains the power asymmetry enriches the account.

Questions too can be described as using the speaker's frame of reference (Stiles, 1992). Vehviläinen shows how *why*-questions can misalign with the action initiated by the client and shift (in effect) to the therapist's frame of reference. Similarly MacMartin shows how the "optimistic presuppositions" of solution-focused therapists carry with them a solution-focused frame of reference that constrains the answer to emphasize clients' competencies and successes.

In Antaki's cooperative–combative conceptualization in Chapter 2, the cooperative actions – formulations, elaborations, and extensions – seem primarily varieties of reflections, insofar as they seek to represent the client's perspective, whereas corrections and challenges sound like varieties of interpretations, insofar as they seek to impose the therapist's frame of reference on the client's experience. On the other hand, even formulations (in Antaki's usage, though not in Bercelli *et al.*'s) and extensions involve selecting and recasting, potentially in the service of advancing some therapeutic, institutional, or personal agenda. That is, they may slip into the speaker's frame of reference, albeit subtly, advancing interpretive intents despite their acquiescent form. Person-centred therapists and supervisors, as well as psychotherapy process researchers, are interested in how these alternative types of formulations or extensions differ. What distinguishes interpretative selection and rephrasing from non-directive intent to reflect the centre of the client's experience? What are the observable features of accurate empathy? Cross-fertilization requires CA researchers to consider this problem in terms of therapy theory (distinguishing client and therapist frames of reference) – to adjust CA concepts so they can be integrated.

Conversely, person-centred therapists can profitably adjust to some CA concepts. In his descriptions and examples of how therapists use lexical substitution to make corrections (e.g., making an expression more explicit or more succinct) and convey understanding – further sorts of reflection – Rae (Chapter 4) advances the very interesting idea that at least some person-centred reflections could be assimilated to the CA concept of conversational repair. If the client is struggling to express some imperfectly symbolized experience (this is person-centred jargon), then the progressive disclosures can be construed as flawed communication, and the therapist's empathic reflections could be considered as attempts to repair them. The observed sequelae – more open and explicit client disclosure, for example – are congruent with person-centred expectations.

Of course, these CA authors make finer distinctions than therapy theorists, and they place the actions in conversational sequences. Concepts that help unpack the notion of frame of reference include Peräkylä and Vehviläinen's (2003) notion of stocks of interactional knowledge (describing the content of a frame of reference), MacMartin's characterization of the presuppositions underlying questions, and Rae's observation that whereas some reflections are based just on the expression, others use extensive knowledge of the client's experience. Bercelli *et al.* illustrate the logic of sequences: "therapists' re-interpretations make relevant clients' agreeing or disagreeing with them, rather than simply confirming, disconfirming, or correcting them" (Chapter 3, p. 49). The client's response in turn constrains the therapist's subsequent responses, and so forth. In the ensuing sequence, clients show what they make of the therapists' proposals – whether they change their view of their own experiences.

This volume brings together conversation analysts and practising therapists (sometimes in the same person). Through this juxtaposition of CA with psychotherapy theories and practices, readers as well as the authors can build meaning bridges between the two conceptual shores.

WILLIAM B. STILES

Miami University,
Oxford, Ohio

1 Analysing psychotherapy in practice

Anssi Peräkylä, Charles Antaki, Sanna Vehviläinen, and Ivan Leudar

What are psychotherapies?

The *Oxford English Dictionary* defines modern psychotherapy as "the treatment of disorders of the mind or personality by psychological or psychophysiological methods." Administering electroconvulsive shocks would, however, hardly count as psychotherapy; the common assumption is that, in psychotherapies, the means of healing is talk. Not all talk is therapeutic, and the history of psychotherapy involves not just formulating new psychological theories but evolving new and distinct ways of talking with clients. This book is an effort to describe and to understand these distinct ways of talking.

Many psychoanalytic historiographies locate the invention of psychotherapy in Breuer's work with a patient they called Anna O. (described in Freud and Breuer's *Studies on Hysteria*, 1991/1895) at the end of the nineteenth century. Anna O. found that narrating her worries and fantasies helped to relieve her symptoms and she coined the phrase "the talking cure" to describe what she was doing. Freud used her case retrospectively to document the invention of psychoanalysis, which became the first form of psychotherapy. Rather soon, however, there emerged other ways of doing and thinking about "the talking cure," and at least since the 1950s, the field of psychotherapy has been characterized by the multitude of (often rival) approaches. In psychotherapy with individual patients, client-centred psychotherapy gained influence in the 1950s (see e.g. Rogers, 1951), and cognitive-behavioural therapies have been increasingly popular since the 1970s (see e.g. Dryden, 2007). Alongside psychotherapies with individuals, group and family therapies based on psychoanalytic, system-theoretical, and later on social-constructionist ideas have been influential since the 1950s and 1960s.

Each school of individual, group, or family therapy is characterized by specific theoretical ideas about mind, behaviour, and social relations, and about the ways in which these may change. While, for example, psychoanalysis and psychodynamic therapies emphasize the importance of unconscious mental processes, cognitive therapies focus on adaptive and maladaptive interpretative schemes. In this book, we refer to such theoretical ideas, but they are not the main theme. What concerns us more is this: each different school of individual, group, or family therapy considers some interactional practices between therapists and patients to be the ones that promote change in the patient's mind, behaviour and social relations. Such practices may involve particular ways of asking questions, or of listening to and commenting upon the client's talk. One task of this book is to explicate, in greater detail than has been done before, some of these key interactional practices in specific forms of psychotherapy and group therapy.

There is, however, yet another major task for this collection. It is to point out and describe features of interaction that are part of psychotherapy but which the psychotherapeutic theories have *not* recognized or discussed. Psychotherapy is made possible by therapists and clients exerting their ordinary skills in *social interaction* as speakers, listeners, questioners, answerers, and so on. The contributions in this collection show some ways in which such ordinary interaction practices are made use of when conducting psychotherapy.

For all the contributors to this collection, conversation analysis (CA) provides (in varying degree) the research method and the central theoretical principles. (The details of CA will be described later in this chapter.) In the CA perspective, the features of interaction that are specific to psychotherapies are firmly anchored in more generic features of social interaction which can be found in any human social conduct.

The conviction that psychotherapies are grounded in and related to broader everyday forms of life is not unique to CA. A similar kind of idea, in a rather different context, has been developed by scholars who draw upon the work of Michel Foucault (Foucault, 1967; 1977; Rose, 1996). They point out that psychotherapy depends on certain prior social practices. Relevant practices are those in which the modern reflective self and subjectivity originate. According to Foucault, self-monitoring and introspection are historically contingent, and originate in relatively recent practices of social surveillance. Psychotherapy presupposes these qualities in clients – that the person is divided into two related aspects: one that is public and visible and another that is private. If one is to participate in psychotherapy, one has to be able to inspect the innermost aspects of oneself and to do this just in the way pertinent to psychotherapy. There are concrete historical antecedents of psychotherapy in discursive practices such as confession.

As Foucauldian scholars have sought to show the embeddedness of psychotherapy in other historically contingent practices (such as confession) and competencies (such as self-monitoring), the contributions of this book will show the embeddedness of psychotherapy in generic interactional practices having to do with questions, answers, comments, and the like, and the related interactional competences that therapists and their clients employ.

Studying psychotherapy: From case reports to the analysis of recorded interactions

Since the formation of the first modern psychotherapeutic techniques at the turn of the twentieth century, the case report has been the default way of presenting and discussing data from psychotherapeutic encounters. Freud's case reports, such as "Dora" (Freud, 1905) or the "Rat Man" (Freud, 1909) constitute classic examples. In case reports, all references to interactions between therapist and patient are based on the memory of the therapist. The case report often covers the whole treatment of the patient – i.e., it seeks to encapsulate what happened in possibly hundreds of sessions (plus, in most cases, the key events in the patient's biography).

Conversation analytic studies of psychotherapeutic interaction do not seek to compete with case reports. Rather, they seek to open up another kind of window for observing and understanding psychotherapeutic interaction. Rather than focusing on whole treatments and the ways in which these treatments have sought to redirect the biographical path of the patient, conversation analytic studies elucidate the second-by-second, or utterance-by-utterance, unfolding of psychotherapeutic sessions, with the aim of explicating the actual interactional patterns and practices through which psychotherapy gets done. Rather than relying on the memory of the participants, conversation analysts use audio and video recordings of actual psychotherapy sessions as their data.

However, conversation analysts are not the first researchers to use audio or video recorded data in the study of psychotherapeutic interaction. In the next section, a brief overview of earlier and parallel research will be given.

Linguistic and social scientific studies of psychotherapy interaction

Social scientific and linguistic analysis turned to psychotherapy as early as the 1950s. In fact, psychotherapy and psychiatric interviews provided the very first materials of the study of naturally occurring tape recorded or filmed interaction. The pioneering projects involved some of the leading anthropologists, linguists, and psychiatrists of the time, such as Gregory Bateson and Frieda Fromm-Reichman (see Kendon, 1990, pp. 15–21).

The first major milestone in this line of research was the collaboration between an anthropological linguist (Charles Hockett) and two psychiatrists

(Robert Pittenger and John Daheny). In a book called *The first five minutes* (Pittenger *et al.*, 1961) they analysed in great detail the audio recording of the beginning of an initial interview with a patient of a psychotherapeutically oriented psychiatrist. Pittenger *et al.* describe the aim of their study in a way which is very close to the aims of the present collection. They wanted to "understand and describe what transpires in psychiatric interviews" (Pittenger, Hockett & Danehy, 1961, p. 4). For them, asking the participants to describe the interview after it had been conducted was an unsatisfactory method of observation, because the participants' accounts would be selective, and offer inferences about the actual interview rather than a direct description of it. Instead, Pittenger *et al.* used tape recording, because

> What concerns us . . . is precisely the nature of the behaviour on which the inferences are based . . . We want to know about these things partly as a matter of basic scientific interest, and partly because such knowledge is obviously crucial in training new therapists. (Pittenger *et al.*, 1961, p. 5).

Pittenger *et al.* came up with a detailed description, proceeding utterance by utterance, of the first five minutes of the interview. In searching for the implicit meanings of these utterances, the authors focused in particular on lexical choice (choice of words) and prosody (ways in which the utterances are delivered in terms of tone, volume, and speed). For example, in an exchange where the patient asks "may I smoke?" and the therapist responds "sure," the authors see two exchanges. Alongside the factual question, the patient is asking what kind of a situation they are in and what their relative status is. This other question is carried by the prosodic details of the patient's talk: breathiness, soft voice, high tone, and the specific way in which the word smoke is released (p. 40). Likewise, the choice of "sure" rather than "yes" in the therapist's response, along with its specific intonation contour, carry his response to this second question: he is conveying controlled surprise and implying that "the answer to your second question is that you don't have to ask permission here, and I'm surprised . . . that you should feel . . . that you do" (p. 42).

What Pittenger *et al.* (1961) suggest about implicit meanings is intuitively most appealing. Their study is a genuinely explorative one: it offers insightful, if unsystematic, observations about a short segment of therapeutic interaction, without trying to make any generalizations about recurrent structures or practices in this interview, let alone in therapeutic interaction in general. The conclusions that the authors offer (pp. 228–250) have to do with the (then emergent) general theory and method of research on spoken interaction, rather than psychotherapy. The more systematic unravelling of the practices of psychotherapeutic interaction had to wait for subsequent studies.

Another early research project was started by an anthropologist (Ray Birdwhistell) and a psychiatrist (Albert Scheflen) at the end of 1950s, but the publication of its main results was delayed until the early seventies (Scheflen, 1973). This research focuses on the filmed initial session of an experimental psychotherapy between a schizophrenic patient, her mother, and two experienced psychotherapists. Scheflen was particularly concerned about the uses of body posture and body movement during the psychotherapy session. He shows how the talk of the participants is coordinated with their body posture, producing nine basic positions such as "explaining," "passive protesting," "contending," and "defending" (see esp. p. 33). Likewise, Scheflen showed how the postures and postural changes of each participant are related to those of other participants. Through this work, Scheflen made a major contribution to the social scientific study of gesture. Moreover, he set his observations into the context of psychotherapeutic and family therapeutic theories, showing how the general theoretical principles of psychotherapy are realized through the therapist's uses of posture and body movement suggesting, for example, that rapport between patient and therapist is built largely through postural choices (pp. 237–264).

The next major milestone in the social scientific and linguistic analysis of psychotherapeutic interaction was the publication of William Labov and David Fanshel's *Therapeutic discourse: Psychotherapy as conversation* in 1977. This research was based on collaboration between a linguist (Labov) and a social work scholar (Fanshel). As in the studies described above, Labov and Fanshel examined a single segment of therapeutic interaction, in their case a 15-minute episode from the tape recording of an ongoing psychodynamic therapy with an anorexic patient.

Labov and Fanshel characterize their work as "comprehensive discourse analysis," and their analysis does indeed embrace various layers of the organization of verbal interaction, from phonological detail to overall "frames of discourse." At the core are what they call speech acts: the often implicit, multilayered actions that are performed through utterances. They single out four basic types of actions – metalinguistic action (initiating, continuing, or ending an action), representation, request, and challenge (Labov & Fanshel, 1977, pp. 60–65). Through the examination of the matrix of these actions, they address themes that are pertinent in the professional understanding of psychotherapy, such as emotion and repression.

Labov and Fanshel's study is rich in detail and insight, and the study is referred to time and again in interaction research. It draws a lively picture of the interaction between the patient and her therapist, as well as the patient's family interactions which are described in the patient's narratives. One important distinction Labov and Fanshel introduced was between descriptions of a state of affairs and the kind of knowledge participants are taken to have of it. Thus, an "A-event" is biographical or experiential information that the speaker has privileged access to, while others do not. A "B-event" is a description of a matter in another person's experience, and the speaker thereby has limited access to it. Their system included other categories, but these two have turned out a crucial distinction even outside Labov and Fanshel's own approach. It has proved a central analytic dimension also for conversation analysts, under the title of "ownership of experience" (Peräkylä & Silverman, 1991).

However, like *The first five minutes*, Labov and Fanshel's *Psychotherapy as conversation* does not seek to offer a systematic view of recurrent practices in psychotherapy. The typology of the four basic speech actions is very abstract and would apply to virtually any conversation. Like its predecessor, this study also offers as conclusions suggestions concerning the general theory and method of interaction analysis (Labov & Fanshel, 1977, pp. 354–361).

The linguistic line of research on psychotherapy interaction was further continued and developed by Kathleen Warden Ferrara in her *Therapeutic ways with words* (1994). She points out (p. 4) the continuity between her study and that of Labov and Fanshel. However, unlike the studies mentioned above, she does not focus her study on a single segment of therapy talk, but uses a database of forty-eight hours of therapeutic interaction in the production of which six therapists and ten clients were involved. Ferrara's study explores the linguistic features of a number of recurrent "discourse strategies" in psychotherapy: personal experience narration, dream narration, repetition of the other's talk, construction of metaphors, and joint production of utterances. There is much in common between Ferrara's discourse analytic work and the conversation analytic studies presented in this collection. Ferrara, like most CA scholars, draws upon a large database and seeks to explicate recurrent practices of interaction through meticulous analysis of these data. The authors of this volume also explicate recurrent practices of psychotherapy; but to a greater extent than does Ferrara, they tie their observations to an understanding of the sequential structure of interaction and, hence, they seek to explicate the participants' orientations in producing the basic mechanisms of the psychotherapeutic interaction.

Psychotherapy process research

The studies described above drew the major part of their resources from social science and linguistics. They also contributed to these fields, by methodological and theoretical proposals concerning the study of spoken interaction. There is, however, also another current in the study of psychotherapy interaction. Rather than seeking to contribute to social science or linguistics, this stream of work seeks to address psychotherapists' concerns more directly. Basically, it seeks to find ways to describe how the change in the client takes place in and through the psychotherapeutic interaction. This line of investigation is often referred to as psychotherapy process research.

One traditional avenue to describe psychotherapy process involves coding and counting the participants' actions. Perhaps the most sophisticated undertaking in this direction is "verbal response mode" (VRM) analysis developed by Stiles (1992). The VRM coding scheme makes a distinction between eight types of utterance (such as "question," "reflection," or "interpretation") and yields global quantitative descriptions of psychotherapeutic sessions or segments of them. It has been used to document differences between psychotherapeutic approaches (such as "explorative" and "prescriptive") (Stiles, Shapiro & Firth-Cozens, 1988), but researchers have failed to show correlates between the outcome (success) of the therapy and the therapist's verbal response modes (Stiles & Shapiro, 1994; Stiles *et al.*, 1988;). Hence, the usefulness of research based on correlations of category frequencies with psychotherapy outcomes has been called into question by its main developer himself (Stiles, 1999). A good therapist is assumed to be responsive to the client's specific and momentary behaviours and this responsiveness cannot be measured by a fixed coding instrument.

The difficulties in attempting to describe therapeutic interactions in successful and less successful therapies have led psychotherapy researchers to seek other routes for understanding what happens in psychotherapy. These other routes seem to be more sensitive to the specific nature and tasks of psychotherapy, as well as to the specific characteristics of each patient. The assimilation model, developed by Stiles and his associates (Stiles, 2002; Stiles *et al.*, 1990) seeks to understand psychotherapy as a process in which the client's relation to his or her particular problematic experience gradually changes. The problematic experience can involve, for example, painful memories, destructive relationships, or traumatic incidents. The model suggests that during the course of therapy, the clients "follow a regular developmental sequence of recognizing, reformulating, understanding and eventually resolving" such problematic experiences (Stiles 2002, p. 357). The assimilation model offers a way for categorizing segments of speech regarding the level of assimilation that they represent.

Many contemporary approaches in psychotherapy process research are similar to the assimilation model in terms of using recorded psychotherapy material as an index of the psychological change in the patient. Hence, for example, the "core conflictual relationship theme" method (CCRT)

(Luborsky & Crits-Christoph, 1997; Luborsky & Luborsky, 1995) operates through coding the patient's accounts of his or her interactions with others. The coding is done by experienced clinical judges and aims at identifying patterns in how patients relate to others. The Referential Activity Scale (Bucci, 1995) seeks to describe the connections of the patient's emotional and other nonverbal experience with language, and operates through judges' ratings of properties (such as concreteness and imagery) of the patient's speech. Computerized analysis of speech (based on word counts) can also be used.

As a whole, psychotherapy process research involves an impressive effort to understand how psychotherapy works. Its practitioners have been both insightful and self-critical, and there is a constant search for more adequate ways for describing psychotherapy. Some studies have sought to give global characterizations of psychotherapeutic sessions, while others have focused on the ways in which the client's talk on specific topics indexes his or her inner state. Both approaches have successfully brought into light new aspects of the psychotherapeutic process. However, it seems that neither global characterizations (like VRM) nor methods which describe the change in the patient (like the assimilation model) are sensitive to the process through which the patient and the therapist *together*, and *moment by moment* create their psychotherapeutic sessions. This is where conversation analytic studies can make their contribution.

Conversation analysis

In this section we want to introduce the conversation analytic way of investigating social interaction – methodology through which we can develop new insight into the dynamics of psychotherapeutic practice. Conversation analysis (CA) was initially developed by Harvey Sacks (1992a; 1992b) and his colleagues (see e.g. Sacks, Schegloff & Jefferson, 1974) at the University of California in the 1960s and early 1970s. It arose from, and is still closely connected to, the sociological tradition known as ethnomethodology (Garfinkel, 1967) which seeks to explicate processes of inference upon which the everyday social order is based. We will start by pointing out some issues that CA *shares* with at least some of the earlier approaches in psychotherapy research. Thereafter, we will outline the aspects of CA which make it a *new* and *different* approach in psychotherapy research.

The focus on action and a concern for detail are things that CA shares with earlier research on psychotherapy. For example, Labov and Fanshel (1977) studied "speech *acts*" such as representation, request, and challenge, and Stiles' (1992) "verbal response mode" analysis employs an action-oriented coding system that includes categories such as question, reflection, or interpretation. CA studies (in this collection and elsewhere) typically focus on specific actions, such as questions and answers (see chapter 5 by MacMartin), formulations (i.e. actions in which participants say in their own words what they understand that the others meant by their preceding utterances, see chapter 2 by Antaki), or therapists' interpretative statements and their patients' responses to them (see chapter 3 by Bercelli *et al.* and chapter 6 by Peräkylä). With the help of qualitative analysis of numerous instances of such actions, conversation analysts seek to explicate in detail *how* these actions are performed and responded to: what kind of words and syntactic structures are involved in them, what kind of presuppositions about the participants are created through them, and how the participants align or misalign while producing them.

Concern for detail is, as we say, an important feature that CA shares with many earlier studies on psychotherapeutic interaction. The analyses of Pittinger *et al.* (1961) and of Labov & Fanshel (1977) were particularly rich in prosodic detail, and those of Scheflen (1973) in kinesic detail. Likewise, CA studies involve an effort to attend as much as possible to vocal and (when available in the data) visual aspects of the actions that are being studied. So, if you look through the pages of this book you will see that there is much concern for the fine detail of talk, ornamented with a filigree of notational symbols. The transcription symbols used in CA were initially developed by Gail Jefferson in the 1970s and involve notation for intonation, silence, sighs, hesitations, and the like. (The symbols are explained on pages 198–199.) The actions people perform in conversation are complex, so it is no surprise to find that the details of the talk that produce those actions are complex to a corresponding degree.

Besides sharing some central concerns with earlier research on psychotherapeutic interaction, CA studies also attend to something that the earlier studies did not deal with systematically. An effort to understand the *sequentiality* of social action is the core of CA. CA studies attend to the ways in which single utterances are intrinsically related to the utterances that precede them and the utterances that come after them. Or, to put it more precisely, CA studies how interactants design their utterances in such a manner that makes these utterances intrinsically related to preceding and subsequent utterances. Utterances that arise from what happened just before and create conditions for what can happen next form social actions. "Questions" and "answers," "requests" and "responses," or "assessments" are examples of social actions in this CA perspective. CA studies on psychotherapy seek to understand how therapists and clients perform such sequentially organized social actions by designing their utterances in particular ways that establish particular relations between the co-interactants' utterances.

CA has now built up – after forty years of effort since the pioneering work of Harvey Sacks – a collection of structures organizing the relations between actions which we can identify in almost any interaction. The most basic concept that CA uses to illuminate talk, is the "adjacency pair" (Schegloff & Sacks, 1973). The idea is that by launching something that strongly projects a certain class of response (as, for instance, a question projects an answer and a request an acceptance) a speaker shows the next speaker what they are both doing at the moment, and will direct (or limit) what the next speaker can do next.

If the adjacency pair is the basic unit of talk, then how it is exploited is the first resource that we can study if we are interested in what people do (rather than simply in what words they speak). After the first part of an adjacency pair has been launched, the next speaker is at liberty to respond appropriately or not; but if they do not (and inspection finds that non-normative responses will be marked by hesitation, a pause, and perhaps something like "well . . .") then they will suffer – or exploit – the implications of so doing. Hence answering the question "Can you lend me that book?" with a brief pause and a "well . . ." will mark the answer as not the expected one, and economically signal that the answer is "no." Empirical investigations demonstrate many such regularities in talk (across many languages) and indicate that, in Sacks' resonant phrase, there is "order at all points." Announcements get receipts, questions get answers, invitations get acceptances, and so on; the second utterance depends for its meaning on what has preceded it, and departures from these "expectables" are marked displaying orientation towards the normative order of conversation.

Many chapters of this book focus on actions which involve the structure of the adjacency pair. In a number of chapters (e.g. Chapter 5 by MacMartin and Chapter 8 by Halonen) what are analysed are questions and answers. In some other chapters (e.g. Chapter 2 by Antaki, Chapter 3 by Bercelli *et al.*, Chapter 6 by Peräkylä, Chapter 7 by Vehviläinen, and Chapter 9 by Leudar *et al.*) the analytic interest lies in the therapists' statement-formatted utterances that serve as "first-pair parts" and project an acceptance or rejection from the client. In all these chapters, any properties of the action of one participant (such as its word choice or the presuppositions about the participants that it carries) are examined in their relation to the actions of the other participants.

An adjacency pair involves a strict relation between two utterances. The sequential analysis of psychotherapy (or other type of interaction), however, encompasses relations that go beyond this basic structure. *Any* utterance in interaction – even when it is not produced as an element of an adjacency pair – "proposes a here-and-now definition of the situation to which subsequent talk will be oriented" (Heritage & Atkinson, 1984, p. 5). Schegloff and Sacks (1973) named this generic property of utterances their "sequential implicativeness." Thus, for example, when a therapist is formulating (saying in his or her own words) what he or she understood that the patient was saying in his or her preceding utterance (see Chapters 2 by Antaki and 3 by Bercelli *et al.*), or when the therapist continues (extends) an utterance that the patient has started (see Chapter 6 by Peräkylä), the therapist's action is intrinsically tied and oriented to what the patient did in his or her utterance and also projects a delimited range of next utterance as the client's part. It is such retrospective and prospective relations between an action and its surrounding actions that the chapters of this book seek to explicate.

CA is, however, not only about relations between utterances that immediately follow one and precede another. The sequential implicativeness of individual utterances gives rise to, and serves as resource of, patterns that span over several turns (see Schegloff, 2007). Long and complex sequences can be built *around* a single adjacency pair through what Schegloff (2007) calls *expansions*. For example, in a *pre-expansion*, a particular adjacency pair serves as preparation for another adjacency pair to occur. A paradigmatic case involves a "pre-invitation": the question "are you free tonight" may serve as a preparation for an invitation to be issued (should the addressee be free). The delivery and reception of stories (Sacks, 1974) involves another example of a pattern that spans over several turns. Furthermore, in what Schegloff (pp. 195–216) calls *sequences of sequences*, successive sequences are linked – chaining of questions (Sacks, 1972, p. 343) where one party asks a series of questions of the other party is an example of this. In this book, patterns that extend over several turns are discussed, for example, in Chapter 3 by Bercelli *et al.* which explores the relations between therapists' questions, patients' answers, and the therapists' reinterpretative statements that sometimes follow the answers. In a similar vein, Chapters 6 by Peräkylä and 7 by Vehviläinen touch upon the ways in which therapists may prepare for their interpretative statements through a number of actions that precede them.

There is a yet larger scale of organization operative in interaction. Sequences that take place within a given encounter can be produced in such ways that connect them with past or present encounters (Button, 1991). For example, in openings and closings of conversations the participants show, in various ways, their orientation to what their relation has been and is expected to be. Moreover, a particular topic – e.g., a specific problem that is spoken about – can have a history over several encounters during which the participants' positions may change (Heritage & Lindström, 1998). Such extended connectedness of encounters is of utmost importance in psychotherapy. In this collection, process of change over several sessions is addressed in Chapter 9 by Leudar *et al.*

The analysis of sequentiality of action is thus *the* contribution that CA can make in psychotherapy research. But why should psychotherapists and psychotherapy researchers be interested in that contribution? It is the conviction of both the editors of this book and the authors of the chapters within it that sequential relations of actions are a major vehicle of the psychotherapeutic process. Any action of the therapist – be it a question, a statement, or something else – expresses an understanding of the patient's experience, and an understanding of how that experience can and possibly should be related to. (It does, of course, also propose an understanding of the therapist's own experience, which is of utmost importance for psychotherapy, but need not concern us at the moment.) These expressed understandings are achieved, mostly, through turn design – selection of words, descriptions, syntactical structures, as well as the perspectives and presuppositions that are built in the utterances. For example, Chapter 5 by MacMartin analyses therapists' questions in constructivist therapy, and shows how they are designed so as to convey an optimistic view about the patients' capacity to manage their lives. Likewise, the patients' actions – be they stories, answers, responses to interpretative statements, or the like – express comparable understandings of their own experiences. In MacMartin's Chapter 5, the patients' answers take stance to the questioners' optimistic presuppositions (and in her data, mostly misalign with them). Because the participants' actions are tied together by sequential implicativeness, the participants inevitably have to orient to and work with the understandings that they each bring about through their actions. The next action *has* to orient to the understandings that the first action brought forward. This work with understandings unfolds, literally, utterance by utterance. If things go well, this interplay of the participants' actions brings about a favourable change in the patients' ways of understanding and relating to their experiences. Sequential analysis is the microscope through which we will observe that process.

Study of institutional interaction

When Harvey Sacks and his colleagues started CA, they understood it as a programme for studying the properties and structures that underlie *any* social interaction. In the past twenty years or so, however, many conversation analysts have been involved in trying to understand *specific* kinds of interactions, ones in which the participants accomplish their specific, institutionally ascribed tasks. CA has been applied fruitfully to a variety of such institutional encounters: not only to the medical consultation, the news interview, and the classroom lesson, to list three of the more routine settings of everyday life; but also to such relatively unusual scenes such as the emergency call-centre, the police interrogation, and the psychic séance, among others (for overviews, see Arminen, 2005; Boden & Zimmerman, 1991; Drew & Heritage, 1992). Unlike everyday conversation among co-equals, such "institutional" talk works to a more fixed order of talk in the design and distribution of turns (who gets to say what, when). What CA wants to do when analysing such interactions is to show how the people involved use these rules to transact their business, be it to pursue the answer to a question from an evasive politician (Clayman & Heritage, 2002), to assess the caller's need for assistance in emergency calls (Zimmerman, 1992) or even to summon the presence of the dead from beyond the grave (Wooffitt, 1992).

Psychotherapy is one particular kind of institutional interaction. Before moving on to an account of earlier CA studies on psychotherapy, it will help if we examine in a bit more detail what CA studies have revealed about another specific type of institutional interaction. So, we will take the medical general practice consultation as an example for illustration. Like psychotherapy, general practice consultation involves interaction between a highly skilled specialist and a client who has come to seek help for personally meaningful problems that he or she cannot manage on her own. Unlike psychotherapy, medical consultation has been studied quite extensively by CA over the years. Heritage and Maynard (2006) provide us with an excellent review of the CA research on medical consultation, which allows us to see what kind of contribution CA might be able to give for understanding the encounter between a client and a professional.

The *overall structural organization* of the consultation is one of the key concerns in CA studies on medical consultation. Building upon the earlier work of Byrne and Long (1976), conversation analysts have shown how the clinician and the client orient themselves to an expectation that the acute consultation proceeds through a number of distinct phases: *opening, presenting complaint, examination, diagnosis, treatment,* and *closing*. This phase structure is not the analyst's stipulation of what ought to happen, but something that the participants themselves demonstrably orient to. For example, during the problem presentation, the patient may take actions that are associated with physical examination, diagnosis, or treatment (for example by asking about the possible cures), and thereby may indicate that the problem presentation is complete (Heritage & Maynard 2006, p. 15).

Understanding the overall structural organization of the medical consultation has helped conversation analysts to set their questions and to contextualize the more detailed phenomena in consultation that they are studying. A large number of individual studies of general practice consultation have indeed explicated the ways in which the participants' conduct is organized in a particular phase, or at the juncture between particular phases. These studies focus on particular sequences through which different phases are accomplished. So, for example, Robinson (2006) describes doctors' uses of different question formats at the *presenting complaint* phase, Maynard and Frankel (2006) compare the ways in which good and bad news are delivered and responded to in *diagnosis*, Stivers (2005) describes the ways in which parents of patients who are children respond to the *treatment recommendation*, and West (2006) explicates some aspects of the collaborative *closing* of medical encounters. As a whole, in CA research on medical consultations, the studies on overall structural organization have provided, as it were, a large-scale map of the consultation, and many individual studies have provided smaller scale maps on key sites (the key sequences of each phase of the consultation) on that large-scale map. In result, these studies amount to a cumulative programme leading to an increasingly detailed and increasingly unified picture of the primary care consultation. Besides the social scientific interest, these studies also arise from practical concerns: their results have been useful in medical education as well as in interventions that seek to improve existing medical practice (Maynard & Heritage, 2005).

CA studies on psychotherapeutic interaction

Harvey Sacks' life work formed the cornerstone for conversation analysis. He examined both so-called everyday conversations and institutional interactions: among them helpline calls received at a suicide prevention centre as well as an eleven-minute stretch of a group therapy session for four teenage boys (see Sacks 1992a, pp. 3–20 and pp. 268–280 respectively for his initial comments on these data). Sacks used everyday conversations and institutional interactions as data side by side, to examine the underlying structures and properties of all social interaction and social life therein. Sacks' lectures, using various data, show glimpses into corners of the social world that are more than relevant to psychotherapeutic settings. For instance, he explicated ways in which we organize our ways of referring to other persons in terms of their responsibilities to help us and others, means by which we maintain the fundamental presupposition of "ordinariness" of our experience, and how we deliver and respond to stories. However, Sacks' studies on these phenomena were not, at that time, presented under systematic rubrics such as "institutional talk" or "therapeutic interaction." His observations were not focused on the institutional character of the particular data he discussed. It was only many years after Sacks' untimely death that the conversation analytic research seeking to unravel specific psychotherapeutic practices began. In what follows, we will review some of the highlights of earlier CA studies on psychotherapy and related practices such as counselling and self-help groups.

The first major study using CA to understand psychotherapy as a particular type of interaction was by Kathy Davis (1986) and took as its topic the therapist's ways of formulating clients' talk. Davis suggested that by such formulations, the therapist renders what was initially presented as a social or other "non-psychological" problem into a psychological one calling for psychotherapeutic intervention. Unlike most of the subsequent CA research on therapy, Davis then adopted a normative and critical stance towards the interactions that she studied. Therapists' formulations have remained in the CA researchers' agenda ever since; Chapter 2 by Antaki in this volume offers a summary.

The studies on formulations have tended to deal exclusively with one-to-one psychotherapies. Group, family, and couple therapies have equally been of interest for conversation analysts. Also in this context, ways in which problems are described has been one of the key analytical issues. Thus, Edwards' (1995) analysis of talk in couples' counselling provides an angle on the way in which clients' talk is constructed for particular therapeutic purposes. He shows how clients present overtly disagreeing versions of their troubles to the counsellor, whose task it is to receive these versions impartially in order to find solutions to the problems. Edwards identifies a number of linguistic resources by which the speaker may describe another person's action in such a way as if it were following what he calls a "script," that is, as stemming from a culturally familiar routine with normative implications. He shows how couples design these script-like descriptions so that they carefully attend to their partner's counter-descriptions. Similarly, Edwards shows how speakers can choose among various categories of person in their narratives, so as to blame the other person, or head off blame for themselves. For example, a wife may shuttle between saying she was at a "girls' night out" (with its hint of fun and licentiousness) and describing the same event as "we sit around, one table full of *married women*" (1995, p. 30). Thus, as Edwards points out, speakers are very much aware of each other's countering versions and design their own versions so as to undermine them and defend their own version. Thus, there is a "rhetorical symmetry" between opposing versions of relationship troubles.

Systematic advances were made, particularly in the 1990s, in the study of counselling interaction. An important set of counselling studies deals with HIV or AIDS counselling and guidance in Britain and the US (Kinnell & Maynard, 1996; Peräkylä, 1995; Silverman, 1997). In HIV counselling, the main aim is to deliver information about HIV and AIDS, to advise people about safe sex and, thus, to prevent transmission of HIV. Another, more therapeutic, purpose of counselling is to help clients cope with related fears and problems. Due to this double function, the issues of advice-giving and delivery of expert views have a central role, but there is also a concern over how to create a space for the client's perspective and how to design the interaction so as best to serve the client in whatever situation she or he is in. One of the overarching themes in these studies is *talk elicitation*.

A core task for counsellors is to elicit personal narratives from their clients, often about delicate issues such as sexual behaviour or fears connected with HIV. Discreet exploration, studied initially by Bergmann (1992) in the context of psychiatric interviews, is prominent in many counselling settings and reported by several studies (Kinnell & Maynard, 1996; Peräkylä & Silverman, 1991). Devices of professional caution are typically used so as to downgrade the epistemological status of descriptions of issues that are "owned" by the recipient. This means that professionals speak cautiously and tentatively on matters that concern the client's experience, and imply in their talk that their knowledge is not authoritative. In counselling with children, talk elicitation poses a particular challenge. In a study focusing on counselling with children facing their parents' divorce, Hutchby (2002; cf. Potter 2006) showed a child used the claim "I don't know" strategically, "as a means for attempting to close down an undesired line of counsellor questioning" (p. 158). In Hutchby's data, the counsellor dealt with this resistance by modulating between playful and serious orientations to the repeated "I don't know" (see also Antaki, Chapter 2 this volume; Hutchby, 2007).

Peräkylä and Silverman (1991; Peräkylä, 1995) have examined talk elicitation in a setting in which counselling involves not only clients but also their partners or family members. These counsellors have adopted the Milan school family systems theory, which is a therapeutic theory about individuals and their problems as located in networks of relationships or "family systems." The counsellors use a particular interviewing technique called "circular questioning" to engage clients and their significant others in discussions about various issues. The authors show how all participants orient to the particular relationship that persons have to those experiences they "own" (Peräkylä & Silverman, 1991), and how counsellors use particular questioning techniques to invoke ownership of experience and thus elicit client talk (Peräkylä, 1995).

Interaction in self-help groups such as Alcoholics Anonymous (AA) may share some key features with group and even individual psychotherapies. Clients' narratives are a central action in probably all therapies; particularly in AA. The sharing of monological stories and responding to others' stories through "second stories" (i.e. narratives that are presented as occasioned by prior stories and demonstrate similarity to them) are the interactional resource by which the recovery from addiction is accomplished (Arminen, 1998; 2004). Thereby, the sharing of personal stories constitutes a therapeutic practice. In the openings of the monological contributions in an AA meeting, there is a strong tendency to refer to other speakers' contributions, and thereby to show that one's topic is occasioned by a previous speaker's topic. Claiming similarity of experience, and demonstrating this similarity through providing an occasioned story are therapeutic practices by which AA members share their experiences, maintain sobriety, and construct their identities as recovering alcoholics (Arminen, 1998; 2004).

Arminen's work on the AA meeting also explicates the way in which the distinct, formal turn-taking order (1998, pp. 49–79) is oriented to and maintained by the participants, and how that, too, becomes the vehicle for therapeutic sharing. In the formal turn-taking order of AA, each speaker is entitled to one turn to talk about personal experience. Other speakers' turns are not countered or challenged. This format, with some variation, is known also in various group therapy settings where the participants orient to the expectation to share and identify with each other's experiences, although in settings where a professional is involved, he or she typically has different speaking rights than the clients and may perform various interventions so as to control the allocation of turn, to shape the narratives according to the therapeutic relevancies, or to confront the clients (Arminen & Leppo, 2001; Jones & Beach, 1995; Halonen, Chapter 8, this volume; Wootton, 1977).

Even this selective review of some key CA studies on psychotherapy and related practices probably indicates two things. One is the applicability of the CA method to research on psychotherapy. The researchers have been able to pin down and explicate some facets of interaction through which understandings of, and ways of relating to, experience are being worked with. Thus, the studies on formulations have demonstrated one particular practice for the therapist to subtly redirect the client's understanding of his or her problems; the studies on couple therapy have shown how the different versions of shared experiences are dealt with and made use of; the studies on HIV counselling have shown ways in which the clients are encouraged to verbalize their fears and worries; and studies on AA have shown how the similarity of the participants' experiences is interactionally demonstrated. The sequential analysis indeed seems to be capable of uncovering key aspects of the therapeutic process.

However, our limited review also shows that the progress of CA in the field of psychotherapy has, thus far, been somewhat unsystematic. No overall account of psychotherapy has been generated – that is to say, the CA research on psychotherapy has not produced anything that is comparable to the CA researchers' scheme concerning the overall structure of medical consultations. With regards to psychotherapy, CA researchers have investigated separate practices without gaining much understanding about the ways in which different practices are related to each other so as to produce a psychotherapeutic session as whole. There may be three reasons for this limitation of the research thus far. The most obvious one is that this line of research is in its infancy – CA researchers have, for the most part, concentrated their efforts on other institutional settings. The second reason is the fact that psychotherapy is indeed a very varied practice. Unlike medical consultation which is rather uniform throughout the Western world, psychotherapy is characterized by a multitude of (often competing) approaches. The ways in which psychotherapists of different schools engage the patients vary and, therefore, it is not likely that any single overall structure or other organizing principle of a psychotherapeutic session, applicable to all therapies, could be found. Finally, it is also possible that psychotherapy, or at least some psychotherapeutic approaches, is not organized in terms of distinct phases that would recur more or less similarly in each session. The key sequences – such as questions and answers, narrations and reception, formulation and response, and so on – may afford different ways of assembling them so as to form an entire session. But that is just one possibility. Basically, we do not know yet, and therefore new research, to be presented in this book and elsewhere, is needed.

This book will contribute to the enhancement of our understanding of psychotherapy by explicating a number of practices that are central for some central approaches of psychotherapy with individuals or groups. Some of these practices are ones that have been described in earlier research (for example, formulations analysed in Chapter 2 by Antaki) and the contribution of the book is to further and systematize the understanding. Others (such as the therapist's "noticings" about the patient's action analysed in Chapter 7 by Vehviläinen or lexical substitutions analysed in Chapter 4 by Rae) are such that have not been addressed in earlier CA studies. At the end of the book, in Chapter 11, the observations of the different practices provided by the individual chapters will be drawn together. The summary presented in that chapter takes us, we believe, as far as empirical research can at the moment go towards an overall picture of psychotherapeutic interaction.

Conversation analysis addressing the concerns of psychotherapists

In recent papers, Peräkylä and colleagues (Peräkylä & Vehviläinen, 2003; Peräkylä, Ruusuvuori & Vehviläinen, 2005) have suggested that for conversation analysis – as both a theory and an empirical investigation of interaction – it is relevant to recognize the existence of other theories of interaction and the way these theories may bear on the practices examined by CA. Professionals who meet clients – and treat, counsel, help, teach, or examine them – have theories, concepts and ideals that are related to their interactions with their clients. Practitioners understand their work (as well as related practices such as training or development) in terms of these theories, and much of the research around professional fields is conducted by reference to such theories. Therefore, it is essential that CA research has a grasp of these theories and ability to enter into a dialogue with them.

Peräkylä and Vehviläinen (2003) suggest that some of these theories can be conceptualized as "professional stocks of interactional knowledge" (SIKs). SIKs consist of organized and codified knowledge that concerns social interaction between professionals and clients. They can be found from professional texts, training materials, and codes of conduct. Peräkylä and Vehviläinen also propose that conversation analytic (CA) research can enter into a dialogue with the SIKs – extending, specifying or correcting the picture of interaction given by them.

In some contexts, a clear distinction can be made between theories or models that inform the interaction process ("interaction theories"), and other theories that seek to describe and assess other (non-interactional) aspects of the practice at hand, for instance, treatment theories within medical practices. In medicine, for instance, the interaction theories might involve propositions concerning ways of interviewing the patient or sharing information (e.g. "a patient-centred way of asking questions"). The treatment theory, on its part, involves propositions regarding the aetiology and cures of illnesses (Peräkylä *et al.*, 2005; Peräkylä, Ruusuvuori & Lindfors, 2007). In other types of settings, however, such a distinction is not as clear. For instance, in psychoanalysis, the propositions concerning the dynamics of psyche and the professional–patient interaction are *intertwined and inseparable*.

When CA results are put into dialogue with SIKs, in some cases the main contribution of CA turns out to be that of showing how a particular task or activity – recognized also by the SIK – is carried out in the turn-by-turn interaction and to explicate the interactional dynamics of the devices and structures used in that context. Chapters 6 by Peräkylä and 9 by Leudar *et al.* (regarding interpretations), 7 by Vehviläinen (regarding resistance) and 5 by MacMartin (regarding optimistic questions) represent such contributions. At times, the task of CA has been to explicate the workings of an action – or aspect of an interactional device – that the SIK had *not* recognized. In this book, such a contribution is made, for example, in Chapter 2 by Antaki (regarding formulations) and Chapter 4 by Rae (regarding therapists' lexical substitutions). And sometimes the findings of CA show that the actual practices and task of the institution in focus are quite different from the ones described by the SIK. CA can, thus, point at mismatches between the SIK and the interactional practices (Peräkylä & Vehviläinen, 2003; Peräkylä *et al.*, 2005).

Conversation analysis and questions about the outcome of the therapy

Psychotherapists, their clients, and the funding agencies are inevitably concerned with the effectiveness of psychotherapy. The methods of evidence-based medicine (EBM; see, e.g. Wessely, 2001) nowadays offer the standard way to address the questions concerning effectiveness. EBM typically involves operationalizing the desired outcome of therapy by means of independently defined variables and comparing experimentally how different interventions affect them. EBM has successfully renewed somatic medicine, but as applied to psychotherapy, it has its limitations. EBM is concerned about the (measurable) outcomes of specific therapeutic interventions, but not about what these interventions in themselves consist of. It treats psychotherapeutic interactions themselves as given, or as a black box, without trying to say what it is out of all that happens in these interactions that produces the change. Leudar *et al.* (2005) have argued that in imposing common operationalizations, EBM ignores unique aspect of different psychotherapies and in using statistics in comparing average outcomes in groups, the method ignores the central tenet of psychotherapy – that clients are individuals. Moreover, as Stiles (1999) points out, skilful therapists adjust their interventions to the momentary contingencies of the therapeutic process, and hence, the assumption about a standardized psychotherapeutic "input" is unjustified.

Perhaps partly for the aforementioned reasons, an index of the outcome of psychotherapy has not been centrally involved in the design of CA studies, in this collection or elsewhere. However, we can point out some ways in which CA research has been, or could be, relevant also in terms of outcome, and hence could also contribute to a more adequate approach of "evidence based psychotherapy." First, many CA studies are concerned what might be called the *internal* outcome of psychotherapeutic interventions. As they explicate recurrent sequences of actions in psychotherapy (such as questions and answers, formulations and responses, or interpretations and responses) they also elucidate the ways in which the therapists' actions in these particular contexts produce an effect in the patient. This does not lead to an overall picture concerning the success of the particular therapies or types of therapies, but it does involve a new insight into the specific mechanisms through which the change in the patient in these therapies takes place.

It could also be possible to use CA as a complementary method in evidence-based studies. The "black box" limitation of those studies could be remedied by using CA to describe objectively the interactions that took place in a trial, and then using this information to warrant the conclusion that the therapy in question was indeed the kind of specific therapy that it was supposed to be. A more radical alternative is to use CA to describe the change in the pattern of interaction that may take place as the therapy progresses. Here the ethnomethodologically informed CA that works with case studies is particularly useful. Chapter 10 by Streeck proposes this kind of approach, and Chapter 9 by Leudar *et al.* demonstrates some of its potential. Conversation analytic case studies focusing on entire therapeutic processes (dyads or groups) could show *what*, in terms of the patterns of interaction, changes in a successful therapy, thus complementing the more global, population-based picture sought after by evidence-based studies. Case studies of that kind, and possible collaboration with policymakers, are prospects for the future. At the moment, CA is establishing a distinct perspective on the fundamental interactional basis of psychotherapies, and beginning to show what can be learnt by its methods.

2 Formulations in psychotherapy

Charles Antaki

Psychotherapists want to find out how clients see things, and then, at some point, get them to see things differently. In ordinary talk there are lots of ways of offering someone an alternative to what they believe. This chapter concentrates on one way – on how one person might *formulate* another's words. I am using the term "formulate" here as it has passed into conversation analysis from the work of John Heritage and Rod Watson (1979; 1980): that is, as a reference to the practice of proposing a version of events which (apparently) follows directly from the other person's own account, but introduces a transformation. Extract 1 shows an example from therapy.

Extract 1 JP/R 5-1-2000.[1]
(Cl= client, Th= therapist. The client is describing how he reacted to the end of a relationship.)

```
     Cl:  .hh Er, but ↑anyhow, I mean she did seem
          sortuv - m- my reaction was one of - instead
          of poor me this time it it was more one of
          sortuv like anger it- oh damn the woman she doesn't
          want to go out with me.
     Cl:  Erm y'know I don't care an I sent her a
          message back an ( ) she's got an answerphone
          y'know like "thanks for tellin me" which- I was
          glad that she'd at least got that far, rather
          than ( ) more sortuv tricks ( ) (s-   )
     Th:  mm
     Cl:  S' >I-jus'sortuv< left it at that y'know ( )
  →  Th:  so you ↑don't feel rejected.
          (1.0)
     Cl:  ((dry cough))
     Cl:  no, no not poss- not badly, no fi:rst of all I did,
```

The arrowed line shows the therapist formulating what the client has said. She seems merely to be summarizing, but in doing so, ignores a great deal of

[1] I'm grateful to Jean Pain for access to recordings marked "JP" in this chapter.

material, and replaces the client's own description (that he felt "sort of like anger", line 4) by hers – that he "does not feel rejected." In the bulk of this chapter, I will try to show how deletion, selection, and transformation serves therapists in three aspects of their work: history-taking and diagnosis, interpretation, and the mundane interactional management of the therapy session.

More and less combative ways of offering an alternative to the client's account

I will lead up to formulations by first listing four other practices, three of which are described and analysed by other contributors to this book. Therapists might display their grasp of, and present an alternative to, the client's account of their experiences by turns which are formatted as: *challenges; corrections*; *extensions*; and *reinterpretative statements*. Of course therapists may do many other things besides these, in their bid to understand their clients and to offer them new ways of thinking, but these four are discretely identifiable (one further practice, that of asking questions, is too complex for easy précis). In their format (though not necessarily in their local force) challenges, corrections, extensions, and elaborations form a gradient, descending from a more combative to a more cooperative way of offering the client an alternative view. At the bottom of the slope are formulations, which, as we shall see, are the most (ostensibly) cooperative practice of all. I say "ostensibly" advisedly; while the format of these practices may apparently tend one way, their interactional force may tend in quite another.

Challenges and corrections

We start with these two practices as they are the most overtly combative, in format at least. Challenges are not extensively described elsewhere in this book, but Rae's chapter includes a systematic analysis of "repair" by which a therapist may handle correction of something the client has said. In both challenges and corrections, the therapist more or less explicitly contradicts the client and claims to reveal a truer state of affairs. Challenges may be more hostile; indeed in certain sorts of therapy, the therapist may be explicitly mandated to "pull the client up short." For example, in therapy groups for convicted sex offenders, Lea and Auburn (2001) show that a group facilitator may respond to a client's account with a blunt correction as to the legally established facts of the matter. One example they give shows the response of a facilitator to an offender-client's apparently evasive description of his actions.

Extract 2 From Lea and Auburn, 2001, p. 27; line numbers altered. ("Off" = offender, "PO(M)" = male facilitator.)

```
     Off:   Yeah I do alright the (insti-)
            what I'm saying is that we accepted
            that we didn't find girls that we
            left the club gone and got a kebab
            parked up in a dark and lonely spot
            eady to sleep the night
            (1)
     Off:   so at that moment in time sex was not on my
            mind (0.7) at that moment in time
 →   PO(M):  (unclear) sex wasn't on your mind then
            why did you grab the girl
            (2.3)
     Off:   I don't know (Harry)
```

The offender's report (line 8) that "at that moment in time sex was not on my mind" is met with the facilitator's straightforward challenge: "(if) sex wasn't on your mind, why did you grab the girl?" This may be disaffiliative, but would be consistent with the kind of therapy being conducted in this setting, which is meant to correct client's "cognitive distortions."

On the other hand, corrections may be done with more sympathetic cast. In Extract 3 from a one-to-one humanistically oriented therapy session, the client is a teacher who is talking about her worry that her pupils may take advantage of her.

Extract 3 JP/S 23:20.

```
     Cl:  the kids >who're=very-< (.)°>tsew<° (5.0)>ahk-< I
          don't know: (will) they?- (1.1) >well she w's all<
          righ:t, (.4) she's (.6) o:kay:?
          (.9)
     Cl:  ERm- (2.4) we can do what we like with her. [.h
 →   Th:                                              [but
 →        they don't do what they [(like  )
     Cl:                          [no:::
 →   Th:  so >I mean< you know it's not true.
```

The client voices what her pupils might think about her ("we can do what we like with her"). The therapist uses a disjunction ("but") to raise the objection that in fact the children (as had been reported earlier in the session) don't do what they like, and the therapist is licensed to correct the client: "you know it's not true." We might note that although ostensibly *combative*, the therapist's intervention could be seen as in fact benign, insofar as she is proposing a milder, better, description of the situation than the extreme case described by the client. But, as with direct contradictory challenge, the therapist is offering a direct alternative to the client's understanding of the situation.

Reinterpretative statements

Outright challenges to, or corrections of, the line of client's accounts may be comparatively unusual. It is probably more common for the therapist to use more cooperative devices. One of these is for the therapist to provide a *reinterpretation* of what the client means, as Bercelli *et al.* show in Chapter 3. Consider this example:

Extract 4 From Bercelli *et al.*, Chapter 3, p. 54.

```
      Cl:  and: so hm: instead as concerns my hu- my father
           (1.2) hhhh he ((Cl's husband)) is delimiting his
           territory (0.4) more and more.
  →   Th:  which with your dad (0.5) it seems to me isn't an
           operation (.) all that easy.
      Cl:  no.
```

In this example, and the others that Bercelli *et al.* discuss, the therapist offers an understanding of something not quite fully expressed by the client herself. It brings out what may be a fundamental, but so far unspoken, concern about the client's relations with her father. Notice that the therapist makes a point of signalling that this is his own view (line 4: "it seems to me"). However, in spite of speaking for himself, he nevertheless designs the intervention to sound as if it is a mere extension of the client's turn ("which with your dad . . ."). This shades into the next practice.

Extensions

As Vehviläinen (2003a) observed, extensions have long been known to CA as a method of displaying intersubjectivity: a way of a speaker "proving to the person they're talking with that they're hearing and understanding what he's saying" (Sacks 1992a, p. 58). It may be used to promote a further, and possibly rival, account of what the client is saying. Here is an example from Vehviläinen's analysis of the psychoanalytic use of extensions of the client's words:

Extract 5 From Vehviläinen, 2003a, p. 582.

```
      Cl:  .hhhhhhnfff so (it comes) >could one think that if<
           we think about it like this that we have a-
           we have this feminine side and we have this
           this masculine side but >somehow this< my feminine side
           now is, (0.5) very much is (0.8) °is sort of° (0.8)
           ehhhhh <activated>.
           (3.2)
  →   An:  .hhhh and is somehow very hostile.
           (.)
      Cl:  ye::s.
```

The analyst uses the conjunction "and" to signal that what he is doing is (as it were "merely") extending what the client is saying. But, of course, in doing so, the analyst imports a therapy-laden interpretation into the account: that the client's feminine side is "somehow very hostile." That provides a more therapeutically informed understanding than was overtly present in what the client said.

Formulations

So far the practices we have seen have been increasingly affiliative – each successive example (correction; questioning; elaborating; and finally merely extending the client's words) is more clearly designed to show that the therapist is cooperatively following the line of the client's account. Now we can turn again to *formulation*, which is a yet more marked display of such (ostensible) cooperation. We saw back in Extract 1 how a therapist could draw out from her client's words that he "didn't feel rejected," implicitly merely summarizing his own account that he "felt sort of anger." Now consider another example where a therapist replays to the client what are ostensibly the client's own words. But note again that the therapist has deleted some material, selected what suits the interests at hand, and edited its design and terminology. A clinical psychologist is getting a sense of her client's life history:

Extract 6 CBT UV&JR 110698.[2]

```
     Th:  .hhh So you work out yer months notice
     Cl:  [Yeh                     [(an we got
     Th:  [Can we look at that [bit of time
          (0.5)
     Cl:  An we got made redundant
     Th:  Yeah
          (0.9)
     Th:  .phhh an you so you're you've just finished work
          (0.4)
     Th:  You must have not known what to do with yourself
          after twenty years
     Cl:  I didn't do
          (1.1)
     Cl:  I came (.) came to (0.4) eh I found it very hard I
          don't (.) get on with that
          (1.5)
  →  Th:  So you found it very difficult [to ]adjust
     Cl:                                 [yeh]
     Cl:  Yeh
```

2 I am grateful to Ivan Leudar for access to data marked "CBT" in this chapter

At line 17, the psychologist offers back to the client what is ostensibly a simple summary of all that he has said: but notice that, in doing so, she has deleted some parts of the account (most obviously, her own Socratic questioning at lines 8 and 10–11) and has rephrased his experience so as to be more articulate, and to accord better with a psychological concept. Instead of his halting delivery at lines 14–15 which ends with the idiomatic "I don't . . . get on with that," she offers the psychological reading "you found it very hard to adjust."

In explaining formulation I have been following the analysis of Heritage and Watson (1979; 1980): that the signal characteristics of formulating the someone's words are that the formulation comes after that person's account, and is heard as giving the gist of it, or as picking out one of its natural upshots; but that the formulation deletes a certain part of the account, and, in selecting another part, transforms it to some degree.

A brief history of the technical use of the term *formulation* in discourse studies

Let me break off temporarily at that point. I shall spend the bulk of the rest of the chapter on how this sort of practice is used in psychotherapy. But it is worth making a brief digression to see where the term *formulation* comes from. The term starts with Garfinkel and Sacks' observation (1970) that people in an interaction have the option, at any point, of making explicit to each other just what it is that is going on – they can *formulate* the talk so far: they can make what linguists might call a meta-pragmatic observation ("this is great isn't it?" or "now you're cross with me" and so on). For Garfinkel and Sacks, formulations were a public display of agreed intersubjectivity, a kind of sociological glue.

Interest in Garfinkel and Sacks' observation about such wholesale descriptions of *where-we-both-are-in-the-conversation* has dropped away in favour of Heritage and Watson's more tightly specified version of the phenomenon. It became not so much one speaker announcing *where-we-both-are,* but rather observing to the other: *so-you're-saying-that-X.* By inspecting examples of talk, Heritage and Watson saw that a formulation did the three things we have already had occasion to list: it deleted some part of a previous speaker's turn, selected a certain other part to reproduce, and transformed the selected material into a (supposed) summary of what the previous speaker had said, or brought out a seemingly natural implication. I have already mentioned the power of the formulation to delete, select, and transform, but now let me emphasize what Heritage and Watson identified as its sequential power – its projection of *agreement.*

Extract 7 From Heritage & Watson, 1979, pp. 134–135.
(Upshot formulation (arrowed). Lines renumbered.)

I: If occasion - if occasion 'rises again will you take
similar action?
R: Well we have never hesitated so far to er take action
where er freedom is being abused.
→ I: So there might be another occasion on which you will use
→ the law against unions
R: Not necessarily against unions but against any body or
which has become over mighty er and is abusing its
responsibilities er if that happens to be a trades union
so be it but we're not I repeat not er looking out er for
trouble to bash the trades union er the unions have their
proper role to play [. . .]

In line 5 the interviewer picks out something that seems to follow naturally, perhaps even to be logically entailed, from the interviewee's own words. This is just what we saw in our example from the psychologist in Extract 1 and just now in Extract 7, where the client's account of his troubles was met with the psychological summary "you found it very hard to adjust." In both case, the formulation projects an agreement, which the speaker has actively to provide (as the client did in Extract 6), or (as in Extract 7 above, line 7) combat in the next turn.

While there is plenty of work on the Heritage and Watson version, we ought to note that Garfinkel and Sacks' more general observation is still visible in conversation analysis and more broadly in discourse analysis, though in very dilute form. Formulation is available to those researchers who want a term for descriptive practices which promote versions of events in whatever format: assertions, questions-with-implied-answers, statements, hints, definitions, and so on, whether they appear in response to a previous speaker's utterance, or in one's own monologue, or anywhere else. To be sure, very few people use the term to refer to Garfinkel and Sacks' notion that it is the whole interaction that is being glossed; the *where-we-both-are-in-the-conversation* sense has all but disappeared. What has survived is the notion that the speaker is making a bid to define, or perhaps redefine, some topic of concern to both parties.

In such generic uses of the term formulation, the researcher's interest is in what the descriptive practice accomplishes as a general gloss on a topic, without much resort to its local interactional implications and consequences. That use of formulation is not specially interested in its local placement as a summary or implication of the previous speaker's words, for immediate ratification. Indeed, the very first use of formulation (and reformulation) in a CA-inspired analysis of psychotherapy (Davis, 1986) used it in that sense. Description and redescription is, of course, a powerful resource, and when it refers to that, formulation has a secure place in the list of rhetorical practices available to any student of therapy talk, and discourse more generally. It has migrated into such useful terms and concepts as *extreme case formulation* (Pomerantz, 1986), or *script formulation* (Edwards, 1994) with great benefit. But there the term formulation does a service that could be equally well done by a term like *representation* or *description.* I am in favour of limiting the term to the sense suggested by Heritage and Watson, for the reasons which are implicit in the analyses of the extracts above, but which are worth making explicit.

The benefits of limiting the term "formulation" to local editing

What elevates Heritage and Watson's version from the general run of rhetorical tropes is their insistence on the intimate relationship between what someone has just said, and the formulator's account of it. That allows us to see three specifically directive editorial features: the formulator's claim to find the new description in the very words of the previous speaker; their transformation of those words; and the presumption that this new description is to be agreed with. The formulator times her or his words to come relevantly after the first speaker's, designing a version of them to sound as if they are a mere summary or natural upshot – and projecting agreement. Such locally implicative force is a powerful resource for the speaker who wants to get an alternative, and possibly rival, version of events on record. The advantages become clear when we start to look at what interests rival accounts may serve.

What formulations do institutionally

In retrospect, it must have seemed to Heritage and Watson significant that of the twenty or so overlapping examples of formulation in their two papers (1979; 1980), all came from institutional settings, and none from the sort of mundane telephone conversation among friends that was proving to be the staple of contemporary CA work. Heritage and Watson's examples came from broadcast news interviews, crisis intervention calls, a medical social worker consultation, and the like. Heritage was later to recognize that "Although it [formulating]is relatively rare in conversation, it is common in institutionalised, audience driven interaction [where it] is most commonly undertaken by questioners" (Heritage, 1985, p. 100). But it fell to Drew (2003) to probe what might account for such an imbalance.

In looking through a corpus of non-institutional telephone talk, Drew reports that that so-prefaced formulations are indeed comparatively infrequent in ordinary conversation. This suggested that they were doing some institutional job. Drew finds that when used by a radio talk-show host, a formulation may propose a tendentious reading of what the caller has said, prompting or obliging them to have to argue their case; by news interviewers, it may be a neutral alternative to an "oh" news receipt, and so serve the need to appear impartial while clarifying issues for the broadcast audience; and in industrial negotiations, though ostensibly reporting the other's position, a formulation might also manipulate it to one side's own advantage (Drew, 2003). The common thread that ties these together is that the institutional agent's formulation picks out something in the other's words, and while putting it forward as a mere neutral summary or implication, uses the opportunity to edit it in ways that will help the speaker's own institutional interests.

What specifically therapeutic interests might formulations promote?

In the rest of this chapter, I shall describe what has been said about three uses of formulation in therapy. Most research (for example by Davis, 1986; Hak & de Boer, 1996; Madill, Widdicombe & Barkham, 2001) has been done in its therapeutic service as a way of *interpreting* the client's talk psychologically (though we need to remember that interpretation is a core feature of much, but not all, therapy). Formulations can also be used to manage the *interactional progress* of the therapeutic interview (for example, by closing down certain avenues of talk), and as a means, in *diagnosis and history-taking*, to cast the client's symptoms into a shape more suitable for later interpretative work.

Formulations in the service of therapeutic interpretation

Perhaps two of the clearest examples of CA work on formulations which start from a principle of therapy, and look to see how it actually cashes out in talk, are Vehviläinen's work on interpretations in psychoanalysis, and Hutchby's work on formulations in child counselling. Vehviläinen makes the point (about psychoanalysis, but it is generalizable) that if the therapist is to make an interpretation, it would be more persuasive, and more in keeping with the intersubjective contract with the client, to "indicate that what they are saying is based on something that has *already and essentially been there in the patient's talk*" (Vehviläinen, 2003a, p. 580, emphasis in the original). We shall return to Vehviläinen's work in a moment, but let us begin with Hutchby, as the kind of therapy he describes is more common than the psychoanalysis studied by Vehviläinen, and the formulations more accessible in lay terms.

Hutchby starts by noting that *active listening* is a core skill for child counsellors, according to their own manuals and texts. But, as he observes, although the texts are firm in their recommendation that the counsellor or therapist listen actively, they are less helpful in saying quite what this means and how it is to be done. A strong, if under-specified, theme in the in-principle account is that the therapist summarize and reflect back the child's experience. This seems to imply what CA might call formulation, but the texts – perhaps inevitably, given their concern with the teachable principles, and not the ephemeral detail, of therapy – are vague on practical specifics. They advocate using formulas like "What I hear you saying is . . ." but inevitably, given the shifting sands of the conversational ebb and flow, these stand out as starkly idealized models. Here, then, is a chance for CA to step in. As Peräkylä and Vehviläinen (2003) point out, when the practitioner has an underspecified account of their interaction with the client, CA can reveal detail (or, indeed, discover unsuspected phenomena). How do the therapists actually "listen actively," and what are the consequences for the interaction?

Hutchby points out that if active listening breaks down into summarizing and reflecting back, then it opens the way to non-neutral reshaping of what is heard. He adds the significant detail that, when the client is a child, special circumstances come into play: children may or may not so readily volunteer their worries to strangers, prompting the counsellor to use questions to get them to talk; and what they then say might not be consonant with adult scripts of psychological hurt and trouble. So the therapist has a useful routine of question + answer + formulation (ostensibly a mere *summarizing* and *reflecting back*) which will elicit material and then reshape it into recognizably therapizable terms. The extract below illustrates how this is done:

Extract 8 From Hutchby 2005, pp. 312–313.

```
     C:  How does your mum get your dad to hear what she
         wants to say.
     J:  Oh she shouts:.
     C:  Does your dad hea [r her.
     J:                    [She shouts really loudly cuz
         she's a teacher and she shouts sort uv .hh she's got
         thisuh really lou [d voice ((squeals))
     C:                    [.h A:hh.
  →  C:  So she's good at sort of shou [ting like, like she's=
     J:                                [Yeh.
     C:  =b[eing a teacher.
```

Hutchby directs us to the subtle shift that the counsellor accomplishes by reworking the child's description. Jenny accounts for her mother's shouting as being *because* she's a teacher (which would explain the shouting without blame; that's what teachers do), and goes on to develop the topic of the voice quality of such shouting. That seems infertile ground for therapy. The counsellor, however, proposes (under the guise of a summary) that the mother is "good at" shouting "like being" a teacher; that drops the issue of the squeally voice as a topic, puts the focus back on Jenny's mother, raising the question of why she chooses to shout like a teacher when at home. when arguing with her husband. One can see the therapy-relevant scene that is implied (the child facing the upsetting sight of her parents shouting angrily at each other) and the formulation has been remarkably efficient at getting it into view.

In summary, Hutchby finds that formulations such as the one in Extract 8 serve the counsellor's interests in making the conversation lean towards the therapeutic: the therapist reshapes the talk to refer to the child's feelings and makes a link between those feelings and the issue that brought the child into therapy in the first place (marital break-up, for example, as in the case above). Where the client is specially vulnerable, the practitioner is under greater obligation not to lead or coerce them into agreeing to a version of their experience. Formulations, by finding that version in the child's own talk, are specially useful ways of finding an agreed path towards the ends of therapy.

For the psychoanalyst, formulations can "verbalize a layer of the unconscious meaning of the patient's talk," as Vehviläinen puts it. Consider Extract 9:

Extract 9 From Vehviläinen, 2003a, p. 585.
(Original in Finnish. Cl is the client, An the psychoanalyst.)

```
    Cl:  I have worked in a children's home you know and (.)
         I've been with small °children°.
         (2.2)
    An:  which is somehow clearly feminine.
    Cl:  =ye?a:h.
         (1.0)
    Cl:  but at this< (.hhhhhhhhh) this point erm:: (1.0)
         (but if<) (.) one works with these labor↓ious (0.2)
         antisocial (0.6) difficult aggressive (0.4)
         >adolescents< ↑then< then there is .hhhhhhhh clearly
         a place for a man there.
         (0.6)
    Cl:  and and he has his duty (°there°).
         (2.0)
→   An:  so it is a point from which the father cannot leave.
    Cl:  =yeah:.
```

In line 9 the analyst uses a turn extension to interpret the patient's story as a matter of male–female difference; the client concurs, and adds that the work clearly needs a man. The analyst comes in with a formulation that (for the first time, according to Vehviläinen) introduces the figure of "the father" (line 20). The link between the formulation and the client's previous talk is much less commonsensically clear than is the case in more mainstream therapies, such as the deliberately non-technical counselling that we saw analysed by Hutchby (above). That may give the psychoanalyst more of a task in getting the client to accept the formulation, but again the yes-expecting format comes to the therapist's aid; it is difficult to disagree, without paying an interactional cost.

Formulations in managing the progress of the session

So far we have been seeing formulations do the canonical business of psychotherapy (or, at least, the kind of therapy which favours interpretation): finding, in the client's words, evidence of some psychological state of affairs that will bear profitable examination. But there is more to therapy than that, and interpretation is not the only place in which formulations turn up. Antaki, Barnes and Leudar (2005) notice that formulations can also do traffic-management work (by formulating what the client has said as *not* being psychologically interesting, for the moment, and allowing the therapist to move on to other business); and they can, in the history-taking phase of proceedings, gently edge the client's experience to what can, later, be treated as properly psychological and ready for interpretation. We shall see more of that latter, history-taking use of formulations in a moment. First let us look at how formulations can be used to manage the therapeutic session as a mundane institutional interaction, where the therapist tries to control the ebb and flow of the talk.

Consider what the therapist is doing in Extract 10 to formulate the client's report as *not* specially worthy of therapeutic attention (at least, not at the moment). This is at the polar opposite to the canonical use of formulation to pull out a psychologically interesting meaning or implications from what the client says. Nevertheless it does a job: it helps the therapist manage what needs to be heard, at what point.

Extract 10 CBT AG&HD session 1.

```
     Cl:  b't it j'st seem to be a nasty °voi°-I might feel a bit
          (.)bit better, when soon's=I (.6) er y't- (1.0) >wunnit,
          wunnit< wite (.) wite- why'it says summi' like er
          (.3) (.) er (bitch) or ° (tick=or) summin' like° 'at °
          °>n'ye-<°° (.4) .h (.) but ee- ee- it does (.) °(*or dog
          or whatever*)° ((*croaky*)) (.) it's very er- it's
          menacing, you know,
     Th:  °°m:: °°=
     Cl:  =doesn't seem to:: er go away, (.5) ('n)'it's very nasty.
→    Th:  so it's not long   [sentences then is it. (.) it's  [not
     Cl:                     [ (yeh snog-)                    [no
```

```
→  Th:  er (.3) it's saying the odd [ wo:rd °and° (.) repeatin' it]
   Cl:                              [ (    s'm words and y'r      ]eh)
        (peatin' 'ole) sentence °somthin'=like° (.3) 'ittin' someone
        or wha'ever or [w- losin' me temper an' that, (.6) lo:sing
   Th:                 [°°yeh°°
   Cl:  me rag or something [ (but it jus' has- tee-) it does .h
   Th:                      [ °°m°°
   Cl:  ahw- ah
   Cl:  w- the man' times I write down the (teams) it's that kind
        of thing.
        (.3)
→  Th:  °yeah° (.) [so you've been doing a lot of writin' down.
```

This client has a diagnosis of schizophrenia and hears voices. Although this session is an introductory one, in preparation for the start of therapy proper, it is important that the psychologist gets a sense of the client's history as he sees it. The therapeutic imperative of "hearing the client out" is in play. Where his description of the voice he hears is clear, it is troubling: the voice is "nasty" and "very menacing." The client allows the therapist a possible turn at line 10, which would commit the therapist to orient to the description "it's very nasty." Instead, she formulates the issue as being (merely) one of sentence length: "it's not long sentences then, it's not er it's saying the odd word and repeating it." This skirts round the nastiness of the voice. The client at first plays along ("yeh repeatin' 'ole sentence") but then he adds more detail, again of a troubling sort: "'ittin' someone or wha'ever or losin' me rag" (an idiom for "losing my temper," in British English). Again the therapist formulates the trouble away: "yeah so you've been doing a lot of writin' down."

These two formulations do not do *active listening*, by any stretch of the imagination. Yet they serve a purpose. They keep the client's descriptions *non-therapizable* until this stage of the session is complete. The therapist could have closed down the client's account of his symptoms in some other way (compare, for example, medical practitioners' rather more brutal non-response to what they take to be patients' irrelevant description; see, for example, Beach, 1995; Robinson, 2001). The formulations format is good for picking out something useful (to the therapist) while seemingly being attentive to something in the client's own words.

Formulations in history-taking

The last sort of service that formulations have (so far) been shown to do in therapy is in making some sort of record the client's circumstances. This might be done in some formal stage of the proceedings like an explicit history-taking at first interview, or might be occasioned by some uncertainty that arises from the client's account at any time. Ostensibly, the therapist is simply *getting the story straight*. But in doing so, the therapist has the opportunity to prune away the irrelevant material and shape the remainder in therapeutically more fruitful directions, ahead of the interpretative work which waits further down the line.

Here is an example of a psychotherapist getting the history of the client's experience of being talked about by other people:

Extract 11 From Antaki, Barnes & Leudar 2005, RS and AB session 1.

Th: [how do all these
people know that you've had er (.) >sort of mental<
health problem or (.) whatever.
(1.2)
Th: °how d'they° (.7) how do they know:
(.4)
Cl: well I know (remember one) van that drives past me
that's (y'l builders) .h (.4) a:n' they (thin' there
buildin') to me ouse.
(.3)
Th: ri:ght.
(1.4)
Th: and when they were at yer house, did th- f- did you talk
to them or somethin, °or,°
(.5)
Cl: No:, me mum did, but me mum talks to er-=bleedin' everyone
(tsat "ve tol') (.5) t- (.4) told them all me business
like I've been in hospital [(all](times) and all this shit.
Th: [I see]
→ Th: so people actually lean out of the windows when you go past
→ 'n (.6) shout abuse at you.
Cl: yeh.
Th: what sort of people just anyone in particular, or (.)
c- (.4) .h you know is it just one or two people or a
lot of peo°ple°

As Antaki *et al.* point out, the therapist could have done quite a lot of interpretation at any point in this extract. The client's troubles are vivid and seem to be keenly felt. But the therapist does not orient to the client's negative assessment of what his mother does. Instead, at lines 20–21 he offers a formulation of the client's experience of being harassed: "so people actually lean out of the windows when you go past 'n shout abuse at you." This formulation – seemingly a mere summary of what the client has said – appears to be a check of the reality of the client's possibly delusional beliefs, or at the least a retopicalization of those beliefs, leaving aside the mother's allegedly wanton indiscretions.

The formulation is couched in terms that invite the client to recast what he has said as an exaggeration, but he does not. In a further bid to see how wide this delusion extends, the therapist goes on to ask how often the client experiences it – "just one or two people, or a lot of people?" Getting a sense of the diagnostic implications of the client's experiences and circumstances is a very different use of formulation for finding a psychological interpretation, or managing the progress of the interaction; but, like those two, it is part and parcel of the therapist's job.

Resistance

In the sections above I have laid out the three most researched uses of formulations. The common thread is that they allow the therapist to suggest a tendentious reading of the client's situation, and expect it to be confirmed. But the client may demur. Extract 12 is an example of a client giving what seems to be a rather half-hearted agreement to the therapist's summary, or gist, of the experience he is describing. In lines 1 to 8, the client is expressing a conflict he feels between, on the one hand, delaying gratification, and, on the other, "living in the day."

Extract 12 JP/R 280200.

```
     Cl:                     [y'know,= w'I'm thinking- (.4) tha-ther
           there's a lot of (>s'v'< thin- th) conflicting in me,
           (.)one is that (.5) oh yes, it's- (.) >er-<it's (mature
           y' wa' >y'know<) I b'l've it is mature tuh- (.)
           delay gratf-gratification.
     Th:   °>yeh<°
     Cl:   the oth- the other- s- the >s't've spiritual side< of
           me says (.)b't I want to live in *the °da::yh°*,
           ((*loud whisper*))
           (.3)
     Cl:   [y'kner]
     Th:   [m (.)  ]mi.
     Cl:   erm:-
           (.8)
→    Th:   .h OH::: I see- (.) h so you're interpreting wanting
           to live in the day in a certain way.
           (.9)
     Th:   °right?°
           (2.0)
     Cl:   er::m
           (1.6)
     Cl:   yes.
```

The distinction between instant and delayed pleasure that the client draws in lines 1–8 is available for comment. The therapist takes a moment, then delivers her upshot formulation (line 13) as a realization ("oh I see"). Her version of what the client is experiencing deletes the contrast the client sets up, and the side he would prefer to be on; she distils out of his talk only the consequence that he's "interpreting wanting to live in the day in a certain way." To an observer (and seemingly the client) this is rather an obscure moral to draw out of what he has just said; in any case, the client does not immediately jump to fill the projected agreement-space. There is 0.9 of a second's worth of pause at line 15 (and one second is the "standard maximum" according to an early experiment by Jefferson, 1988). The therapist prompts an affirmative response with a confirmation check (*right?*), but there is a still more marked pause (now two seconds) before the client issues an "erm"; then, finally, after a further 1.6 seconds, a "yes." The client does not actually disagree with his therapist's formulation; but the trouble he has agreeing is there for both parties to see, and to interpret as they will.

For a more explicit disagreement – indeed, a flagrant one – we can go back to Hutchby's analysis of children's counselling. In Extract 13 below, the counsellor is trying to draw out the child's feelings about his changing family circumstances.

Extract 13 From Hutchby 2005, pp. 324–325.
(C is the Counsellor.)

```
     C:  Dju think it should stay the sa:me, .h or dju think it
         should be diff'rent tuh how it is.
         (1.0)
     P:  °Diff'rent.°
     C:  Diff'rent.
         (1.8)
 →   C:  So you know it needs to be diff'rent.
         (.)
 →   P:  DON'T KNOW!
         (.)
     C:  No no- n listen you know it needs t'be diff'rent,
     P:  Don't kno    [w,
     C:               [But dju know how it should be.
```

The counsellor has got the child to say that he thinks things should be different (line 5). His formulation in line 7 is an invitation to get this "on record" as something the child "knows," presumably an upgrade on what the child "thinks." As Hutchby observes, if he *knows* that things should change, that commits him in a way that merely *thinking* they ought would not. Perhaps it is this implication which the child so strongly resists, with his very loud "DON'T KNOW!" What is interesting for us is to carry on the analysis a bit longer than Hutchby does, and see what happens next. The counsellor does not immediately abandon the formulation format entirely, but he gives it a curious spin: he repeats it (line 11). but this time prefaced with "no, no listen . . ." Merely neutral, bland reworkings of what the speaker has said would hardly need such insistent backing. The counsellor has been pushed into it by the child's (unusual) resistance, but his "no, listen . . ." unmasks the combative, perhaps even coercive, message behind the cooperative face of formulations. (For resistance, see also Halonen, Chapter 8, this volume; MacMartin, Chapter 5, this volume; Vehviläinen, Chapter 7, this volume.)

Concluding comments

To formulate a state of affairs (in the sense identified by Heritage and Watson, which I have followed here) is obviously a powerful rhetorical move, and therapy is shot through with therapists and clients each offering their own understanding of events. It is worth holding on, as I have tried to do here, to a specific sense of the term *formulating* to pick out just those times when the therapist summarizes the client's own words, or draws out a seemingly natural implication from them, while nevertheless editing them in a tendentious way. It is the ostensibly cooperative link between the formulator's version and that of the previous speaker that makes the move extra powerful. Unlike corrections (see Rae, Chapter 4, this volume), reinterpretative statements (see Bercelli *et al.*, Chapter 3, this volume) or even extensions of the patient's turn (see Peräkylä, Chapter 6, this volume; Vehviläinen, Chapter 7, this volume), this way of doing it promotes the sense that one has listened to the other speaker and has extracted something that they themselves might have said. In that sense, formulations are wholly in keeping with the respectful and attentive culture of therapy. While "hearing the client out," they serve the therapist's interest in a variety of ways – shaping symptoms, closing down troubles and tending interpretations towards the psychological.

3 Clients' responses to therapists' reinterpretations

Fabrizio Bercelli, Federico Rossano, and Maurizio Viaro

This chapter is based on a corpus of about a hundred sessions, mainly audio taped, run in Italy by cognitive and relational-systemic therapists. We have identified a type of action, which we call *reinterpretation*, by which the therapist proposes his or her own version of the client's events and experiences, the therapist's version being grounded in another version of them previously provided by the client. We locate the placement of therapists' reinterpretations in the overall structural organization of the therapies of our corpus. We also briefly compare them to *formulations* (Antaki, Chapter 2 this volume) and *psychoanalytic interpretations* (Peräkylä, 2004a; Vehviläinen, 2003a). This leads to the main concern of the chapter, which is clients' responses to reinterpretations. We identify some types of clients' responses and a corresponding array of procedural features, and discuss their importance in the therapeutic process.

In recent conversation analytic research on psychotherapy, clients' responses to therapists' interventions have often been analysed in terms of acceptance vs. rejection or resistance. This has been the case where clients respond to formulations (Antaki, Chapter 2, this volume; Antaki, Barnes & Leudar, 2004; 2005; Hak & de Boer, 1996; Hutchby, 2005) and to psychoanalytic interpretations (Peräkylä, 2005; Vehviläinen, Chapter 7, this volume). The same tack has been followed in research dealing with other similar phenomena, e.g. clients' responses to experts' formulations in medical settings where mental-health talk routinely occurs (Beach & Dixson, 2001). Our tack is slightly different. Beyond the still-useful dimension of clients' acceptance vs. rejection or resistance, our findings point to a different dimension: we distinguish more active clients' responses, which contribute further relevant content to the ongoing elaboration of their own events, from more passive ones, which do not (cf. Peräkylä, 2005; Chapter 6, this volume). Special analytical attention is given to a kind of clients' responses, namely *extended agreements*, through which clients provide autobiographical material as evidence accounting for their agreement with the therapists' reinterpretations. We discuss how both participants orient to such responses and how clients' actions achieved through them contribute to some important tasks of the therapeutic work.

Some organizational features

Our corpus consists of sessions run by therapists adopting two different clinical approaches: cognitive and relational–systemic. Though there are differences in the contents of therapists' turns, related to the specific approach they adopt, many organizational features of these sessions are similar (Bercelli, Viaro & Rossano, 2004; Viaro & Leonardi, 1983). In this section, we offer a sketch of the turn-taking pattern prevailing in the sessions, the main courses of action occurring and some aspects of their overall structural organization. This will allow us to place the phenomenon here examined – clients' responses to reinterpretations – within a larger sequential pattern.

As for turn types distribution and turn order, a uniform asymmetric pattern is observable throughout all the sessions of our corpus:

a) therapists can ask questions about clients' personal events at any transition relevant place in the sessions, and generally ask many questions in every session;
b) clients do not usually ask questions, except repair initiation questions;
c) apart from questions, therapists mainly make statements about clients' events, grounded in previous clients' talk, be they *formulations* or *reinterpretations* (see below);
d) clients regularly respond to such statements (in minimal or non-minimal ways) (again, see below).

These turn-taking features, shared by both kind of therapies in our corpus, are quasi-conversational (Peräkylä, 1995), rather than being normatively set as in more formal institutional settings (Drew & Heritage, 1992). Such a pattern accommodates two main courses of action, inquiry and elaboration. Inquiry is a series of question/answer sequences, through which therapists gather information from clients about their events and experiences, whereas elaboration is a series of therapists' reinterpretations and clients' responses to them, through which therapists, by offering their views, and clients, by responding to them, elaborate on what has been reported by clients.

Inquiry regularly precedes elaboration. Further inquiry can follow or be inserted into elaboration. In any case, elaboration is generally based on previous inquiry. The overall structural organization of these sessions is very schematically outlined in Figure 3.1 (the arrows indicate which type of action can follow another type of action; Th=therapist, Cl=client).

A sequential organization of this sort affects topic development: therapists can initiate new topics, while clients generally do not; clients can however shift topics step-by-step through extensions of their answers and

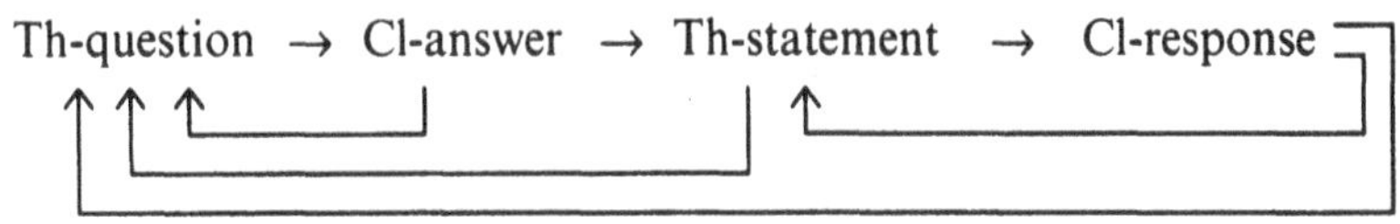

Figure 3.1 Sketch of question–answer–statement–response sequential patterns in therapy

responses, as far as therapists allow. Let us briefly illustrate some of these organizational features in Extract 1. (All extracts are translated from Italian original data. In all extracts, Th is the therapist, Cl the client.)

Extract 1 G/P.

(Th is reconstructing with Cl the first lecture Cl gave in an undergraduate class; q→ indicates questions, r→ indicates reinterpretations.)

```
1   q→ Th:  [. . .] this sense of not being up to it how is it?
2           (0,5)
3   q→ Th:  how's it going?
4           (0,5)
5      Cl:  eh, it's going well.
6           (1,0)
7   q→ Th:  i- in what way is it °going well°?
8      Cl:  that I feel that- hm (.) I have less and less of
9           this::sensation
            . . .((a few turns of Th-questions and Cl-answers omitted))
16  q→ Th:  =their faces what are they like during the lesson?
17     Cl:  they're interested, because:::: (.) they ask me
18          questions, so they want examples, so the lesson also
19          becomes very (.) open
20     Th:  hm
21     Cl:  I like this type of interaction [between (°      °)]
22  r→ Th:                                  [(eh yes you then-) ] you
23  r→      really go in- in tandem with the faces of the
24          (0.8)
25     Cl:  well    [°n(h)o° (they're) o(h)nly hohohoh]
26  r→ Th:          [no?               because at first-]
27     Cl:  [(they're) only:   hhh]
28  r→ Th:  [at first you give- at fi]rst you give an introduction,
29  r→      th[ey] appeared smiling, [you feel] accepted.
30     Cl:    [yes]                  [hm: hm: ]
31  r→ Th:  then you go on, their faces are interested,
32  r→      you     [you feel] like a teacher.
33     Cl:          [hm: hm   ]
34          (1,0)
35     Th:  >okay, < (then the lesson finishes)=
36     Cl:  =hm hm=
```

q→ Th: =the feeling you have when it's finished? ( )
[( ) what do you do, do you go home?]
Cl: [( ) that's to say ni] ce <u>satis::fied::</u>=
q→ Th: do you go home or go to-?
Cl: no no I go to::: I have the surgery, after that.
q→ Th: °hm.° and do you remember how you- how you felt just
after you go out of- (.) this lecture room and
you're going towards the surgery?

In Extract 1, after a series of question/answer sequences (lines 1–19), the therapist provides his reinterpretation of the client's experience (lines 22–32) manifestly grounded in the client's previous answers (for instance, Cl's "interested" at line 17 is repeated by Th at line 31). In this case, the client disagrees with the therapist, though she does so in a mitigating way by inserting laugh tokens (lines 25, 27); the therapist goes on overlapping her response and gets some acknowledgment tokens from her (lines 30, 33). Then, after this short elaboration segment (22–33), the therapist turns to inquiry through another series of questions (lines 37–44).

Extract 1 illustrates how the turn-taking features (a)–(d) allow the therapist to direct both topic development and sequential organization of actions, by alternating inquiry and elaboration, as schematized in Figure 3.1. In this paper, as we have already indicated, we shall focus on elaboration. Before dealing with clients' responses to therapists' reinterpretations, we will compare reinterpretations to a similar conversational object, formulations.

Two kinds of therapists' statements on clients' events: formulations and reinterpretations

Therapists' formulations have been a major theme in recent conversation analytic research on psychotherapy. Generally, through formulations speakers can offer their candidate understandings (Schegloff, 1996a), interpretations (Drew, 2003), or candidate representations (Hutchby, 2005) of what their interlocutors can be taken as having said or meant in previous talk. Furthermore, according to Heritage and Watson's influential characterization, "Formulation of the topic, 'gist' or 'sense' of a conversation may further be accompanied by formulations as to the 'gist's' 'upshot' or further 'significance' (which may or may not be retrievable from the 'rest' of the conversation)" (Heritage & Watson, 1980, p. 249). We have found that, at least in our corpus, therapists can deal with such "further 'significance'" in two different ways:

(i) as something that was implicitly meant by the client, so claiming that they are still offering a candidate reading of the perspective expressed by the client;

(ii) alternatively, as something that, though grounded in what the client has said, is caught and expressed from the therapist's own perspective – therefore something possibly different, and ostensibly so, from what the client meant.

In the first case, and only in the first case, we maintain the term *formulation*, which is therefore used by us in a more narrow sense than the one sometimes adopted in the literature (see the discussion in Antaki, chapter 2 this volume). In the second case, we label the therapists' utterances *reinterpretations*. As we will show in the next two paragraphs, this distinction reflects a different orientation by the participants towards these two kinds of therapists' actions and what these actions make relevant next by clients.

Therapists' formulations

Formulations, in the narrow sense, are devices by which therapists manage to express what has been previously meant by clients. They are so designed, through framing expressions such as *you mean, you say, you told me*, or by largely mirroring the content and form of the prior client's talk, as to manifestly offer a candidate reading of it. These or similar design features convey the therapists' claim that they are not altering the point, sense or gist of the client's talk, though formulations can select, highlight, delete, or transform parts of it.

As for sequential aspects, therapists' formulations make relevant clients' confirming (preferred), disconfirming or reformulating responses. Therefore, even though formulations are contingent on clients' prior turns, they are also first pair parts of a specific sequence, the formulation/decision sequence (Heritage & Watson, 1979). A formulation sequence often occurs after a question/answer sequence: the therapist formulates some aspects of the client's previous answer(s) and the client confirms, disconfirms, or corrects the formulation. In our corpus, a client's confirming decision generally consists of a minimal confirming token (such as *yes* or *hm*, with falling intonation) and is not post-expanded, or only minimally post-expanded (Schegloff, 2007), by therapists. Here is an illustrative example.

Extract 2 V/S, 11.

(Cl is describing, through her answers to Th's questions, what happened during a visit to her parents.)

```
     Cl:  [no, there] and then I saw my father who::: who
          hm:: (.) was protecting my mother.
          (0.3)
     Cl:  and n[ot
     Th:       [you read this thing as (0.3)
  →       protection of your mum=
```

```
Cl:  =yes
Th:  okay explain to me how.
```

In Extract 2, the therapist's utterance (lines 5–6) largely mirrors the form and content of the prior client's talk (lines 1–2) and thus offers a candidate understanding of what she meant. It transforms a component of the client's turn, "I saw" (line 1), into "you read" (line 5), which can still be heard as maintaining the client's perspective on the described events, though a subtle shift from the client's sensorial perception to the client's interpretation is here proposed by the therapist.

As for sequential aspects, the client's confirmation is promptly provided and followed, after closure (line 8: "okay") of the formulation sequence, by a question contingent on the previous (confirmed) formulation. In this way, some aspects of the client's previous report are fixed by the sequence, and, thus fixed, they become available for subsequent exploitation: by formulating the client's description of her past noticing (lines 1–2) as an interpretative one (lines 5–6), the therapist paves the way to the next request (line 8) for an account of such a reading.

Our analysis of Extract 2 is in accordance with the results of current research on formulations in psychotherapy: formulation sequences do (important) preparatory work towards subsequent therapists' actions (Antaki, Barnes & Leudar, 2005; Hutchby, 2005; Vehviläinen, 2003a). As we will show in the next section, therapists' reinterpretations differ from formulations and perform a different type of work.

Therapists' reinterpretations

Therapists' formulations and reinterpretations both offer readings of clients' events grounded in prior clients' talk. But, differently from formulations, through reinterpretations therapists forward their own perspectives, ostensibly shifting the point of prior clients' versions of their own events or possibly forwarding some divergence from them. Therapists' reinterpretations share this feature with psychoanalytic interpretations (Peräkylä, 2005; Vehviläinen, 2003a). In Peräkylä's words, "in interpretations, the analyst says something to the patient about the things that the patient has been telling the analyst about, and suggests that some of these things mean something different or something more than what the patient has said" (Peräkylä, 2005). The difference between therapists' reinterpretations and formulations is generally displayed in our corpus by both design and sequential features.

Design features. While formulations are generally designed and marked as candidate readings of what clients have meant, reinterpretations display some *independency* from clients' talk. This can be achieved through epistemic markers referring to the therapists' perspectives (for instance: "I think"; "I mean"; "let us say"), *neutral* perspective markers ("from this point of view"; "in some aspects"; "in a sense"), evidential or speculative markers ("it seems that"; "all things considered"; "perhaps"; "maybe"), evaluative components, figures of speech, metaphors or psycho-professional terms, and many others. Some of these devices can be noticed in all reinterpretations occurring in our excerpts. For instance, in Extract 1, the metaphorical expression "in tandem" together with a lack of formulation markers, designs the multi-unit statement lines 22–32 as a therapist's reinterpretation of the client's events.

Sequential features. Therapists' reinterpretations, like formulations, are B-event statements (Labov & Fanshel, 1977): they deal with clients' personal events and experiences, which clients have wider access to. Therefore, both reinterpretations and formulations make clients' responses relevant, but in different ways. Formulations make relevant clients' deciding whether formulations fit with what clients themselves have meant: clients' confirming responses are generally minimal and are not post-expanded, or minimally post-expanded, by therapists (see above). Therapists' reinterpretations make relevant clients' agreeing or disagreeing with them, rather than simply confirming, disconfirming or correcting them: even when clients agree, they can account for their agreement, and therapists can post-expand clients' extended agreements (or disagreements) in non-minimal ways.[1] These sequential features are documented below.

Moreover, therapists' reinterpretations can propose views, possibly unexpected for clients, to which they can have difficulty responding. This engenders (and is reflexively indexed by) a further sequential feature: clients sometimes provide no response, not even an acknowledgment token. In such cases, therapists regularly pursue some response through subsequent increments of their re-interpretations, until they get one, as illustrated by Extract 3.

Extract 3 B/F, 7.

(At the beginning of this extract, Th comments on an episode previously described by Cl: Two colleagues of his had complained about his shortcomings at work and one of them, Marco, had then excused him for his shortcomings because of his current psychological problems. Arrows indicate transition relevant points where Cl could, but does not, respond to Th.)

```
    Th: You're not well, which is even worse isn't it? like
        saying I can't cope, I'm collapsing I can't handle it,
        but I'm not capable (0.5) of doing this job.
→       (0.5)
```

[1] Confirming is a special kind of agreeing (Schegloff, 1996a) and has sequential properties partly different from other kinds of agreeing, as shown by the recent literature on epistemic rights (for instance, Heritage & Raymond, 2005).

```
     Th:  it's a real nice slap
→         (1.0)
     Th:  you got.
→         (9.0)
     Th:  also (.) this (.) thought ( ) of Marco's
          (1.3) is also a cop-out, I mean (.)
          the fault's not mine
→         3.0)
     Th:  I'm (.) I'm risking going mad, ( ) it's an
          illness.
→         (2.0)
     Th:  or not?
     Cl:  yes.
```

In Extract 3, a therapist's reinterpretation is progressively produced through a series of consecutive and connected turn constructional units (lines 1–3, 5–7, 9–14: the latter is connected to the previous ones through the turn-initial "also"). Though grounded in previous client's talk, which is reproduced in direct speech format (lines 2–3, 11, 13–14), the therapist's utterances are designed so as to propose the therapist's own perspective on the client's events (line 1: "even worse," which is a therapist's evaluation; line 1: "like saying," marking the therapist's reading of the client's experience; line 5: "slap," a metaphorical term; line 10: "I mean," framing the therapist's view).

At the completion of every unit of his progressively constructed reinterpretation (lines 4, 6, 8, 12, 15), the therapist gives time (a rather long one at lines 8, 12 and 15) for a response, which is not provided by the client, until the therapist explicitly solicits and gets it (lines 16–17). Such a sequential pattern – which has also been observed in psychoanalytic sessions (Peräkylä, 2005) – contrasts with the one generally applying to formulation/decision sequences in the narrow sense, where clients can, and generally do, readily provide their decision about the sense of their own previous talk (as in Extract 2 above).

Through such design and sequential features, therapists' formulations and reinterpretations can be distinguished. Even though boundary cases can occur, generally in our corpus both therapists and clients orient differently to, and thus differentiate, these two activities. In the next paragraphs, we will outline, describe and discuss some kinds of clients' responses to reinterpretations.

Clients' responses to reinterpretations

While formulations make relevant confirming, disconfirming or reformulating responses, reinterpretations make relevant – for reasons touched upon in the previous section – a wider range of clients' responses. Some of them are listed below:

a) acknowledgment tokens;
b) mere agreements – from minimal agreement tokens to repeated claims of agreement – doing no more than agreeing;
c) agreements + descriptions/narrations of evidence accounting for agreement and corroborating the previous therapist's reinterpretations – we name them *extended agreements*;
d) qualified agreements or disagreements + descriptions/narrations of evidence accounting for the qualification or disagreement;
e) any of (a)–(d) beginnings + disjunctively introduced autobiographical material somehow relevant to the previous therapists' reinterpretations, though not clearly working as confirming or disconfirming evidence.

In the following paragraphs, we will discuss and illustrate cases (a)–(c). Analysis of cases (d) and (e), though equally important, will be provided in future publications.

Acknowledgment tokens

Some reinterpretations can propose views which clients may not be ready to respond to. In psychotherapy, there are specific reasons why a therapist's reinterpretation, though carefully grounded in material offered by clients' previous talk, might not be easy for the clients to accept: therapists have the professional task of providing clients with views on their personal problems not available to clients themselves in their life environments. This entails some therapists' views being possibly dissonant with clients' cognitive habits and therefore uneasily adoptable by them (Guidano, 1991; Haley, 1963). If clients do not succeed in agreeing or disagreeing with reinterpretations, they can still resort to more neutral or uncommitted responses, such as acknowledgment tokens, i.e. responses displaying they have heard and understood the previous turn without taking any agreeing or disagreeing stance on it. Therapists, in their turn, can (a) go on with further increments of their reinterpretations in pursuing an agreeing or disagreeing response until they get it, or even (b) start a new course of action without (further) pursuing anything more than an acknowledgment token. Both these cases occur in our corpus, and are illustrated, respectively, by Extracts 4 and 5 below.

Let us firstly consider a case where the client responds only with acknowledgment tokens (indicated by the arrows) and the therapist, through increments of his reinterpretation, pursues and finally gets an agreeing response.

Extract 4 B/F.

(Cl has just narrated a recent disturbing experience: when sitting at dinner with his wife and 4-year-old son, he was repeatedly visited by the thought of assaulting his wife with a dinner knife, a thought felt by Cl to be utterly unmotivated. Th works this out.)

```
     Th:  and another thing could be that you're sitting there
          and- (0.7) it's a bit (1.2) like a cage
          (0.4)
          right? because sitting at table (0.6) is a bit like
          being caged
          (0.5)
→    Cl?: [(hm)
     Th:  [you can't get up, however: in short
          (0.3)
→    Cl:  yes
          (0.3)
     Cl:  °hh°=
     Th:  =like now as well you're a bit like that there
          (0.2) right?=
→    Cl:  =hm
          (0.5)
     Cl:  yes=and actually it's a bit the sensation of:::
          ((continues))
```

At the beginning of this excerpt, the therapist forwards his reinterpretation (designed as a speculative one, line 1: "could be"; and formulated through a metaphorical assessment, line 2: "like a cage") of the client's events, previously reported by him, through a series of incremental units (lines 1–2, 4–5, 8, 13), which are punctuated by the client's acknowledgment tokens (lines 7, 10, 14). This progressively incremental construction (which also contains two response-soliciting tag questions: lines 4, 13) repeatedly allows for a more extended response from the client, which he finally provides (lines 16–17).

Such a sequential pattern often occurs in the elaboration phases within the sessions of our corpus, and has also been observed in psychoanalytic sessions (Peräkylä, 2005). Its occurrence suggests that therapists welcome more committed responses than mere acknowledgment tokens from clients. Yet clients' acknowledgment tokens can be and sometimes are treated by therapists as somehow acceptable responses to their reinterpretations, as illustrated by Extract 5.

Extract 5 G/P.

(Th here provides an increment to his reinterpretation of Cl's worries, previously described by Cl herself, about a lecturing task she has been assigned by a senior professor – mentioned at line 2.)

```
     Th:  yes (.) on the one hand it's as if- (.) also while
          lecturing, you always referred to him
```

```
            (.)
        Cl: hm
            (1.0)
        Th: right? this is [the] theme
        Cl:                [hm ]
        Th: on the other hand it seems to be quite a comparison
            that you really- what comes out is that you are
            always a sort of a loser.
   →    Cl: hm
   →        (5,0)
   →    Th: and now this prospect of: doing it also in
            December:: is it open or not?
```

In Extract 5, the therapist's reinterpretation (lines 1–10: marked by the *analytical* marker "on the one hand . . . on the other hand," at lines 1 and 8; the professional term "the theme," line 6; and the evidential "what comes up," line 9) is received with the client's two acknowledgment tokens during its construction (at line 4; at line 7 after a tag question at line 6) and a third one at its hearable completion (line 11). After this last acknowledgment token, a rather long silence ensues (line 12), in which the client provides no further response nor does the therapist solicit one, merely allowing for it by remaining silent. Then, in the absence of any further response, the therapist starts a new course of action, through an and-prefaced new question as a further step in his inquiring agenda (Heritage & Sorjonen, 1994). Although a response beyond the client's previous acknowledgment token (line 11) is allowed by the therapist's rather long silence (line 12), its lack is not treated here as a problem by the participants, insofar as the interaction, by resuming the topic of the future lecture, then proceeds smoothly (lines 13–14).

In this sense, acknowledgment tokens can be treated by therapists as acceptable responses to their proposals. This can be linked, on the one hand, to the possible unexpectedness of some reinterpretations for clients, and, on the other hand, to the overall structural organization of the session itself, which allows therapists to forward such reinterpretations again and again, in ways and at times which depend on their clinical judgement about clients and clients' responses to their actions.

Through our analysis of Extracts 3, 4, and 5, we have shown how reinterpretations make clients' responses relevant: if no response at all is provided by clients, therapists pursue some response until they get it (Extract 3); although responses other than acknowledgment tokens can be and often are pursued by therapists (Extract 4), mere acknowledgment tokens can be treated as acceptable ones (Extract 5). These sequential features fit with the epistemic character of therapists' reinterpretations and their difference from formulations: when responding to the latter, clients have to decide about the sense of their own previous talk; when responding to the former, they have the possibly more difficult task of choosing if and how to take a position on the experts' reading of their own events.

Mere agreements

When clients' responses consist of mere agreements, therapists can either (a) deal with them as sufficient responses and proceed to other courses of action or (b) progressively increment their reinterpretations of clients' events and thus pursue a more extended response from clients. Extract 6 illustrates the first possibility.

Extract 6 V/S, 4.
(The client is describing how she and her husband coped with some of her father's repeated intrusions in their married life.)

```
      Cl:  and: so hm: instead as concerns my hu- my father (1.2) hhhh
           he ((Cl's husband)) is delimiting his territory (0.4) more and
           more.
      Th:  which with your dad (0.5) it seems to me isn't all that easy
           (.) an operation.
  →   Cl:  no.
           (0.8)
      Th:  .h at the moment your dad where is he?
      Cl:  here. ((continues))
```

In Extract 6, the therapist starts a new sequence and changes topic (line 8) just after the client's mere agreement (line 6) with his own short reinterpretation (lines 4–5: marked as such by "it seems to me") of the client's circumstances. The next extracts (7a–b) illustrate the alternative option, i.e. the therapist pursues something more than a claim of agreement.

Extract 7a V/X.
(In previous talk Cl reported on recent developments in her intricate private life: though not succeeding in getting from her lover, Antonio, the daily attention she gets from her husband, and not having with the latter any of the passionate sex she has with the former, she feels better. In the excerpt below, Th forwards his reinterpretation of the situation reported by the client.)

```
      Th:  °that's to say° putting the two things together, hhh perhaps
           you feel less (1.5) let's put it this way, (0.7) dependent
           on Antonio BECAUSE you have this [other o[ne who
      Cl:                                   [yes    [yes
      Th:  after all gives you what [you'd look for
      Cl:                           [yes
      Th:  (.) from Antonio, >which however maybe if you had it from
           Antonio would frighten you more.<=
  →   Cl:  =ah yes=yes certainly
           (0.5)
  →   Cl:  certainly, certainly.
```

```
              (1.0)
  →    Cl:    this man frightens me, °he frightens me.°
       Th:    and so all in all you're calm for this reason
              (0.5)
       Cl:    °yes°=
       Th:    =because he doesn't call you, ((continues))
```

In Extract 7a, the therapist's reinterpretation (lines 1–8, where "putting the two things together," at line 1, marks the therapist's perspective) is firstly interjected by the client's three agreement tokens (lines 4, 6) and then, at its completion, responded to with an emphatically repeated agreement (lines 9–11). After a silence (line 12), the client adds a twice-repeated utterance (line 13: "this man frightens me, he frightens me") which, by reproducing the design pattern of her previous agreement (line 11: "certainly, certainly") and repeating the last part of the therapist's reinterpretation (line 8: "would frighten you more"), though in a modified way, is hearable as a further claim of agreement, and is so treated by the therapist in the next turn: he ignores the modification and goes on with an increment to his reinterpretation (line 14), which receives a further, though much weaker, agreement (line 16), followed by a further increment of the therapist's reinterpretation.

Here again, we find a sequential pattern through which the therapist, by incrementally producing subsequent units of his reinterpretation and then leaving conversational space to the client, repeatedly allows for and pursues a more extended response than the claims of agreement initially provided. In fact, a more extended response finally ensues (see extract 7b below), which dramatically contrasts with the client's previous claims of agreement, though the point of the reinterpretation seems to be the same throughout its progressive construction: some aspects of her situation make her feel better (line 2: "less . . . dependent"; line 14: "calm").

Extract 7b V/X.
(Continuation of 7a.)

```
       Th:    =because he doesn't call you, but you have another one
              who calls you, he thinks of it (0.5) hh (0.5) let's say as an
              overwhelming passion hhhh
              fr[om the point of view of [attrACTIOn] and this other
  →    Cl:      [hm                      [I don- I don't know]
       Th:    (.) so far hasn't succeeded in overwhelming you=
  →    Cl:    =how can you have a- an overwhelming
  →           passion for someone and not call her?
              (0.7)
  →    Cl:    is it possible?
              (1.5)
  →    Cl:    >I don't believe so<=
```

In Extract 7b, the last increment of the reinterpretation (lines 17–20, where the therapist further makes explicit the opposite, yet complementary, attitudes of the two men as something possibly explaining why she feels "calm") is firstly interjected with an expression of doubt (line 21) and then, at its completion, responded to by the client with a countering argument (lines 23–28): by doubting Antonio's passion, she counters a substantial part of the reinterpretation she previously apparently agreed on. Furthermore, her two rhetorical questions (lines 23–24, 26) and the answer to them provided by herself (line 28) are hearable on the whole as a complaint about Antonio's conduct. Such a complaint is misaligned to the point of the reinterpretation, which puts in the foreground the positive side of her situation. So, an agreeing response (lines 9–13) is turned into misalignment and, indirectly, disagreement (lines 21, 23–28).[2]

This case demonstrates the possible unreliability of clients' claims of agreement with therapists' reinterpretations – such unreliability being oriented to by the participants throughout the course of action in which the claims are produced. In this case, for instance, by insisting on explicating his view despite the client's repeated claims of agreement, the therapist deals with them as if they were not sequence-closure relevant and thus treats them as possibly unreliable.

This can be a reason why therapists often extend their reinterpretations through subsequent turns or turn constructional units and thus provide further space for clients' responses. In Extract 7a–b, by progressively extending his reinterpretation (from lines 1–8 to 14 and lines 17–22) and providing many opportunities for the client to respond (lines 10, 12, 15, 25, 27), the therapist allows her the possibility of turning an initial emphatic and seemingly full agreement with his reinterpretation into an altogether different response to it.

The emergence of such clients' contradictory stances towards therapists' reinterpretations is a major phenomenon from a clinical perspective (Guidano, 1987). And it points to the importance of the different kinds of clients' agreeing responses to which the last section of this chapter is devoted.

Extended agreements

In our corpus, after having agreed with therapists' reinterpretations, clients sometimes account for their agreement by offering evidence, which can take

[2] Such a reversal of the client's stance can be better understood by taking into account the paradoxical character of the therapist's proposal: he has been suggesting (1: *perhaps. . .*) that a somehow awkward and complainable attitude of the client's lover (passionate, yet absent) gives her some emotional benefit.

different forms. In some cases a personal narrative is offered (Bercelli, Rossano & Viaro, forthcoming). In other cases, the evidence is offered in a non-narrative form.

After both kinds of extended agreements, therapists regularly expand the elaboration sequence through comments (often favourable ones), follow-up questions, further reinterpretations, or a combination of these, and thus show that such clients' responses are valuable contributions to the therapeutic work. Though we do not extensively deal with therapists' treatment of clients' responses in this chapter, it is an important theme for future research (see Peräkylä, 2005; this volume). Here is an example of the second kind of extended agreeing response: agreement + evidence in a non-narrative form.

Extract 8a B/F, 8.
(This extract comes shortly after Extract 4 and refers to the same symptom dealt with in Extract 4.)

```
     Th:  (so) what's come up as well (0.5) is this- h (.) interesting
          thing.=so then (0.3) the fact of being at ta:ble, (1.0) and
          being a bit (.) caged (.) at ta::ble
→    Cl:  at this point, thinking back it might be.
     Th:  it might be that you feel- then you resolve it
     Cl:  by getting up=
     Th:  =by getting up and getting out (.)
     Cl:  o[f
     Th:   [of the cage.
→          (3.0)
→    Cl:  °yes.°
→          (5.0)
```

In Extract 8a, an increment to a previously started reinterpretation is shown (lines 1–9). It is marked as a therapist's view by the inferential "what's come up" (line 1), the evaluative component "interesting" (line 1), the metaphorical term "caged" (line 3), the speculative "it might be" (line 5), and again "the cage" (line 9), referred to the family or family routines. The therapist had previously linked the client's disturbing thought (of assaulting his wife with a dinner knife) to a feeling of being "caged" in family life, and is now suggesting that a feature of the narrated episodes fits with his explanatory reinterpretation: by getting up and leaving the table, the client manages to "resolve it" (where "it" can be interpreted as both the feeling of being caged and the previously mentioned aggressive thought).

The client first interjects the therapist's reinterpretation with an agreement, though expressed in terms of possibility (line 4: ". . . it might be"), and then, at the completion of the therapist's statement and after a silence (line 10), responds to it with an agreement token (line 11), followed by a lapse (line 12). By abstaining from talking during these silences, the therapist allows for a more extended response from the client, which is finally provided – as shown in Extract 8b below.

Extract 8b B/F, 8.
(Continuation of Extract 8a.)

```
12          (5.0)
13  Cl:     h °at this point right? (0.5) I think that the birth° of my
14          second son right? because then (.) not- he'll gr[ow
15  Th:                                                     [heh heh
16  Cl:     it: it: makes me:: feel this aggressiveness because:: it cages
17          me °in my opinion, even more.°
18          (1.5)
19  Cl:     °I don't know.°
20          (1.0)
```

After having agreed with the therapist, in Extract 8b the client accounts for his agreement with him. He refers to a life event, his wife's pregnancy, which was not mentioned in the previous therapist's reinterpretation, and forwards it as supporting evidence (lines 16–17: "because it cages me . . . even more"). It is, moreover, a kind of evidence that was not considered by the therapist, who referred only to current family routines and commitments, rather than to the future prospected by this major change in family life.

Notice another feature of the client's response: the evidence in support of the therapist's reinterpretation is presented by the client as something that he has considered from this perspective right at this moment, just after the therapist's last increment to his reinterpretation (line 13: "at this point right? I think . . ." uttered in a low voice).[3] This makes the previous rather long silences (lines 10, 12), before and after the low-uttered agreement token, retroactively hearable as silences during which the client's idea has emerged. And the client's hesitations and low voice utterances throughout his response (lines 10–20) convey the same sense of an idea under construction. Such design features are not unusual in talk in interaction and can have various functions. But here, together with the other topical and sequential features described above, they characterize the client's response as displaying a change of perspective about the talked-about matters, and moreover a change triggered by the therapist's previous reinterpretation.

Let us now consider how the therapist takes up the client's response. As already noticed, he leaves large conversational space to it: he remains silent

[3] A similar phenomenon has been observed in a client's response to a psychoanalyst's interpretation (Peräkylä, 2005, p. 170). Notice also how both Th and Cl subsequently refer to what Cl says he thinks (lines 13–17) as something that came to Cl's mind (line 24: it came to you; line 26: it couldn't not come to me), thus describing it as sort of a "sudden thought" occurring to Cl.

in four successive transition relevant places (lines 10, 12, 18, 20), produces a short laughing affiliation (line 15) to a notably ironic passage of the client's response (line 14: "he'll grow"), and then, at its completion, emphatically aligns to it, as shown in Extract 8c.

Extract 8c B/F, 8
(Continuation of Extract 8b.)

Cl: °I don't know.°
(1.0)
Th: let's put a °question mark on it, <my second child (0.8) cages
me?>° ((articulating the words))
(1.0)
Th: it came to you eh?
(0.8)
Cl: y:es, because:: it couldn't not come to me, the first made
me feel::: in- in a state of terrible agitation,
Th: oh: (.) yes, it's true!=

The therapist, here, openly displays his appreciation of the client's *co-elaborative* contribution: he formulates it (the formulation being prefaced by a reservation at line 21: "let's put a question mark on it," which matches the previous client's reservation at line 19) and most probably writes it down, as suggested by his way of slowly uttering the formulation (lines 21–22); explicitly credits it to the client (line 24: "it came to you eh?");[4] and then responds to an increment of the client's contribution with an emphatic assent (line 28; "yes, it's true!").

Moreover, the assent is "oh"-prefaced. Through this "oh," which usually indicates a change-of-state of its utterer (Heritage, 1984a), the therapist displays both his change of orientation after the latest information from the client and an independent access to it (Heritage & Raymond, 2005): in fact, that information had already been given by the client in an earlier session. In this way the therapist displays his appreciation of the client's response, by showing that without it he would not have remembered that relevant information.

Such an uptake of the client's response fits with the way the client has responded to the reinterpretation: both participants deal with the response as something worth special consideration. And, in fact, the subsequent last part of this session and a large part of the next session will be devoted to the contents of the client's response (data not shown).

Our analysis of this example illustrates how clients, through their extended agreements with therapists' previous reinterpretations, can accomplish a variety of tasks: Firstly, they can show how they understand

[4] Which is hearable as a positive comment insofar as in previous sessions this therapist has often positively valued the "free" expression of views by this client.

and agree with the reinterpretations they are responding to. Showing understanding and agreement is quite a different kind of action from simply claiming them (Schegloff, 1984). We have previously argued that, in psychotherapy, therapists' reinterpretations can be hard to agree or disagree with for clients, and for this reason, clients' acknowledgment tokens can be treated as acceptable responses. This is also why mere claims of agreement from clients can be unreliable, and more extended responses can be usefully pursued by therapists – as shown by our analysis of Extracts 7a–b. Therefore, the distinction between claiming and showing understanding and agreement is of special importance in psychotherapy.

Secondly, through the evidence provided by accounting for their agreement, clients can corroborate the views proposed by therapists. Thirdly, clients can develop the therapists' proposals by extending their validity to a wider range of life events and experiential fields: in our illustrative example, for instance, the evidence provided by the client regards a major life event and field of family life which had been utterly ignored by the therapist in his previous reinterpretation.

Finally, we can note that through their responses to reinterpretations, clients can display a change of perspective on their own events and experiences, and display it as triggered by the therapists' utterances. Such changes are, quite obviously, precious stuff in psychotherapy, especially when manifestly triggered by therapists' interventions. Indeed, one of the institutional tasks of therapists' actions is to facilitate such changes.

In an other kind of clients' extended agreements, where the accounting evidence is provided through personal narratives, similar achievements can also be attained (Bercelli, Rossano & Viaro, forthcoming). Our analysis of this particular case, however, does not claim to do anything more than illustrate what can be done through clients' responses to therapists' reinterpretations.

Conclusions

In this chapter, we have focused on clients' responses to an important kind of therapists' action, achieved through statements which are grounded in previous clients' talk and propose therapists' reinterpretations of clients' events. We have argued that the design and sequential features of these actions are distinct from formulations, as generally understood in the CA sense, and make relevant a wider set of clients' responses.

Our analysis of a single example of "extended agreement" has illustrated some tasks that can be accomplished through such responses. In particular, we have shown how clients can actively contribute to the elaboration initiated by the therapist. Rather than simply claiming acceptance of therapist's reinterpretations – a kind of clients' uptake we have shown to be of dubious value – clients can do much more. They can display their understanding of and agreement with therapists' reinterpretations, provide evidence supporting them – evidence possibly unknown or ignored by therapists – and thus develop, enrich and partly modify therapists' reinterpretations. We have also shown how therapists, for their part, firstly allow for and even pursue such extended responses, and then, when they are provided by clients, welcome and deal with them as important contributions to the therapeutic work. Future research will focus on how therapists deal with and possibly exploit disagreeing or other relevant extended responses from clients.

We hope to have shown that something more than accepting the therapists' proposals, on the one hand, or rejecting or resisting them, on the other hand, is at stake in this specific juncture of psychotherapy interaction: namely the possibility for clients to show what they make of the therapists' proposals, and how, by extensively responding to them, they possibly change their perspectives about their own events and experiences.

4 Lexical substitution as a therapeutic resource

John Rae

Introduction

This chapter examines a counselling psychology psychotherapy session and reports on how the therapist occasionally produces turns that correct, or more generally offer alternative words for, just-prior expressions produced by the client. These proposals may rephrase something that the client has said in a contrasting way or in a more explicit way.

This chapter, in common with other contributions to this book, draws on conversation analysis (CA). Specifically, it draws on CA work on the organization of repair to show that, structurally, some of the corrections used are amongst the stronger forms of repair types that occur in talk. Although such choices might appear unexpected in psychotherapy, the analysis shows how these repair formats are in fact appropriate to certain tasks within the psychotherapeutic session; in particular encouraging the client to talk more explicitly and openly about her feelings (the client in the data I will present is female, and the therapist is male[1]). Two dimensions can be identified in talk that recomposes just-prior talk: a dimension that corrects that prior talk and a dimension that shows an understanding of it. Both these dimensions may be present in the therapist's articulation of alternative ways of saying things: he displays that he is monitoring the client closely, but he also suggests that the client should express her feelings more explicitly. I compare and contrast the use of such proposals with talk that challenges or disagrees with things that the client says.

Whether or not psychotherapists should take issue with client's talk has been tackled in different ways by different therapeutic models. Ellis' Rational Emotive Therapy (one of the major influences on cognitive behavioural therapy, Beck, Rush, Shaw & Emery, 1979), grew out of Ellis' impatience with classical psychoanalysis, and is explicitly founded upon

[1] I am grateful to the client and the therapist for making their session available for analysis. Examination of a number of points considered here has benefited very much from discussions at CA and Psychotherapy conferences in Manchester and Helsinki and at a panel at the IPrA meeting in Riva del Garda.

the principle that the therapist should argue with clients when they say things that the therapist believes are incorrect or problematic (Ellis, 1962). By contrast, some other therapeutic models are less confrontational; indeed one of the core principles of person-centred therapy is that the therapist should adopt a perspective of "unconditional positive regard" towards the client.

The data examined in this chapter come from a single therapy session that was video recorded for training purposes. The therapist in this session is in Extracts 2 and 7 referred to as "Michael." He is a very experienced counselling psychologist who uses a model known as integrative psychotherapy, which seeks to draw on features of the major psychotherapeutic models. The model places particular emphasis on the therapeutic relationship; practitioners of this approach are often said to work "relationally." However, rather than attempting to relate specific variables to theoretical orientation (see for example the analysis of psychotherapy supervision conducted by Holloway, Freund, Gardner, Lee Nelson & Walker, 1989), the psychotherapist's model will only be commented on when concrete specifics of the interaction suggest its relevance. In the session the client reports that the anniversary of her husband's death is approaching. The session explores the client's grief and feelings of responsibility.

Preliminary sketch of the phenomenon

Extracts 1, 2, 3 show cases in which the client produces an expression and, in the next turn, the therapist produces talk which (in addition to whatever else it does) proposes an alternative word, or a modification to a word, produced by the client.

(1) replacing a qualifier before an adjective:

Extract 1

```
Cl:  It feels a little uncomfortable
Th:  Or a lot uncomfortable.
```

(2) replacing an adjective

Extract 2

```
Cl:  It's hard talking about this Michael
Th:  Yeah I can s:ee: that (.) w- when you say har:d
     I think you mean painful
```

(3) inserting a modifier before a verb

Extract 3

```
Cl:  Tis the season to be jo:lly y'know an I say
     y'actually
```

```
24           (1.0) tis the season to be jolly and y'know
25           I can play
26 →         I can do jo- I can do jolly
27 →   Th:   Pretend jolly
28     Cl:   I can pretend jolly I can just be out there
29           y'know oh Jane she can (.) y'know she can:
30           em she can y'know arrange tha
31           (u) dinner for the team she can make sure
32           everybody gets
```

The therapist's proposal of alternative, or modified, expressions can be contrasted with cases such as Extract 4. Here, though targeting a specific word ("funny"), he is not proposing an alternative or modified expression. Rather (though conceding that there is a humorous dimension to the image) he is disagreeing that it is funny.

Extract 4

```
27 →   Cl:   Isn't that funny that just that visual image just
28           comes
29           ((glitch))
30 →   Th:   Well it's kind of funny and kind of not it seems to
31           me
```

In Extracts 1–3, then, the therapist proposes alternative words to those just used by the client, a practice I shall refer to as "lexical substitution." This practice can be considered one instance of a larger class of practices in which a speaker proposes a different version of something presented by a prior speaker.

The relevance of lexical substitution to the psychotherapeutic situation

In Extract 5 (an expanded version of Extract 1), the therapist proposes a correction to the client's description of how she is feeling in the psychotherapy session.

Extract 5 Case 1 [Or a lot uncomfortable].

```
07     Cl:   I am surviving and I am
08     Th:   But it feels (.) doesn't feel right
09     Cl:   It feels a little uncomfortable
10 →   Th:   Or a lot uncomfortable.
11     Cl:   It feels a l(hoh)ot unc(huh)omfortable actually
```

With reference to how she feels at that moment, she has said "It feels a little uncomfortable." By starting with "or," the therapist's turn shows, from its inception, that it is undertaking some form of divergence from what has just been said. Such turn-design features are an important resource through which speakers display how the turn-in-progress relates to previous talk, and how it should be heard with respect to that previous talk (see for example Schegloff, 1996b, and Schiffrin, 1987 for an alternative approach). The therapist reproduces part of the client's prior turn but substitutes an opposite qualifier namely instead of "a little uncomfortable" he proposes "a lot uncomfortable." He thus proposes that her conventional understatement can, and should, be replaced by a freer expression of feeling.

The client's description of her own experience is a paradigmatic example of what has been called a Type-A event; that is an event which is in the personal knowledge domain of the speaker (Labov & Fanshel, 1977). The position that individuals have privileged access to their own thoughts is a very widely held position in the philosophy of the mind, indeed it has been proposed as the anchor of all knowledge (Descartes, 1911/1641); though of course it is perhaps less self-evidently true in everyday action (Antaki, 2004). Within psychiatric and psychotherapeutic discourse the taken-for-grantedness of privileged access has been problematized; see for example the classic psychoanalytic discussion in Tausk (1933), and Sacks' discussion of it (Sacks, 1992a).

Another context where a speaker produces a description and another speaker then produces a second description is in the assessments of events to which both parties have access. Pomerantz (1984) shows that one way of agreeing with an assessment is by producing an "upgrade" (through a stronger evaluation term [e.g. "beautiful" > "just gorgeous"] or though an intensifier ["fun" > "great fun"] (pp. 65–66).

Extract 6

```
01 J:    T's- tsuh beautiful day out isn't it?
02 R:    Yeh it's jus's gorgeous
```

In Extract 6 though, R is producing their own assessment of the day whereas in Extract 5 the therapist is not describing how he is experiencing the psychotherapy session but is proposing a redescription of how his client is experiencing it. Thus although the client is describing how *she* feels in the current situation, the therapist corrects her. In other words, the therapist shows that, not merely does it occur to him that he can express her feelings better than she can herself but, that he is apparently engaging in remedial action: proposing an alternative, preferable expression. These features are also present in Extract 7 (an expanded version of Extract 2).

Extract 7

```
03     Cl:  °hh And then there's a part of me thinks well
04          actually it was his time to go an you can
05          philosophize you can sit
```

```
06                with it an you can say okay °hhh yi know he was
07                in pai::n he was having a h- y'know it was his time
08                to go °hhh but there's a part of you:: that just
09                feels I don't know it's pt ohhh shhh
10        (Th):   °hhh
11                (.)
12          Cl:   It's hard talking about this Michael
13    →     Th:   Yeah I can s:ee: that (.) w- when you say har:d
14                I think you mean painful
15          Cl:   Yeh it's painful talking about this it's actually
16                painful
17                because ( . ) it's real (.)
18          Cl:   It's like the movie's still ↑running
```

The client has been talking about the difficulties of talking about her husband's death and in line 12 she states "It's hard talking about this Michael." The therapist says that he understands this, indeed that he has noticed this, but then proposes that "painful" is better descriptor than "hard." This is elaborately presented as a proposal through the modal expression "I think you mean." As in Extract 5, the therapist proposes an alternative word to one which the client has used and again it is a substitution which describes affect more explicitly.

In the case of Extract 3, expanded in Extract 8 (and to be examined in more detail later); the operation performed by the therapist involves proposing an alternative version in which a lexical item is inserted such that "do jolly" (line 26) becomes "pretend jolly" (line 27).

Extract 8

```
22          Cl:   Tis the season to be jo:lly y'know an I say
23                y'actually
24                (1.0) tis the season to be jolly and y'know
25                I can play
26    →           I can do jo- I can do jolly
27    →     Th:   Pretend jolly
28          Cl:   I can pretend jolly I can just be out there
29                y'know oh Jane she can (.) y'know she can:
30                em she can y'know arrange tha
31                (u) dinner for the team she can make sure
32                everybody gets
33                their bottle of wine she can y'know (.)
```

In these cases, the lexical substitution proposed by the therapist is subsequently adopted by the client. In Extract 5 the client continues with "It feels a l(hoh)ot unc(huh)omfortable actually," in Extract 7 with "Yeh it's painful talking about this it's actually painful because (.) it's real (.)" and in Extract 8 with "I can pretend jolly I can just be out there."

Table 4.1 *The distribution of repair initiation and repair completion amongst different parties*

	Who carries out the repair?	
Who initiates the repair?	Self	Other
Self	SISR (self-initiated self repair)	SIOR (self-initiated other repair)
Other	OISR (other-initiated self repair)	OIOR (other-initiated other repair)

Lexical Substitution and other-initiated other repair and correction

In their seminal treatment of repair in conversation, Schegloff, Jefferson and Sacks (1977) point out that correction itself is one part of a larger entity, the repair segment. In repair segments repair is *initiated* (basically, the progress of a turn or sequence is interrupted). Subsequently *repair* itself may be completed (and the progress of the turn or sequence then resumes). They further point out that that the repair may be initiated by either the speaker themselves or by another party and repair itself may be carried out by the speaker themselves or by another party (pp. 364–365). The resulting combinations of whether repair is initiated by self or other, and whether repair is completed by self or other are shown in Table 4.1 and empirical examples are shown in Extracts 8–11 (reproduced from Schegloff *et al.*, 1977 and drawn from a variety of contexts).
(1) Self-initiated self repair

Extract 9 (10) [NJ:4].

```
      N:   She was givin me a:ll the people that
  →        were go:ne this yea:r I mean this
  →        quarter y'[know
      J:                [Yeah
```

(2) Other-initiated self repair

Extract 10

```
      Ken:    Is Al here today?
      Dan:    Yeah.
              (2.0)
  →   Roger:  He is? hh eh heh
  →   Dan:    Well he was.
```

(3) Self-initiated other repair

Extract 11 (13) [BC:Green:88].

```
→ B:  He had dis uh Mistuh W- whatever k- I can't
      think of his first name, Watts on,
      the one thet wrote that piece,
→ A:  Dan Watts.
```

(4) Other-initiated other repair

Extract 12 (14) [TG:3].

```
  B:  Where didju play ba:sk[etbaw.
  A:                       [(The) gy:m.
  B:  In the gy:m?
  A:  Yea:h. Like grou(h)p therapy. Yuh know=
  B:  = [Oh:::.
  A:    [half the group thet we had la:s* term wz there
      en we jus' playing arou:nd.
→ B:  Uh-fooling around.
  A:  Eh-yeah. . .
```

Schegloff, Jefferson and Sacks (1977) note a "preference for self-correction" in the sense that self-correction is, empirically, more common than other repair. And their analysis of the organization of repair permits them to articulate an explanation for this in terms of structural opportunities for repair: the first opportunity for repair is in the turn in which the trouble source occurs; the next opportunity is just after the completion of the turn in which the trouble source occurs. Thus, the turn-taking mechanism itself has the result that the person who produced the trouble source has the earliest opportunities to undertake repair. The fourth cell in Table 4.1, other-initiated other repair, may be thought of as the least congenial form of repair for two reasons. Firstly, because the other party, though initiating repair, chooses not to allow for self repair. Secondly, because they are able to carry out repair the other party shows that repair was not required in order for them to understand the trouble source. Yet, structurally, it is this form of repair that is found in the lexical substitution (Extracts 1, 2 and 3) from the psychotherapy session.

In another seminal analysis of repair, Jefferson (1987) further examines cases of other repair where one participant corrects another.

Extract 13 (3) [SF:II:7].

```
  Larry:  They're going to drive ba:ck Wednesday.
→ Norm:   Tomorrow.
  Larry:  Tomorrow. Righ[t.
  Norm:                 [M-hm,
  Larry:  They're working half day.
```

Extract 14 (6) [GTS:II:2:ST].

```
01        Ken:  And they told me how I could stick a th-uh:: Thunder-
02  →           bird motor? (0.5) in my Jeep? And I bought a fifty
03              five [Thunderbird motor.
04  →     Rog:       [Not motor, engine.
05        Rog:  You speak of [electric motor and a gasoline engine.
06        Ken:               [Okay
07        Ken:  Engine.     [Okay-
08        Al:               [Internal combus:tion.
09        Ken:  Alright, So[lookit,
10        ?:                [mhhhh
11        Ken:  I moved this thing in the Jeep, yesterday . . .
```

Jefferson refers to such cases as "exposed correction" because the correction, and the activity of correcting, comes to the conversational surface. This contrasts with "embedded correction" where an alternative reference is used by a recipient and is subsequently adopted by the first speaker. Here correction occurs *in passing* rather then explicitly, as shown in Extract 14.

Extract 15 (14a) [GTS:II:60:ST].

```
1  →  Ken:  Well-if you're gonna race, the police have said
2           this to us
3     Rog:  That makes it even better. The challenge of
4  →        running from the cops!
5     Ken:  The cops say if you wanna race, uh go out at
6           four or five in the morning on the freeway. . .
```

Jefferson reports that commonly in cases of exposed correction, the turn that carries out the correction is largely occupied with carrying out correction rather than progressing the interaction in other ways. Thus in Extract 14, line 4 Rog's "Not motor, <u>en</u>gine." offers a correction whereas in Extract 15 substitution of "cops" for "police" occurs within a turn "That makes it even better. The challenge of running from the cops!" offering his own assessment of a matter that Ken has referred to. Jefferson also shows that instances of exposed correction engender accounts and acknowledgments (Extract 13, line 3; Extract 14, line 7 in contrast to Extract 15 where Ken continues to progress his talk about what the police – "cops" – said).

In terms of previous research into repair then, the cases of lexical substitutions shown in Extracts 1, 2, and 3 involve the proposal of substitutions in forms that are isomorphic with other-initiated other repair and with exposed correction. These might be thought of as the more explicit and authoritarian forms of repair, yet this kind of organization is appropriate, I suggest, to the work of the psychotherapeutic session.

Lexical substitution as a resource for displaying understanding

Consider, as a point of departure, that other-initiated repair is one form of action in which a prior action is targeted. (Schegloff [2007] has termed such sequences "retro-sequences.") Other examples are derision and certain cases of laughter. Here an event – not necessarily designed to be laughed at or derided – becomes the target of subsequent action. Such actions operate by virtue of the pervasive sequential phenomenon that next position is a place to show what has been made of what just happened (Sacks, 1987). Generally then, subsequent action (such as subsequent talk) can hear, or claim to hear, something that has happened in a certain way and can make something of it.

In Extract 8 above the client refers to the line from the Christmas carol "'Tis the season to be jo:lly" and says that "I can do jolly" (line 26). The therapist responds with "pretend jolly" (line 29). Whilst "do jolly" certainly implies jollity as an accomplishment rather than a spontaneous authentic state, this expression is not as clear-cut as "pretend jolly" which explicitly evokes something feigned. So one practice that the therapist can engage in is restating something that the client has said but putting it in bolder relief. The client then subsequently adopts this expression in her next turn (line 28). In fact her use of the therapist's expression is marked by her producing the ungrammatical expression "I can pretend jolly" as a result of substituting the therapist's "pretend jolly" for her own "do jolly" in her "I can do jolly." The occurrence of an inexplicit expression, a more explicit rendering by a recipient, and the subsequent endorsement of that expression has been reported by Schegloff (1996b) and described as "confirming an allusion."

Extract 16 Schegloff, 1996b, p.183.
(Interview with Susan Shreve on National Public Radio concerning her recent novel.)

```
01 Edwards:   Why do you write juvenile books.
02            (0.5)
03 Edwards:   ['s that- b- (0.?) [hav]ing [children?    ]
04 Shreve:    [Because I love child[ren]. [I really do: ]=
05            =°hh I enjoy children:, °hh I started writing: (.)
06            juvenile books fer entirely pra:ctical reasons, °hh
07            (.)
08 Shreve:    [u- u-
09 Edwards:   [making money::.
10 Shreve:    Making [money
11 Edwards:          [yes ((+ laughter))
12 Shreve:    that- that practical reason hhh
13            (.)
14 Shreve:    I've been writing juvenile books for a lo:ng..
```

In Extract 16, the novelist Shreve (line 06) cites "entirely practical reasons" in her answer to Edwards' question about why she began writing certain books. Edwards responds to this by saying "making money"; thus displaying her understanding of the "practical reasons" that have been alluded to. In her subsequent turn, Shreve repeats Edwards' expression thereby confirming it as the matter to which she had alluded somewhat inexplicitly. Here, then Edwards is concerned not so much with *correcting* a prior expression, but rather in using an alternative expression to show that the prior expression has been understood and has been understood to be an allusion. In general, when a speaker produces an alternative expression to one used in immediately prior talk two dimensions are potentially relevant: one to do with understanding, the other to do with correction. (And a third dimension, concerning knowledge, may be present too: thus Ken's proffering on "engine" is, addition to being a correction, also a display of knowledge.)

In Extract 7, however, when the client says "It's hard talking about this Michael" (line 12) and the therapist responds with "Yeah I can s:ee: that (.) w- when you say har:d I think you mean painful" (lines 13–14) shows some limitations to lexical substitution as resource of showing understanding. Here the substitution is only carried out as a second action following acknowledgment and agreement with what the client has said.

Although "I can do jolly" is not an inexplicit allusion, the phenomenon of confirming an allusion shows how alternative expressions may be offered – and adopted – not so much because a prior expression was inadequate but rather to display understanding.

In the course of their discussion of other repair, Schegloff, Jefferson and Sacks (1977) point out that one reason for this format being comparatively infrequent is that for it to occur, the recipient of the trouble source understands what has been said and consequently could proceed to a next action rather than carrying out repair. They further note that the occurrence of other correction may constitute certain kinds of relationships between the speakers and the matters being talked about. The specific example that they consider is the case of joint story-telling, that is where two (or more) parties are jointly reporting something. Here, Schegloff *et al.* (1977) point out that by carrying out other correction, one party may constitute the relationship of being in a team with the other story-teller. What seems to be at issue in the expressions that are implicated in cases of confirming an allusion is another form of relationship between speaker and recipient: not one of constituting a team but rather one of being an understanding recipient.

In Extracts 5, 7, and 8 then, the therapist is showing that although he has heard the client say one thing, he considers that what the client has said could, or should, be formulated differently. An alternative repair organization would be for the therapist to initiate repair (that is to propose that an alternative expression is appropriate) but to leave it to the client to supply it. However such an organization would not permit the therapist to accomplish the action of offering a different perspective; it would be a matter of implicating that the client should find an alternative expression. This would simply propose something about the adequacy or appropriateness of the expression that the client had used.

Nevertheless there are cases where the client does respond to the therapist by producing a different expression, for example in Extract 17.

Extract 17

```
     Cl:  °(t)hh %Yeah%[2] and you know I don't want to come
          here and cr:y: %about it you know because actually
          (.) °hh that's not (.) what I'm here for really I'm
          here to I don't want to be here to (.) to
          actually (.) poor me.
          I don't want to sit here in poor me (.) cos I'm a
          strong woman (.)and you know I: I'm a survivor
→    Th:  So if I see you cry then (.) [(what)
→    Cl:                               [Then I'm weak
          (1.2)
```

Having been tearful, the client says that she has not come to the session to cry and she asserts a resourceful, non-pitiable identity: "I'm a strong woman (.)and you know I: I'm a survivor." Whilst this might be seen as a positive assertion, and something perhaps to be endorsed, the therapist does not encourage this upbeat trajectory. Instead, he chooses to examine the implications of her crying: "So if I see you cry then" and what this means for her. Nevertheless, although she offers a different characterization of herself, the therapist's talk appears to be oriented to unpacking what she has said rather than with getting her to correct it.

By offering an alternative expression, whilst there may be dimension of correction, the therapist is able to display that they have understood what the client has said. Thus offering alternative expressions contributes to the therapist's identity as an attentive and active recipient of the client's talk.

Two further points should be noted. In some cases details that the therapist is drawing on – and thereby invoking in proposing alternative expressions – do not reside solely in the local features of the client's talk as is the case in Extract 15. Here, "pretend jolly" can be offered as an alternative to "I can do jolly" without any particular knowledge of features beyond that phrase. However, by contrast Extracts 1 and 2 ("a little uncomfortable" > "a lot uncomfortable" and "hard" > "painful") involve alternative expressions based on broader features of the client's conduct (i.e. other things they have said and, perhaps, aspects of their nonvocal conduct).

Secondly, it can be noted that the therapist's alternative expressions involve more explicit or extreme versions of things that the client has referred

[2] % signs indicate tearful voice.

Table 4.2 *Summary of therapist's substitutions*

Extract	*Client's expression*	*Therapist's substitution*
1	a little uncomfortable	a lot uncomfortable
2	hard	painful
16	I can do jolly	pretend jolly

to, as summarized in Table 4.2. This suggests that the therapist is showing that the client may, and should, state her feeling explicitly rather than, for example, using the kind of conventional understatement shown in Extract 1.

There is some evidence that the therapist's redescriptions are associated with more explicit expressions of feeling from the client. In Extract 8, following the therapist's redescription, the client proceeds to a much more vivid version of what is glossed by her saying "I can do jolly." In particular, she moves from "I can" to "he can" and she lists responsibilities involving arrangements and ensuring things for significant numbers of people – "the team" and "everyone": "she can y'know arrange the dinner for the team" and "she can make sure everybody gets their bottle of wine." Thus doing jolly involves meeting rather onerous expectations that appear to be placed on her by other people.

One feature of repair in general is that commonly the progressivity of the sequence in progress (or in some cases even the turn in progress) is suspended while repair is carried out. This is one reason why repair can be delicate in everyday talk and it lies behind Sacks' celebrated analysis of how the initiation repair might be a way of avoiding giving your name (Sacks, 1992a, pp. 6–7). Nevertheless one interactional motivation for repairing a client's lexical choice, or proposing a word substitution, might be to facilitate a certain form of talking. There is a comparison here with certain kinds of language-learning environments, for example where a language teacher will engage in repair and correction rather than allow a sequence to progress (Seedhouse, 2004). By contrast though, Wong (2005) shows how native speakers of a language may withhold the correction on non-native speakers' errors thereby "side-stepping" grammar. Kurhila (2001; 2004) shows how native speakers' corrections of non-native speakers' grammatical errors often occur *en passant* thereby avoiding them becoming the focus of the interaction. She proposes that native speakers may use other-correction formats because these do not open up repair sequences, which would delay the progression of the sequence in progress and which would suggest a teacher-like identity.

To summarize, on occasion the therapist produces talk that proposes alternative expressions to the lexical choices that the client has made. Such talk

(a) occurs in the next turn to the talk that it targets
(b) occurs in a turn that is occupied largely with carrying out that proposal rather than progressing the talk in other ways
(c) is followed by talk from the client that adopts the proposal.

These substitutions appear to accomplish three things: (a) they show that the therapist is monitoring the client's talk very closely; (b) they show that the therapist is making sense of the client's talk (and perhaps other conduct) very closely; (c) they propose clients should express their feelings in an more explicit, unvarnished, way.

Clearly the design of the therapist's substitutions is far from confrontational; it contrasts with such contexts as courtroom cross-examination (Drew, 1992) and "talk radio" (Hutchby, 1992). Rather, the talk observed is an example of a system that permits the expression of contrary positions in a non-disputatious way (see Garcia, 1991, on mediation hearings).

Disagreements and formulations

Whilst therapists' practices invariably trade off clients' talk, in particular through proposing alternative versions to one produced by the client, there are two groups of practices which show important contrasts with lexical substitution. These are (a) the use of the client's word choices in the way in which a therapist may build a disagreement and (b) the use of formulations.

So far, the analysis has considered therapists' substitutions involving specific lexical choices. However, as briefly shown in Extract 4, reproduced with more context as Extract 18, the therapist may, in a next turn, target a specific word "funny," but does not propose an alternative redescription.

Extract 18 Case 4 [kind of funny and kind of not].
(The client has described how, as a little girl, she fed some younger siblings.)

```
     Th:  I don't know what Gerbers are
     Cl:  It's like baby food (hih) [(hah)
     Th:                            [ah
     Cl:  An just feeding one and feeding the other
          yiknow just
          like having to be mum at four (hih)(hah)
     Th:  (gh)mm
  →  Cl:  Isn't that funny that just that visual image just
          comes
          ((glitch))
  →  Th:  Well it's kind of funny and kind of not it seems to
          me
          (.)
  →  Cl:  W[ell
  →  Th:   [Its all very well if your turn comes to be
```

fed
(1.0)

The client says, of "a visual image" of a past event; or perhaps of the coming to mind of that image: "isn't that funny." The therapist says "Well it's kind of funny and kind of not." This proposes that whilst there is a humorous dimension to the image there are features of the situation depicted that are not at all funny. Here the therapist is displaying a problem with the client's assessment rather than proposing an alternative description or proposing that the description stands in need of remediation. By starting with "well," the turn which accomplishes this challenge is designed to show that a stance is being adopted which is different to the stance adopted by the prior turn. Furthermore it ends by using a modal expression "it seems to me" to relativize that stance (Rae, 2005).

Extract 19 shows a further case where a modal expression is used in the construction of a disagreement.

Extract 19

Cl: ab(h) out (huh)! (0.6) and um for me Christmas is a
sad time.
(.)
(t) %co:s% my husband ↑died three days after
Christmas.
Cl: °hh So I have a lot of pai:n there °hhh an I
want I don't want to go there (.)
I don't wanna talk about that because (.)
that's done that was before
→ Th: But my sense is that (.) you are there (.)
right now.
→ <just having (.) touched on it
(.)
→ Cl: Yeah.
Th: [An that you would like it to be (.) done
Cl: [(An d'you know)
Cl: I'd like it to be finished I'd like to be over with
I'd like that °hh okay that story's over now
°h an I'm in a new story °h but that story is
still impacting on me at this point in time
°h cos I'm saying okay

In this extract the client says, with reference to her husband's death "I don't want to go there (.) I don't wanna talk about that" and then says "because (.) that's done that was before." However the therapist challenges this by saying "you are there (.) right now." This is a particularly significant formulation since it is one that seeks to characterize aspects of the client's situation (see Antaki, Barnes & Leudar, 2005). Again, a turn-initial element, in this case "but," shows that this turn is going to undertake contrastive work. In addition, the contrastive assertion "you are there" is delivered through a modal expression "my sense is that" such that the assertion is presented as something coming from the therapist's perspective.

In Extracts 18 and 19 then, lexical features of the client's talk are used in the therapist's intervention. The client's lexical choice may be reproduced, for example "funny" as in "isn't that funny" > "Well it's kind of funny and kind of not," or a contrast may be built to reflect their choice of words, for example "right now" contrasting with "that's done that was before" in "I don't wanna talk about that because (.) that's done that was before" > "But my sense is that (.) you are there (.) right now." However here, unlike the cases of lexical substitution, the therapist is drawing on the client's talk in order to disagree with what the client has said, rather than to propose an alternative phrasing of what she has said.

The use of formulations (Garfinkel & Sacks, 1970; Heritage & Watson, 1979) by psychotherapists has been studied extensively (for example Davis, 1986; Hak & de Boer, 1996). One feature of formulations is that, though responsive to the clients' talk, they routinely use expressions not present in that talk – or as Davis 1986 points out – they may reformulate the clients' talk in such a way as to delete political issues and transform them into matters of individual psychology (see also Antaki, Barnes & Leudar, 2005; Antaki, this volume). In his analysis of therapy with children, Hutchby (2005) has shown how, in summarizing a child's answer to a previous question, the therapist may modify the child's talk to arrive at a more therapeutically relevant formulation. Formulations are present in the session analyzed here. Before the talk transcribed in Extract 20 the client has been describing her feeling that she could have prevented her husband's death. She goes on to describe feelings of guilt about this, and about her not being there when he died (lines 21–24). The therapist's response to this involves articulating a belief that he implies can be inferred from the client's talk.

Extract 20

(The client has been describing how she feels that if she had been with her husband she could have prevented his death.)

```
21        Cl:  °hh So I'm left holding that guilt around
22             the fact that (1.6) he died
23             (.)
24        Cl:  [an he died with me me not being there:
25             (.)
26        Th:  [s-
27   →    Th:  So in your mind you (2.6) you should (.) have the
28             power of life and death
29             (1.5)
```

```
Cl:  °snh No::. that's that's I don't mean that it's not
     like (0.5) I'm just holding something there (.) °hh
     (.) an I
     feel a huge guilt (.) a h:u::ge guilt °h that (.) I
     couldn't make it better
```

As with Extracts 18 and 19 the therapist's turn contains a turn-initial element that proposes that his turn stands in a specific relationship to the client's talk to which it is responsive. Here, by starting with "so" the therapist proposes that what he is about to say draws on what the client has just said. In addition, the turn is constructed with a perspective-marking expression "in your mind." The therapist's response constitutes a challenge to the client's prior talk because it formulates what the client has just said as a belief but does so in a very exaggerated version: he suggests that the client is subscribing to a position which is absurdly strong.

In addition to challenging specific lexical items then, the therapist on occasion challenges beliefs ascribed by (or attributable to) the client. These challenges to beliefs have a Socratic character to them: confronting the client with the implications of what they have said. However, they show a further therapy-related feature. In Extract 19, the modal expression "my sense is that" formulates the subsequent description "you are there" (i.e. in the painful "place" to do with her husband's death) as a description that is offered from his perspective. To this the therapist adds "right now" thus invoking a sense of the current situation and to how her talk in the situation is connected to events in her past "just having touch on it." Such reference to the current situation also occurs in Extract 19 where the therapist formulates her belief about herself with respect to crying in terms of "if I see you cry." He thereby invokes the here-and-now relationship. These features are consistent with the relational orientation of the therapist. Put prosaically, the relationship between client and therapist in the current setting reflects and invokes other relationships within the client's experience.

Compared to practices of disagreement (Extracts 18 and 19) and reformulation (Extract 20), lexical substitution may seem a rather minor practice: the operations of the therapist's work appear to be very local indeed (concerning just one lexical term) and the therapist's advances very little in terms of his own perspective. Nevertheless the economy and limited scope of lexical substitution is consistent with them being a resource to facilitate the client's expression of her feelings. They provide a resource for helping to establish (a) what kind of talk is possible or appropriate in a psychotherapeutic setting – and how it might differ from talk in everyday settings; (b) the therapist's mode of participation and thereby the aspects of the relationship between client and therapist.

A central feature of the practice of proposing alternatives to the client's lexical choices is that the client's talk, indeed her very words, are a resource for the therapist to design his turns. Peräkylä (2004a) identifies how talk that delivers a psychoanalytic interpretation can be built to include the client's lexical choices, a phenomenon that he refers to as the "circulation of figures," thus establishing "a match between the different domains of experience" (p. 289). However, in the case of lexical substitution the incorporation of client's prior talk can be extremely economical – for example just one word from the client's talk, such as "jolly" can be replaced by "pretend jolly." This economy is possible through the sequential organization of lexical corrections: namely in the turn immediately following the talk that they target. As therapeutic interventions, they thereby contrast with another practice that has been identified in psychoanalytic therapy, namely the delivery of an interpretation through an "interpretative trajectory" which extends over several turn-constructional units (Vehviläinen, 2003a).

Conclusion

A general feature of interactions between members of institutions and members of the public, or users of the services of that institution, concerns how talk should be designed and organized. For example *advice giving* has been examined in a number of contexts such as call-in radio (Hutchby, 1995); interactions between health visitors and first-time mothers (Heritage & Sefi, 1992) and AIDS counselling (Silverman, 1997). Peräkylä and Vehviläinen (2003) have proposed that whilst sociological and everyday thinking often considers members of institutions to be equipped with domain-related knowledge, doing their work also draws on "professional stocks of interactional knowledge."

A key sector of the interactional knowledge drawn on by psychotherapists concerns a diversity of practices in which alternative versions of talk produced by the client are presented. For example, psychoanalytic interpretations, formulations and reformulations, and disagreements all involve making proposals which are responsive to a client's talk but which differ from it in a range of respects. This chapter has examined a counselling psychology psychotherapy session and reported on how the therapist produces turns that propose an alternative word to one that the client has used and which thereby redescribe something that the client has said. This may be used to redescribe affect in a more explicit way. I identified two dimensions in talk that proposes different expressions to prior talk: a dimension that corrects that prior talk; and a dimension that shows an understanding of it. Both these dimensions may be present in the therapist's articulation of alternative formulations: he displays that he is monitoring the client closely, but he also suggests that the client should express her feelings more explicitly.

Although seeing a therapist propose rephrasings of a client's talk might be an unexpected feature of the kind of psychotherapy that draws on a person-centred approach, such respecifications can be a vehicle for conducting aspects of the psychotherapeutic work (in particular, facilitating the client's expression of her feelings). Furthermore, respecification brings to the surface of the interaction the terms in which a matter raised by the client can be restated. Consequently it is a means by which "active listening" can be accomplished by the therapist. Respecification is thus one way in which interaction furnishes the means through which the participants' therapy-relevant identities are established and the therapeutic relationship is constituted.

5 Resisting optimistic questions in narrative and solution-focused therapies

Clare MacMartin

In a recent paper, McGee, Del Vento, and Bavelas (2005) wrote about how therapists' questions constitute a form of intervention. By that, they mean that therapists' questions often carry with them a framework of presuppositions that constrain the client to answer in such a way as to ratify, and hence to affiliate with, the presuppositions informing the questions. Such affiliation involves the co-construction or sharing of the perspective of the therapist. But sometimes clients resist sharing therapists' perspectives, a situation known to even highly experienced therapists: "What therapist is not familiar with the experience of feeling his or her body tense as a client replies with 'yes, but' to everything that is discussed?" (Lipchik, 2002, p. 17).

How much more stressful, then, might it be for training therapists to manage such resistance? The impetus for the particular study on which this chapter is based was provided by a masters student in a university-based programme in couple and family therapy. As part of their internship, students in this programme work as individual therapists, and sometimes as co-therapists, providing counselling that is supervised by a programme faculty. This student was participating in a research project I was conducting using conversation analysis (CA) to study therapy interactions between training clinicians and their clients. When handing me the small audio recorder on which her most recent session with a client had been taped, the student remarked with discouragement that she had found that session especially challenging but could not exactly put her finger on what had been so difficult. I promised the student that I would try to identify the trouble.

What I uncovered in my analysis of that session turned out to be part of a wider phenomenon in a sample of ten individual counselling sessions involving four clients and five trainee clinicians. Clients often disaffiliated with certain questions posed by their trainee therapists. These questions asked clients about their strengths, abilities, and successes in addressing the issues that brought them to therapy. I called this class of questions "optimistic questions" due to the optimistic cast of the presuppositions embedded in them.

Although any therapy or therapist may ask optimistic questions, my study focused on questions grounded in the constructive psychotherapy models of narrative therapy (e.g. D. White, 1993) and solution-focused therapy (e.g. Lipchik, 2002), two of the clinical models learned by interns in the programme. In these frameworks, which de-emphasize a problem-centred orientation in order to stress clients' competencies and successes (Hoyt, 1994), optimistic questions are used frequently and hence are routinized. To see if CA might be of assistance in future training, I decided to explore the design of such questions and the misalignment of clients' responses with their optimistic presuppositions. One by-product of this exploration was the identification of what I see as broader concerns at the interface between CA and psychotherapy, even those forms of therapy that do not employ optimistic questions of the exact types appearing in my corpus.

Questions and their presuppositions

There has been longstanding discussion in the pragmatics literature of the constraining nature of presuppositions in language generally and of question presuppositions more specifically. A presupposition refers to "propositions whose truth is taken for granted in the utterance of a linguistic expression" (Green, 1996, p. 72). Linguistic structure is the vehicle by which the implied truth status of propositions is conveyed and which makes presuppositions by definition resistant to negation and disagreement (Levinson, 1983). Among those linguistic items that trigger presuppositions are questions, including *wh*-questions (Karttunen, cited in Levinson, 1983). For example, the question "Who is the professor of linguistics at MIT?" triggers the presumption *Someone is the professor of linguistics at MIT* (see Levinson, 1983). But the question also contains other presuppositions associated with its assertive counterpart, such as the existence of a linguistics department at MIT. The lawyers' question "When did you stop beating your wife?" is the quintessential presuppositional or loaded question exemplifying a brand of questioning in cross-examination designed to be resilient to witness challenge. The *wh*-format occasions an answer in the form of a date; the change-of-state verb "stop" is another form of presupposition trigger, carrying in this instance the assumption that the recipient used to beat his wife (see Levinson, 1983). Such a "quandary" question (Nevin, 1994) is so described because it is impossible for the recipient to answer the question without implicitly agreeing with the hostile propositions embedded in it. In order to refute those presuppositions, the recipient must refuse to respond to the question's agenda of date verification.

Presuppositional questions and responses of resistance have been studied by conversation analysts in a variety of institutional contexts, including courtroom interactions (e.g. Drew, 1992; Ehrlich & Sidnell, 2006), television and radio news interviews (Clayman & Heritage, 2002), and AIDS counselling sessions (Peräkylä, 1995). Of particular relevance to my investigation in the sections that follow is prior work on the features of question design and evasive answers. This work has studied presuppositions in relation to adversarial questions posed by interviewers in news interviews (Clayman & Heritage, 2002) and therapists' questions about "dreaded issues" in AIDS counselling (Peräkylä, 1995).

The design of optimistic questions

Optimistic questions in my corpus consisted of over fifty queries therapists posed to clients that were built so as to prefer answers from clients that affirmed their agency, competence, resilience, abilities, achievements, or some combination thereof. Projectables invited by such questions included action, event and person descriptions, and mental predicates of various kinds. The verb tenses of these questions referred to clients' past, present, future, or hypothetical experiences and attributes. Most questions appeared in the form of interrogative *wh*-questions (e.g. "What skills helped you be able to do X?"); however, one therapist also used a form of declarative *wh*-question, beginning with the statement "I am curious" followed by an embedded *wh*-clause (e.g. "I am curious about what skills helped you be able to do X"). Both the therapist and the client oriented to this declarative form as a question such that a non-response to it was treated as accountable.

The most frequent interrogative pro-forms employed were *who*, *what* and *how*, especially *what* and *how*. A much smaller subset of optimistic yes–no interrogatives (YNI) (see Raymond, 2003) was also identified. However, YNIs are not reported here for two reasons. First, they were relatively rare (such questions are less open-ended than *wh*-questions and hence do not invite client elaborations integral to constructive psychotherapies). Second, they did not pose difficulties for clients in disaffiliating with an optimistic rendering of their lives. Presuppositions vary in the degree or *depth* to which they are embedded in a question (Clayman & Heritage, 2002). A YNI optimistic question such as "Do you have skills that helped you be able to do X?" permits a type-conforming negative response "No" that manages to answer the agenda of the question while also refuting any of a range of its propositions, such as the possession of skills or the accomplishment of X. In contrast, the more deeply embedded presumption of client achievement conveyed by the question "What skills helped you be able to do X?" can be challenged only by responding in a manner that refuses to answer the question agenda.

Therapists' optimistic questions were delivered in simple and prefaced versions (see Clayman & Heritage, 2002). Simple questions often included propositions, sometimes in the form of clients' exact wording, incorporated from clients' prior turns elicited by preceding non-optimistic therapist questions, descriptions, or formulations. Prefaced questions each contained one or more statements prior to the actual questions, with prefatory statements contexualizing and providing relevance for the question that followed. In some cases in my sample, question prefaces also contained references to the unusual, difficult, or professional nature of the impending questions. These statements appeared designed to secure client cooperation by anticipating and addressing clients' projected resistance to the questions. The features seemed built to create agreement regarding an optimistic interpretation of the client's experience or conduct, essential in establishing the presuppositional ground of the optimistic question. Similarly, in their study of news interview questions, Clayman and Heritage (2002) noted that interviewers' questions rarely came "out of the blue," usually drawing on resources from prior answers to establish their relevance and intelligibility.

An example of a simple optimistic question appears in Extract 1. It involves a male client (Client 2) who has entered therapy complaining of chronic depression and anxiety. Prior to this segment, the female therapist has told this client, a university student living at home with his parents, that she has the sense that he "has had a number of difficult things to deal with" since childhood. She then asks him to imagine how anybody else might have coped with those difficulties. The client states that others probably would have run away from home; he says he does not think "a lot of other people would have been able to deal with it." The ensuing interaction unfolds below, with the therapist's optimistic question appearing on lines 34 to 38.

Extract 1 Client 2 Mar. 8/05 (36:41–37:21)

```
Th:  So they might have (0.2) what-what would've (0.4)
     the >kind=of-< (0.6) average person might=of
     (0.8) done in that situ↑ation
     (1.1)
Cl:  UH:: well honestly try an' (0.3) find somebody
     else to live with?
     (0.2)
Th:  Mm hm
     (0.9)
Cl:  Run away:.
     (0.2)
Th:  Mm hm
     (0.4)
```

```
14      Cl:  #↑Uh::# (0.2) ↑or:: start living on their ↑own.
15           (0.3)
16      Th:  Mm hm
17           (1.9)
18      Th:  >Wha [t (if)<]
19      Cl:        [ Or st ]ay there an:' (0.2) blow off their
20           head (.) hgh
21           (0.3)
22      Th:  Yeah
23           (0.2)
24      Th:  Yeah.=
25      Cl:  =(Man?)
26           (0.6)
27      Th:  Ye[ah]
28      Cl:    [Th]at's about #it.# (.) #Get out er stay:.#
29           (0.2)
30      Th:  Yeah
31           (.)
32      Cl:  An' deal with it.
33           (0.4)
34  →   Th:  .Hg (.) hgh=what do you think it says about you
35  →        that you've-you were able to:, (0.2) to:,
36  →        ↑not ↑leave to stay there (0.5) to make the choice
37  →        to stay: an' kind of deal with (0.2) things that
38  →        were going on.
```

The therapist's *wh*-question invites the client to describe himself in relation to a number of optimistic presuppostions about his ability to cope. The question includes the interrogative pro-form *what* and a subordinate clause in which are embedded particular presuppositions, specifically about his ability to "↑not ↑leave to stay there" (line 35) and to "deal with (0.2) things" (line 37). Both these aspects of the client's behaviour are contextualized with reference to elements that he himself has previously introduced as alternative courses of action that the average person might take in his situation. The part of the therapist's question highlighting the client's capacity to "deal with things that were going on" (lines 37–38) echoes his prior mention, "deal with it" (line 32). The element "stay" (line 37) also incorporates the prior wording of the client (lines 19, 28). This course of conduct was established by the client on lines 5 to 6 and line 14 as an option that the average person would reject in favour of running away from home. The client's previous reference to this alternative permits the therapist further to foreground the client's agency by situating him as "making the choice to stay" (lines 36–37). This decision takes on heroic implications in that the client has previously portrayed this alternative as eventuating in suicide for the average person (lines 19–20), an end to which he has not succumbed.

This optimistic question is recognizable as one associated with narrative therapy which considers alternative ways in which clients' problem experiences can be told or storied (Freedman & Combs, 1996). It invites clients to understand the ways in which problems are socially constructed in accord with dominant discourses that make people synonymous with their problems. Therapists help clients to externalize problems as separate from themselves and to reauthor their lives in accord with preferred ways of being (Freedman & Combs, 1996). The question on lines 34 to 38 is one of a range of "landscape-of-consciousness" questions (White, 1993, pp. 43–45) used to invite clients to create meaning regarding unique outcomes, actions or ideas incompatible with dominant problem-saturated stories of clients' lives. In particular, it is a unique redescription question (see Avis, 2006; Nicholson, 1995) that asks Client 2 to restory himself and his situation in terms of his successful resilience in overcoming adversity; it thereby simultaneously resists a dominant depressive story of failure and limitation.

In summary, the design of therapists' optimistic *wh*-questions included both interrogative and (less typically) declarative forms and preferred optimistically valenced answers from clients regarding their personal attributes, experiences and actions. Simple and prefaced questions were used, wherein both the prefatory statements and the questions themselves typically incorporated clients' prior talk, often repeating lexical elements verbatim (see Peräkylä, 2004a). These features worked to establish the intelligibility and relevance of questions by creating common ground for the optimistic presuppositions they contained.

Client responses that misalign with optimistic presuppositions

Disaffiliative responses by clients were those taken up by therapists as inadequate responsive actions to their optimistic questions. The majority of optimistic *wh*-questions in this sample occasioned misaligned responses from clients. The depth of embedding of the optimistic presuppositions in *wh*-questions made it difficult for clients to challenge their optimistic presuppositions while still cooperating with the powerful expectation that answers to therapists' questions should be provided. Misaligned responses fell into two broad categories of problematic responsive actions: answer-like responses (those that appeared, at least in some sense, to align with optimistic questions) and non-answer responses (those whose misalignment was displayed in the form of clients' unwillingness or inability to answer).

Answer-like responses superficially seemed to affiliate with therapists' questions but were nonetheless treated as problematic by therapists in subsequent turns. Like the evasive answers identified by Clayman and Heritage

(2002) in their news interviews, such answers appeared to exploit the trappings of aligned responding in that they frequently incorporated discursive features that were parasitic on prior questions for their meaning and relevance. Three subtypes of answer-like misaligned responses were identified: optimism downgraders, refocusing responses, and joking or sarcastic responses.

Optimism downgraders

These responses downgraded the optimistic content of the question presuppositions or otherwise sequentially *drifted* from the optimistic agenda set by therapists' questions, as in Extract 2 below involving Client 5. The female client has previously complained to her male therapist that her ex-partner has engaged in controlling behaviour toward her which has left her feeling frustrated and powerless. In the talk prior to this extract, however, she recounts an incident in which she was able to assert herself with her ex-partner and experience some control, an experience that, in line with solution-focused therapeutic practice, the therapist treats as an important exception to the problems the client has previously described. The therapist on lines 1 to 3 then asks an agency question; such questions are designed to underscore the client's experience of control (see Hoyt, 2002).

Extract 2 Client 5 Nov. 1/05 (26:26–26:37).

```
     Th:  How does it feel tuh (0.3) tuh sort of see
          a-where you have been. (0.5) °exerting yer
          influence. an an having control over (him).°
          (0.7)
 →   Cl:  ↑Feels ↑good but then I wonder. °why can't I
 →        apply it to:: (0.6) ↑other ↑areas (0.3) with him.°
```

The telegraphic turn-initial portion of the client's response "↑Feels ↑good" (line 4) appears to align with the question in its structure and its optimistic assessment; however, the conjunction "but" connects to a self-querying *why*-question (lines 5–6) that orients to limitations in the scope of the client's influence. This response thus qualifies or downgrades the positive valence carried by the optimistic question.

Refocusing responses

These misaligned responses occurred in the environment of optimistic questions designed to elicit client self-descriptions and whose presuppositions focused on clients' strengths, abilities, or actions. The open-endedness and multiplicity of elements contained in optimistic questions permitted clients in their responses to shift the focus of the questions to non-optimistically rendered constitutents or to reattribute credit for optimistic constituents to factors or persons other than themselves. For example, Extract 3 is taken from the same therapy session as Extract 1 and shows Client 2's uptake of the optimistic question analysed in Extract 1 (lines 34–38). (The # symbol indicates vocal fry or a "froggy" voice as one hears when a speaker has mild laryngitis.)

Extract 3 Client 2 Mar. 8/05 (37:10–37:30).

```
     Th:  .Hg (.) hgh=what do you think it says about you
          that you've-you were able to:, (0.2) to:,
          ↑not ↑leave to stay there (0.5) to make the choice
          to stay: an' kind of deal with (0.2) things that
          were going on.
          (0.7)
→    Cl:  Because ↑I knew ↑at the #end# my parents did
→         #have# (.) #best intentions for me# in
→         the [ir #hear]ts but.#
     Th:      [ >Mm hm<]
          (0.7)
→    Cl:  The way they-went a#bout things uh:: wasn't.#
→         (1.6) the best #way to=do=it.#
          (0.3)
     Th:  Mm hm.
          (0.4)
     Th:  °Mm hm.°
          (0.9)
→    Cl:  But ↑I ↑knew they #wanted the best for me
→         an'# (°>like<°) (2.6) #↑I dun°no#°
          (0.3)
     Th:  Mm hm.
          (0.6)
→    Cl:  You take the #good with the bad.#
```

The client here does not seem to understand the thrust of the therapist's question. He starts to answer using turn-initial "because" (line 40), which, as a subordinating conjunction, appears to display affiliation with the question. "Because" seems to begin a dependent clause parasitic upon the therapist's prior question. However, "because" is designed to answer a question about *why* the client stayed with his parents, while the therapist's optimistic question is a *what* question inquiring about the personal attributes of the client that enabled him to stay under such difficult conditions. The initial content of the answer, which focuses on the "best intentions" (line 41) of the client's parents, is optimistic in valence, but fails to respond to the therapist's second-person query about what his conduct says about *him*: "what do you think it says about you" (line 34). The client's further elaboration of his *why* response on subsequent lines (lines 45–46, 52–53) continues to topicalize his parents, first in terms of a mild complaint about them (lines 45–46), and then positively again in terms of their best intentions toward him (lines 52–53), an utterance self-aborted in mid-sentence with his admission, "I dunno" (see Potter, 1998). "I dunno" displays the client's orientation to the problematics of his response as somehow inadequate, while perhaps simultaneously managing inferences about his interests in defending parental behaviour that might alternatively be interpreted as abusive or neglectful. The client finally produces the idiomatic utterance, "You take the #good with the bad.#" (line 57) which normalizes his accommodation to his family situation. The use of the generic indefinite second-person "you" is self-referential in its scope and hence may appear to cooperate with the self-focus called for by the therapist's question. However, it turns out that the therapist explicitly treats this response as inadequate.

Joking and sarcastic responses

Occasionally, clients' responsive actions consisted of jokes or sarcastic answers. Some of these were superficially positive in their orientation to the optimistic agenda of therapist's questions. However, such responses ironicized, and hence undermined affiliation with, the optimistic presuppositions of the questions. Other joking responses overtly resisted the optimistic presuppositions of questions but in a way that still appeared to cooperate with the surface requirements of the question. Extract 4 contains Client 3's response to his therapist's prefaced unique redescription question (lines 1, 3–6).

Extract 4 Client 3 June 28/06 (29:56–30:13).

```
      Th:  So so I'm hearing-there's: some [va::]gue like
      Cl:                                  [like]
      Th:  (0.2) some va:lue, can you ex↑pand on that
           >a little bit?=like<
           what-↑what's yer sense of yerself when
           when you have value.
           (2.6)
  →   Cl:  ↑Well, (3.2) ↑I'm an egotist °>(just when I've.)<°=
  →        =↑Hgh-HA HA HA HA HA ↑HA
```

The therapist's question (lines 5–6) presupposes the client's experience of himself as having value, which has been established in his prior talk about his long-term unemployment and his plans to begin part-time work as a salesperson for a pyramid business scheme. The optimistic question thus projects a positive self-description as an answer. Client 3 responds with a self-description as called for by the question, but he undermines the optimistic presupposition of his having value by jokingly using the self-derogating category of "egotist" (line 8), which is ultimately followed by laughter. This response, which equates positive self-descriptions with boasting, seems to orient to the risky identity implications of affiliating with the therapist's question.

Clients also disaffiliated more directly with therapists' optimistic questions by displaying their inability or unwillingness to answer such questions. These strategies of resistance were more overt than the answer-like responses. Non-answer responses included complaints and the refusal to cooperate with some aspects of questions, such as their optimistic presuppositions or their agendas, the actions called for by such questions. Responsive actions sometimes included "I don't know" statements and accounts for not answering the questions as asked. Sometimes clients appeared to resist the optimistic presuppositions of the questions, while in other instances involving self-description questions, clients seemed to challenge the therapeutic relevance of question agendas asking them to articulate explicitly their own strengths, abilities, and accomplishments.

Complaining about optimistic questions

Sometimes, a client resisted answering an optimistic question by complaining about the difficulty of the question or, more infrequently, by turning the conversational tables and focusing the complaint on the questioner. For example, Client 2 refused to answer the question by calling the therapist to account for it. This interaction continues almost immediately after that appearing in Extract 3 in which the client resisted the therapist's inquiry about him by topicalizing his parents. Extract 5 below begins with the therapist's reissuing of her unique redescription question from Extract 3.

Extract 5 Client 2 Mar. 8/05 (37:44–38:11).

```
     Th:  ↑>What ↑would ↑it ↑ (was) ↑it< (0.2) ↑about you:
          that makes: (0.2) °#i-y-#° (0.6) makes it possible
          for you to be able to stay and deal with those
          things. tuh (0.2) recognize ↑you ↑know ↑that, (.)
          ↑yer parents wer:e, (0.3) in fact having yer best
          intentions in mind even though they may not have
          been, (0.3) um going about it in a way that (0.6)
          kind of (.) fit with (0.5) how you would have
          preferred,
          (2.3)
     Cl:  .pt U::M: (1.2) °what does that #say about me?#°
          (0.3)
     Th:  Yeah. (0.4) that- (0.2) .h >you know I'm I'm
          getting the sense too ↑that
          (.)
  →  Cl:  Y'a[sk that ques ]tion °y'ask that question°=
     Th:     [somebody else]
  →  Cl:  =°a lot eh? °
```

An insertion sequence begins when the client responds after a 2.3-second pause (line 73), not by answering the question on lines 64 to 72, but by asking a question of clarification on line 74 ("°what does that #say about me?#°") that incorporates some of the formatting the therapist used in her original optimistic question (Extract 3, line 34). The therapist starts responding (lines 76–77); during a brief pause in her contribution, the client begins to complain, "Y'ask that question °y'ask that question a lot eh?°" (lines 79, 81). This remark is an assessment (note the terminally positioned tag "eh") that invites agreement. It overlaps with and derails the therapist's response to the client's clarificatory question. His complaint about the frequency with which the therapist asks the optimistic question suspends, at least temporarily, the conditional relevance of his provision of an answer by making her accountable for the question. His move thereby disaffiliates with the optimistic question.

Refusing to cooperate with elements of the question

Client 2, in particular, disaffiliated at times not so much with the therapist's positive interpretation of his experiences contained in her questions but with various other elements of the presuppositions or agendas of such questions. For example, in certain instances involving questions designed to call attention to his self-efficacy by asking for personal self-descriptions, he would challenge the therapeutic relevance of those questions asking him to articulate explicitly his own strengths, abilities, and accomplishments.

One of this client's goals was to stop drinking as a way of coping with depression and anxiety. Extract 6 below begins with his joyful announcement reporting how many days it has been since he last consumed alcohol.

Extract 6 Client 2 Feb. 9/05 (27:47–27:55)

```
01      Cl:  It's been thirty-nine days eh?
02      Th:  Wow that's great.
03      Cl:  That ↑is ↑grea[t.]
04      Th:                [Ye]ah. How have you been able ta
05           ↑do this?
06  →   Cl:  ↑£I DON' KNOW:£
07      Th:  .h *HGH ↑HGH* hhh (.)↑Yeah.
08           (0.2)
09  →   Cl:  I don' know I j'st:: I stopped.
```

The client's news announcement (line 1) ends in a tag ("eh?") inviting agreement from the therapist who responds with an enthusiastic positive assessment (line 2) with which the client promptly agrees in the form of an echoic second assessment (line 3). The therapist then poses an agency question (see Hoyt, 2002) that uses the anaphoric deictic "this" (line 5) to back-reference the client's report of his achievement and to invite elaboration on how he has been able to accomplish it. The client's intial "↑£I DON' KNOW:£" response (line 6), delivered loudly in a smiling voice and in the same buoyant tone as his initial news announcement, is responded to by the therapist with high-pitched laughter and then, in a lower pitch and falling intonation, her brief receipt "↑Yeah." (line 7). The humour and high energy now dissipated, the client recycles his "I don' know" which is followed by his preferred account of his accomplishment: " I j'st:: I stopped." (line 9). This minimalist version resists the analysis and reflective self-statements called for by the therapist's optimistic question, even though his earlier contributions (lines 1, 3) clearly display his orientation to his news as jubilantly positive.

Summary

Client responses that disaffiliated with therapists' optimistic questions took one of two broad forms, answer-like responses and non-answer responses. Answer-like responses contained discursive characteristics, such as anaphoric pronouns, that at face value appeared to align with therapists' questions. Responsive actions included clients' downgrading of the optimism of therapists' questions, joking and sarcastic responses, and refocusing responses that resisted questions pursuing client self-descriptions by shifting the focus to non-optimistic aspects or by reassigning credit for optimistic aspects to factors or persons other than clients. Non-answer responses were more directly resistant in that they displayed clients' inability or unwillingness to answer therapists' questions and were frequently accompanied by accounts for not answering. Responsive actions included complaints about the question or the questioner, and clients' refusal to affiliate with aspects of questions such as their presuppositions or agendas.

The majority of optimistic questions in my corpus occasioned client responses that were taken up as inadequate in some way by therapists. However, in a number of instances, clients' answers aligned with the optimistic presuppositions of therapists' questions. A noteworthy proportion of such answers were responses to hypothetical questions. In comparison to non-hypothetical *wh*-questions in this sample, hypothetical questions held a better track record in eliciting type-conforming answers that aligned with optimistic presuppositions. Peräkylä (1995) noted the power of hypothetical questions to elicit client cooperation in addressing potentially difficult future concerns. Such questions created a sequential enclave for HIV-positive clients' responses in the form of hypothetical descriptions that could begin to topicalize such concerns; in solution-focused therapy, this sequential enclave permits clients to risk imagining a future life without pain and to articulate goals that come to constitute the solution to their problems (see Hoyt, 2002).

Therapist strategies for dealing with resistance

Therapists managed clients' disaffiliation in a number of different ways. One strategy used occasionally was to replace one form of optimistic question with another form less likely to elicit misaligned responding. More rarely, therapists would drop their optimistic questions, substituting them with more neutral questions. Another infrequent strategy involved therapists' offers to reframe or replace clients' prior misaligned contributions with more optimistic alternatives. (For psychoanalysts' ways of dealing with client resistance, see Vehviläinen, Chapter 7 this volume.)

The requirements of brevity preclude analysis of instances of these infrequent strategies. Instead, I focus my analysis here on the most common action taken by therapists: reissuing or recycling their optimistic questions, which were lexically and prosodically tailored to invite clients to produce aligned responses. For Example, Extract 7 below involves Client 3. This interaction occurs thirty seconds after the therapist posed an optimistic "therapisty-type question" asking the client to elaborate on how he is able to do things differently than in the past with respect to work. Client 3 disaffiliated with that unique redescription question by assigning credit for his ability to assume employment to its part-time nature. He thereby topicalized the pyramid-scheme business he will soon be working for, explaining to the therapist how the organization shifted its criteria to allow part-time sales people. At the start of Extract 7, he continues talking about the company.

Extract 7 Client 3 June 28/05 (23:09–23:20)

```
     Cl:  I guess they might be (uh) optimistic in their
          growth ↑rate (an' I)
          (0.2)
→    Th:  ↑But what is it? (0.3) ↑I-I'm going to try
→         my therapist question again, .hh ↑what does it
→         tell you about (0.2)↑you. (0.3) right now,
     Cl:  [Okay]:
→    Th:  [That] yer able to (0.2) to do this work. that
→         yer [  able   tuh,::    ]
     Cl:      [↑Well I'm a little] more ↑confident than I was
```

On line 4, the therapist begins asking a what *wh*-question which she self-aborts. She self-repairs her utterance by inserting a preface ("↑I-I'm going to try my therapist question again," lines 4–5) that reprises elements of her original question preface stated thirty seconds earlier. The words "try" (line 4) and the prosodically stressed "again," (line 5) orient explicitly to the failure of her prior question to occasion the sought-for response. This preface signals the recycled status of the question to come. In the reissued question, the therapist reiterates the question elements focusing on the client himself in the present. Brief within-turn pauses set off the key question elements that follow, as does prosodic emphasis on those elements: "about (0.2) ↑you. (0.3) right now," (line 6). Again using prosodic stress, the therapist introduces on line 8 ("yer able to (0.2) to do this work") the focus of the original question: the client's ability to do things differently now than in the past. The client then answers on line 10.

Recycled questions frequently incorporated material from clients' prior disaffiliative turns in a way that acknowledged (while simultaneously transforming) this resistant material in the reissued question (see Antaki, this volume). The incorporated elements often included verbatim portions of clients' misaligned contributions. More instances of the recycling of optimistic questions using elements from clients' prior turns are found in previous extracts in this chapter. For example, Extract 5 (lines 64–72) contains a reissued version of an optimistic question originally posed in Extract 3 (lines 34–38) to which Client 2 had provided a refocusing response about his parents. In the course of his elaborated response in Extract 3, the therapist offers minimal responses in the form of the continuer "Mm hm" (lines 43, 48, 50, 55) and interpolated pauses (lines 39, 44, 47, 49, 51, 54, 56) that subtly display her lack of endorsement of his response to her question. Certain features of the original optimistic question in Extract 3 are reproduced in the recycled version in Extract 5. The emphatic prosody of "you" in Extract 3 (line 34) is reproduced in Extract 5 (line 64) with a slight elongation of the vowel. It should be noted that the implied contrast evoked by "you" in Extract 3 is between the client's abilities and those of the average person, while in Extract 5 the emphasis on "you" makes clear that the question is meant to elicit the client's *self*-attributions regarding his successful coping, rather than attributions to other factors or people. "Stay an' kind of deal with things" (Extract 3, line 37) is carried forward as "stay and deal with those things" (Extract 5, lines 66–67), and in both versions of the question the client's ability is explicitly oriented to by the therapist ("you were able to," Extract 3, line 35; "able to stay," Extract 5, line 66).

Of particular note in the revised optimistic question in Extract 5 is the addition of material taken from the client's initial response in Extract 3 (lines 40–42) to the original optimistic question and his subsequent elaborations (lines 45–46; 52–53). Although the therapist's minimal responses and her subsequent reissuing of the question suggest that there was something problematic about his refocusing response in Extract 3, she incorporates in Extract 5 verbatim and formulated elements of that very response in her revision of the question. She thus acknowledges the client's experiences while employing them to stress his unusual competencies in a way that departs from his self-report. The therapist focuses on the client's perceptiveness in being able to "recognize you know that, (.) yer parents wer:e, (0.3) in fact having yer best intentions in mind" (lines 67–69). "Best intentions" is taken from the client's response (Extract 3, line 41); the gap between his parents' intentions and their actions mentioned by the client in Extract 3 (lines 45–46) is echoed by the therapist in Extract 5 (lines 69–72). "In fact" (Extract 5, line 68) gives a nod to the challenges involved in discerning others' good intentions on the basis of their less than desirable conduct. It implies that it would be understandable if the client did not impute good intentions to his parents. Thus, the therapist reissues her original optimistic question while adding further details, drawn from the client's misaligned prior turn, to underline additional competencies of the client in terms of his capacity to see his parents in a respectful, positive light despite the difficulties of this situation.

Summary

Therapists' strategies for handling clients' misaligned responses to optimistic questions most frequently involved the recycling of optimistic questions. Occasionally, an optimistic question was substituted with another type of optimistic question more likely to occasion an optimistic answer. Other infrequent strategies included the reframing of a client's response in more optimistic terms and the replacement of an optimistic question with a neutral question in which optimistic presuppositions did not figure. In most of these instances, therapists would incorporate material from clients' problematic prior responses in a way that would acknowledge clients' experiences while transforming the trajectory of the conversation in optimistic terms.

Discussion and conclusion

Optimistic questions occurred in both interrogative and, more rarely, declarative forms; these questions were built to prefer optimistically cast answers from clients regarding their personal characteristics, experiences, and actions. The questions were delivered in simple and prefaced forms that often incorporated material from prior turns, particularly those of clients, which worked to establish the questions' intelligibility and relevance.

Clients disaffiliated with the majority of optimistic questions, using answer-like and non-answer misaligned responses. Answer-like responses appeared superficially to cooperate with therapists' questions but were treated as inadequate by therapists. Clients' optimistic downgraders sequentially drifted in their content from optimism to more qualified versions. Refocusing responses occurred in the wake of optimistic questions about clients' personal strengths, abilities, or conduct and involved clients focusing their answers on either non-optimistic self-descriptions or optimistic descriptions of factors or persons other than themselves. Joking or sarcastic responses either ironicized the optimistic presuppositions of the questions or explicitly resisted them in such a way that clients still appeared to cooperate with the surface requirements of questions. Non-answer responses involved more overt displays of clients' unwillingness or inability to answer such questions. These responses usually consisted of accounts for not answering and sometimes included "I don't know" statements. Responsive actions included complaints and clients' refusal to cooperate with the questions, sometimes by challenging their therapeutic relevance, as in the case of questions occasioning clients' self-descriptions.

Therapists responded to clients' resistance most often by reissuing or recycling their optimistic questions, often utilizing lexical material from clients' intervening turns. Less frequently, they might replace one form of optimistic question with another one or with a more neutrally designed question. Another infrequent tack was to reframe the client's misaligned response with a more optimistic formulation.

I want to emphasize that the term "resistance" used throughout this chapter is employed in its pragmatic or conversation analytic sense to represent the responsive action whereby the recipient of a question disaffiliates with it in some manner. This usage diverges from a psychotherapeutic conceptualization of client resistance to therapy, a conceptualization that has itself been challenged by proponents of constructive therapies as the pathologizing of clients (e.g. Hoyt, 2002); instead, therapists are invited to consider how people change (de Shazer & Berg, 1985). Nevertheless, sequential analysis of clients' resistance to optimistic questions clearly shows that such disaffiliation is consequential for the unfolding practice of therapy (cf. Antaki, Chapter 2 this volume; Vehviläinen, Chapter 7 this volume). What can CA offer to psychotherapists working with such questions and the models that underpin them? Is a dialogue possible between CA and the professional stocks of interactional knowledge (see Peräkylä & Vehviläinen, 2003) associated with therapists' optimistic questions?

Following Peräkylä and Vehviläinen (2003), I argue that CA in this instance provides a more detailed picture of questioning practices described in the therapy literature on narrative and solution-focused therapies (e.g. Hoyt, 2002). My analysis helps specify what is problematic about such questions in terms of clients' uptake of them, and how therapists respond in turn. Clayman and Heritage (2002) found that the presuppositions of news interviewers' questions were most visible when these presuppositions were rejected by interviewees in their responses. Similarly, I discovered that the optimistic presuppositions of therapists' questions were especially salient when clients disaffiliated with them. However, the institutional contexts of recipient disaffiliation in these two instances are remarkably different. News interviews involve journalists attempting to display a neutralistic stance while posing adversarial, even hostile questions designed to challenge public figures on the air. In contrast, therapists' optimistic questions were not designed to trip up clients by inviting them to reveal failures of action or of character, but rather projected clients' strengths and accomplishments. Why were patterns of evasive answering or refusals to answer similar to those identified by Clayman and Heritage (2002) found in my corpus of therapy data?

One way in which clients challenged the optimistic content of *wh*-questions was to orient to their struggles, rather than to their competencies and successes, through troubles talk (see Jefferson, 1988; Jefferson & Lee, 1992) and complaining (see Drew, 1998; Edwards, 2005). Troubles talk is a key aspect of the social organization of counselling talk (Miller & Silverman, 1995), which is not surprising given that the canonical account for seeking help is the experience of problems that have not been ameliorated through other avenues. Troubles talk or problem talk, therefore, can be seen as the stuff of which traditional therapeutic conversation is made. That clients in my corpus of data negotiated such versions with their therapists is not surprising. However, proponents of constructive psychotherapies such as solution-focused therapy (e.g. O'Hanlon, 1993) have argued that the reification of problems in traditional psychotherapies, the related conflation of clients' identities with their problems, and the positioning of therapists as experts work to portray clients as damaged and unable to change. The attempt to shift therapy to a more optimistic perspective that is collaboratively achieved seems laudable but can be difficult in the face of clients' disaffiliation with optimistic renderings of their lives.

Interestingly, the basis on which clients legitimized their resistance to optimistic questions resonates with a value that constructive or collaborative therapies uphold: the notion that clients, not therapists, are experts on their own experience. Clients' countering of optimistic questions trades on the commonplace notion in everyday social life that people own their experiences (Peräkylä & Silverman, 1991; Sacks, 1984; Vehviläinen, 2003a; Chapter 7, this volume). Clients could draw on experience entitlements, using their epistemic authority to challenge the presumptions of optimistic questions as incompatible with their own experiences. Therapists would frequently acknowledge clients' entitlement to describe their own experiences as they see fit. Indeed, optimistic questions were often designed using clients' own prior formulations of their experiences, and therapists' reissuing of these questions would sometimes incorporate verbatim elements of clients' previous turns, including their complaints. These were taken up in a way that appeared to validate client experiences of difficulty and yet to reconfigure them in optimistic terms. Such revised questions seemed to instantiate what constructive psychotherapy identifies as the need to balance acknowledgment of clients' felt experiences and perspectives with introducing possibilities for changes and solutions (see O'Hanlon, 1993).

In my analyses, one particular source of difficulty proved to be those optimistic questions occasioning clients' self-affirmations of competence. Clients sometimes disaffiliated with the complimentary presumptions about them built into such questions. For instance, in the same therapy session from which Extracts 1 and 3 were taken, Client 2 later resisted the therapist's embedded ascriptions regarding his exceptionality, countering the premise of such questioning by denying that he was stronger than "the next person"; elsewhere, he tells the therapist that he is "no superman." In Extract 4, we saw how Client 3 affirmed a therapist's version of his abilities by jokingly disclosing his own egotism as a character flaw.

Previous CA research on everyday talk has shown that there are multiple constraints operating when people are complimented by others in everyday talk (Pomerantz, 1978). Typically, the preferred response to a first assessment is agreement. But when first assessments consist of praise directed at hearers, those recipients work to avoid self-praise (Pomerantz, 1978). In my analyses of optimistic *wh*-questions in psychotherapy talk, the preferred response is an answer that aligns with its positive presuppositions; however, in producing such answers, clients could be seen to engage in self-praise, a concern that they sometimes explicitly oriented to in their disaffiliation with therapists' questions. Actions involved in the avoidance of self-praise may be partly constituted in talk about troubles or complaints in psychotherapy, which may work to construct clients as ordinary individuals (see Sacks, 1984, on "doing 'being ordinary' ") in legitimate need of help. In displaying clients' difficulties, troubles talk may thus serve as a call for ongoing therapeutic support, albeit of a particular kind not in line with constructive psychotherapies.

Hoyt (2002) raises the possibility that clients may not be ready for the type of help that the solution-focused therapist is offering, stating that "imposition tends to produce opposition" (p. 340). Narrative therapists who find clients disaffiliating with questions asking them to describe their own strengths and accomplishments might do well to reflect on whether the therapy has moved too quickly to the phase of reconstructing a preferred narrative before sufficient deconstruction of the dominant story, including the dominant version of the client as person, has been successfully accomplished (see Nicholson, 1995). Alternatively, it might be that affirmations of clients' abilities and accomplishments in the past and present project unrealistically high expectations of client conduct in the future, expectations that the client is therefore unwilling to endorse. A bifurcated choice between a preferred story of client competence and success and a dispreferred story of limitation and failure may fail to provide a space for a more moderate self-description somewhere in between those binaries (Jean Turner, personal communication, December 11, 2006).

The CA example of multiple constraints in managing praise suggests that some key challenges in learning constructive psychotherapies may be associated with broader cultural ideas and practices constituted in everyday talk and in traditional psychotherapies. It is no wonder, then, that therapists' training can be challenging. This brings me to a discussion of two limitations associated with my corpus of data. One limitation is that it consists of only training therapists' sessions. To explore further the uptake of optimistic questions, I hope to study therapy sessions of experienced therapists to see how they manage the intricacies of bringing off such questions with clients. Preliminary findings of a discourse analytic case study involving a highly experienced therapist using narrative therapy to assist a male client with a history of intimate partner violence include evidence of the client disaffiliating at times with the therapist's optimistic questions (Denton, 2006); however, more data are needed to explore this phenomenon further. A second limitation involves the study of audio rather than video taped interactions. This precluded my analysis of the ways in which gaze, gesture and bodily alignment may have been coordinated with clients' and therapists' actions (e.g. Peräkylä, 1995).

My work extends previous CA work on constructive therapies (e.g. Gale, 1991) and on disagreements between therapists and clients in other forms of therapy (e.g. Antaki, Barnes & Leudar, 2004). Antaki *et al.* (2004) focused on disagreements about the nature of a client's problem in a cognitive-behavioural therapy session. In my corpus of data, the mismatch involves contestation not about what kind of problem is under consideration, but whether the focus of therapy should be problems at all rather than clients' successes and competencies. This is delicate interactional territory that is not specific to these types of clinical models. I believe that this study illuminates institutional tensions associated with the enterprise of psychotherapy more generally. Given that most forms of psychotherapy have, as their implicit or explicit goal, the transformation of the client's past or current experiences, the tensions between validating clients' pain and inviting more hopeful alternative visions of clients' lives may obtain across different therapeutic modalities. CA provides a powerful tool for examining how these institutional concerns are constituted in actual talk-in-interaction, and takes us one step further in understanding the practice of psychotherapeutic conversation.

6 Conversation analysis and psychoanalysis: Interpretation, affect, and intersubjectivity

Anssi Peräkylä

In this chapter,[1] I will use conversation analysis to explore some themes that are central in the clinical theory and practice of psychoanalysis. These themes include interpretation (which is a central theme in classical psychoanalytic theory), and affect and intersubjectivity (which are central themes in some contemporary psychoanalytic discussions). I will discuss these themes using two kinds of empirical material: clinical notes arising from my own psychoanalytic practice, and transcribed materials coming from a corpus of fifty-eight tape recorded psychoanalytic sessions collected by Sanna Vehviläinen and myself. Clinical notes involve the traditional method of representing interaction in psychoanalysis. The aim of the chapter is to show how the conversation analysis of tape recorded material can radically expand our understanding of the key practices of psychoanalysis.

In theoretical and methodological terms, this chapter draws upon the idea of "professional stocks of interactional knowledge" (SIKs). We (Peräkylä & Vehviläinen, 2003) have proposed that professions dealing with clients have their specific stocks of knowledge which describe and prescribe the professional interactions. We suggested that conversation analysis should enter into dialogue with such SIKs; this chapter is one effort towards such a dialogue (see also Forrester & Reason, 2006).

I should acknowledge my specific position in relation to psychoanalysis and conversation analysis. For nearly twenty years, I have been involved in doing conversation analytic research on therapeutic and medical encounters. Since 2003, I have been involved in psychoanalytic training organized by The Finnish Psychoanalytic Association. Currently, I also practise part time as a candidate psychoanalyst, doing psychoanalytic work with an intensive supervisory backing by a senior analyst. Apart from personal interest, I have been drawn to psychoanalytic training by (a somewhat

[1] I want to thank Sanna Vehviläinen for her long-standing collaboration in analysing psychoanalytic data, and also, along with Johanna Ruusuvuori and Liisa Voutilainen, for their comments upon previous drafts of this chapter.

intuitive) adherence to the ethnomethodological idea of "unique adequacy requirement." Ethnomethodologists suggest that social researchers should "learn to be competent practitioners of whatever social phenomena they are studying" (Rawls, 2002, p. 6). In conversation analysis, such competence cannot be considered as a prerequisite for successful research as, for example, the insightful research on medical consultations conducted by researchers without medical training shows (see Heritage & Maynard, 2006). However, I believe that learning the professional skills can also lead to some additional understanding in conversation analysis.

So, when researching psychotherapy, I am not an outside observer, but a (candidate) member of the psychotherapeutic community. At the same time, my research orientation is strictly conversation analytic. This "dual membership" inevitably involves risks, but I hope it also makes it possible to explicate some aspects of psychotherapeutic practice that might otherwise remain unnoticed. Although it is rather common in some other forms of psychotherapy research for the researcher also to be a practitioner (for examples, see Chapter 1), not many conversation analysts, to my knowledge, have acquired clinical training in psychotherapy. It should be added that "psychoanalysis" as the topic of this chapter is a rather contingent choice. In principle, a similar kind of analysis could be performed on any established psychotherapeutic regime (such as cognitive-behavioural therapy, interpersonal psychotherapy, or the like).

Interpretation

Doing psychoanalysis involves a specific way of hearing the client's talk, a specific way of doing inferences. This specific way of inferring has been institutionalized in the technique of psychoanalytic interpretation. A canonical definition of psychoanalytic interpretation is given by Greenson in his textbook on the technique and practice of psychoanalysis (1967, p. 39): "To interpret means to make an unconscious phenomenon conscious." The analyst hears the client's talk in terms of the unconscious phenomena that it may index, and at times, he suggests to the client what he thinks he is hearing. Greenson indeed considered interpretation as the decisive hallmark of psychoanalysis: unlike in other psychotherapies, "in psychoanalysis interpretation is the ultimate and decisive instrument," as "every other procedure prepares for interpretation or amplifies an interpretation" (p. 39).

Analysts are advised to take clinical notes; usually, as in my case, they are written soon after each session. The notes describe what happened in the session. They are a resource for the analyst's own reflection of his or her work and the client's progress, for supervision, and for case reports and other research that is done with the clinical materials. Due to my conversation analytic background, my notes may be somewhat more detailed and more often in a dialogical form than is typical. But, basically, they are ordinary clinical notes and, as such, they exemplify the way in which clinicians represent their work. Therefore, let us consider an example of an interpretation, taken from my clinical notes. The client works as a janitor in a library. He has recently decided to end the analysis, about ten months after he started it. It should be mentioned that this is a very early termination of analysis, which usually lasts several years. The client is telling a story about an alcoholic using his library. For reasons of space, some sentences have been omitted from the original notes. Cl stands for the client, An for the analyst. All data to be presented (clinical notes and segments from tape recordings) are translated from Finnish.

Extract 1 (clinical notes)

Cl: *Yesterday there was a homeless alcoholic sitting in the reading room. He stayed there from noon until late afternoon. He smelled as the alcoholics smell . . . In my mind, I was worried about him. It was a very cold day and hence I could not kick him out from the library. I was a wondering whether I should call the police. As the closing time came near, he gave me a nice surprise: he went away on his own initiative. He moved very slowly. I was worried how he would manage. Last Friday an alcoholic had been found dead nearby the library . . .*

An: *What comes to my mind is this: The alcoholic, the library, and the idea of kicking him out may have something to do with you quitting the analysis. It is as if there were something unbearable in you, something that forces you to end the analysis.*

Cl: *I don't feel that you would want me to stop the analysis . . . One can think that I myself might have a feeling that there is something so shameful in me, or the like, that I cannot continue the analysis. I don't have the strength to think about that now, I don't feel that this idea is anywhere close to me now.*

In Extract 1, the analyst (remember that these are my notes, but I will be referring to myself in the third person) hears the client's story about the alcoholic at the library in the context of the relationship between himself and the client, as indexing the imminent termination of the analysis. He proposes this hearing to the client. The analyst suggests that alongside its literal meaning, the story also conveys the client's perception of his decision to quit the analysis. The client's response to the interpretation is equivocal. He admits that in principle one could see things in the way that the analyst suggests, but he reports not having the "strength" to consider that possibility "now."

This segment of clinical notes illustrates vividly the analyst's reasoning concerning the client's talk, and concerning the client's state of mind in face of the termination of the analysis. But as a *post hoc* reconstruction of the interaction, the notes do not give us access to many aspects of the actual practices in delivering and responding to the interpretation. For example, the segment does not tell us whether, and in which ways, the analyst possibly prepared the ground for his interpretation before its actual delivery, for example through the ways in which he initially responded to the client's story. It does not reveal the ways in which he possibly chose specific words for his interpretation so as to convince the client that there indeed was a "hidden meaning" in the story that he just told. Or the exact ways in which ways the client combined, in his response, the rejection of the interpretation with its conditional acceptance.

We need more exact data, and a more rigorous method of analysis, to deal with questions like these. In studies reported recently (Peräkylä, 2004a, 2005; Vehviläinen, 2003a) Vehviläinen and I have used conversation analysis (CA) to explore the interactional ramifications of the delivery and reception of interpretations.

Vehviläinen (2003a; Chapter 7, this volume) has described in detail the interpretative trajectory leading up to an interpretation, showing how the analyst's interventions such as extensions of the client's turns and formulations of the client's talk step-by-step create a puzzle, the solution of which is the interpretation. Interpretations sometimes suggest things that would at first sight appear wild – that was also the case in the preceding clinical vignette. Analysts' ways of receiving clients' talk, for example by means of formulations, rearrange the clients' initial stories and descriptions in such ways that make the subsequent interpretations plausible and possible (see also Peräkylä, 2004a). Thus, CA work on interpretations has quite directly specified what Greenson (1976) suggested in general terms: that other procedures in psychoanalysis prepare for interpretations.

Conversation analysis also helps us to specify what happens after interpretations (Peräkylä, 2005). When clients align to the interpretation, they sometimes do that "minimally," by utterances that plainly claim their agreement (e.g. "it is absolutely true"). More often, however, clients respond to interpretation by utterances in which they take up some part of the interpretation and continue it, in the client's own terms as it were. By so doing, the clients show their acceptance and understanding of the interpretation (see Bercelli *et al.*, Chapter 3 this volume). To put it in terms of psychotherapeutic theory, this kind of response can involve such "insights" or "chains of fresh associations" that psychoanalysts consider to be the goal of an interpretation. (See Peräkylä, 2005, for the ways in which it can also involve hidden resistance toward the interpretation.) Extract 2 involves an example of an elaboration from our tape-recorded data. The client's elaboration extends to lines 27, 29, and 32, where she says, referring to her childhood: "Yes just to dance and to sing . . . so that others would be happy and pleased with me." Let us examine how this utterance comes about.

At the beginning of Extract 2, the client talks about her grief after the recent death of her partner. In examining her own feelings, she has realized that she is worried that she might get stuck in her grief. In line 18 the analyst begins an interpretation in which he makes a link between the client's current reluctance to be drawn into grieving, and her "childhood sorrows." Through the design of his interpretative statement (see e.g. "again" in line 19 and "these" in line 21) the analyst shows that he is not suggesting something entirely new but, rather, returning to a theme that the participants had been addressing earlier.

Extract 2 (tape recording).

```
01 Cl:  . . . maybe there is some kind of
02      fear that I . . .
        ((five lines omitted))
08 Cl:  or that I will become like [that
09 An:                             [((coughs)) hmm
10      (.)
11 Cl:  old relative of mine so I will just walk
12      around then and say oh I wish I could get away.
13      (1.0)
14 Cl:  I mean that is no (.) .hhh .hh (0.3) way to live.
15      (0.4)
16 Cl:  You either live or you ↓don't live.
17      (1.8)
18 An:  .hhh I do think that it has (0.5) uh considerable
19      dimensions that thing so that it .hhh again I would
20      indeed connect it to your (0.4) childhood situations
21      to these (.) gre[at sorrows.
22 Cl:                  [Yeah:,
23      (0.3)
24 An:  When >you have the kind of< feeling that they must just
25      (0.4) be left behind right °away°.
26      (0.5)
27 Cl:  ye[:s (just<)
28 An:    [One shouldn't be drawn in[to griev°ing°.
29 Cl:                              [To dance and to sing.
30      (.)
31 An:  Yes,
32 Cl:  So that others would be happy (.) and pleased with me.
33      (.)
34 An:  Yes and you too would feel bet°ter°.
35      (2.3)
36 An:  But there is the problem then that .hhh
37      how much of that grief then goes completely un°grieved°.
38 Cl:  Yes well: now at this moment so far there's not any
39      .hhh .hhh ((coughs)) (0.4) ((coughs)) (0.4) mt .hhh
40      great danger yet that I #would get rid of it#.
```

(3.3)
Cl: But but I (0.5) well I balance things so that,
(1.0) go around (0.5) and do things and. (0.8) .hhh
I went to buy some bulbs of amaryllis and will put them
to the ground . . .

The first part of the analyst's interpretation in lines 18–21 is met by the client's minimal agreement token in line 22. After a brief gap, the analyst then adds an increment to the interpretation in which he points out that in her childhood, the client felt that sorrows have to be "left behind" quickly (lines 24–25). Finally, overlapping with the client's turn beginning, the analyst adds a third component (line 28) which exemplifies the client's attitude.

The first part of the client's elaboration of the interpretation is started by the word "just" after the second agreement token in line 27, then aborted, and completed in line 29. The elaboration is sequentially tied to the second part of the analyst's interpretation (lines 24–25) in which he described the client's childhood scene. The client uses metaphorical language to illustrate the same experience that the analyst was describing: she moved on "to dance and to sing," instead of allowing herself to take time for grieving. After an agreement token by the analyst (line 31), the client expands her description of the childhood scene. She adds an explanatory dimension to the description, referring to the expectations of "others" as a reason for her inability to mourn (line 32). By this two-part elaboration, the client shows her understanding and acceptance of the interpretation.

Usually, in psychoanalytic texts, the interpretation is understood as a two-phase procedure: the analyst's interpretation is followed by the client's response which, when things go well, incorporates new insight instigated by the interpretation. In psychoanalytical terms, the client's elaboration in lines 29 and 32 indeed seems to be an occasion of such insight. The contribution of CA here is to show the linguistic and interactional realization of insight. However, there is more to be said about this case.

Conversation analysis can also show that what happens after the interpretation is very much a co-product of the client and the analyst alike. Insight is not a private business. After the client's elaboration (or other response to an interpretation) there is an opportunity for the analyst to show his stance towards that response. Let us return to Extract 2. In line 31, the analyst agrees with the initial part of the client's elaboration, thereby as it were ratifying it. The client's expansion of her elaboration in line 32 is then produced in this context of agreement. And the analyst not only agrees with the client's elaboration, but he also joins in producing it. In line 34, after an agreement token "yes" (Finnish *nii*, which does affiliative work – Sorjonen,

2001) he produces an utterance that is designed to be a grammatical continuation of the client's preceding turn (line 32). Here, the analyst adds another reason for the client's inability to mourn: by not mourning, the client also made herself feel better. So, in the sequence consisting of the analyst's interpretation, the client's elaboration, and the analyst's further extension (cf. Vehviläinen, 2003a) of the elaboration, the participants collaboratively draw a sketch of sensitive aspects of the client's childhood experience, in the context of the talk about the client's current bereavement. In this case, it is evident that the interpretation is not at all a unilateral act, the analyst interpreting something and the client receiving the interpretation but, instead, is a co-product of both parties.

To sum up, CA research on interpretations explicates the sequential structures, or patterns of activity, that lead towards interpretations, and follow from the interpretations. By so doing, the research reveals some until now unexplicated aspects of the technique of psychoanalysis, and some until now unexplicated ways in which the clients display or reveal the mental events that the interpretations instigate in them. CA also shows how the client's understanding of his or her mind, sought after in interpretations, is a thoroughly dialogical achievement.

Affective communication

Traditionally, interpretation has been regarded as the key technique of psychoanalysis. However, in recent discussions concerning the nature of the change that is supposed to take place in the client in psychoanalysis, the importance of interpretation has been called into question. It has been suggested that instead, or along with, interpretation, the very interaction, especially affective interaction, between the analyst and the client is an agent of change in analysis or therapy (see e.g. E. E. Jones, 1997).

The members of the Boston Change Process Study Group have explicated the grounds for this kind of view (Bruschweiler-Stern *et al.*, 2002; Stern *et al.*, 1998; Tronick *et al.*, 1998). They view mother–infant interaction as a kind of blueprint for the therapeutic relation: similar processes that enhance the infant's mental growth can occur in therapy, enhancing the client's (and the therapist's) growth in that setting. The participants in the therapeutic relation are involved in mutual recognition and regulation of their affective displays, involving moments of mutual affective understanding as well as moments where the understanding gets lost and possibly reestablished (Tronick *et al.*, 1998). This process modifies the participants' "implicit relational knowing," i.e. mostly unconscious expectations regarding the ways of being with other people (Stern *et al.*, 1998, pp. 910–911; see also Streeck, Chapter 10, this volume).

The following extract from my clinical notes illustrates a moment saturated by affect. It is from the very beginning of a session. The preceding day, the client had told me that she would bring to this next session her delayed monthly fee. The passages in italics involve my reflections while writing up the notes immediately after the session. Again, some sentences have been omitted to save space.

Extract 3 (clinical notes).

Cl: *I'm sorry, I was not yet able to organize the money.*
An: *Well what comes now to your mind about that.*
My question comes up very quickly. I'm aware of the tone of my voice when uttering the question; I'm trying to make my voice non-accusatory, and it becomes somewhat brisk.
The question makes Cl somehow embarrassed, struck, or "frozen." Her talk becomes perturbed. I don't remember too well what she says; in any case she tells how di cult the bills are for her to deal with . . .
Thereafter there is a silence for a few minutes. I seem to remember that I feel concern for Cl during the silence, somehow I am afraid of her bad feeling which I consider has been caused by me.
An: *When we talk about money right now, do you become paralysed in the way that you have been talking about quite a lot here in the analysis?*
Cl: *Somehow I do.*
(. . .)
An: *Questions related to money are probably intertwined with many of your experiences. These experiences are sort of summarized in questions regarding money.*
Cl: *Yes. Paying bills is linked with adulthood and with independence.*
An: *And somehow money is also related to the father.*
Cl: *Yes it is related to him.*
(. . .)
Approximately here there occurs a new silence, longer than the previous one, this one might have been about five minutes. During the silence (or at some other point) I am wondering whether Cl could get a permanent job instead of the insecure and badly paid freelance work that she is now doing . . . During the silence I also think about what this silence feels like. I have a peaceful feeling, but I don't know what Cl feels like. I think about the way in which she lies on the couch and breathes, she indeed appears peaceful, not anxious.
Cl: *I cannot get hold of anything.*

The analyst responds to the client's announcement (that she hasn't got the money today) with a "paradigmatic" psychoanalytic question, "what comes to mind." According to the clinical notes, the analyst is quite self-conscious in uttering the question: alive to the moral and emotional implications that it may have. He perceives the client's response to be one suffused with negative emotion. There ensues what appears a moment of mutual discomfort. In the subsequent talk, the analyst links the current emotion with the client's recurrent feelings of being paralysed. This paralysis is indeed a major problem which the client has described during the treatment. During the long silence that follows, the analyst is thinking about ways in which the client's situation could be improved. He is also following his own and the client's emotional states, listening to the client's breathing in a way that a father might listen to his baby breathing.

So, during the episode described in Extract 3, the client's negative emotion is aroused, it gets recognized both verbally and nonverbally, and the participants probably move towards some regulation of that experience. The link, suggested by Stern, Tronick and others, between emotional regulation in early interaction, and that in the therapeutic relation, seems quite plausible here.

As I did when discussing interpretation, I also want here to compare the understandings based on clinical notes with those that arise from conversation analysis. Let me first point out a domain of action that is available in the clinical case material but, as far as I can see, not in conversation analytic data. The clinical notes can give us access to the analyst's account of his or her thoughts and experiences during the interaction. In recent decades, analysts have stressed increasingly the importance of the analyst's subjective experience, as a source of understanding of the client's affective state and the client's relation to the analyst (see e.g. Ogden, 1997). Arguably, these experiences are part of the analytic situation, part of the activity of doing psychoanalysis, especially when it comes to affect. Clinical notes may reveal something of that better than video or audio recordings on their own.

Conversation analysis, in turn, can contribute by specifying the ways in which affect gets expressed and regulated in psychoanalytic sessions. It can explicate one step further the affective interactions that the case reports refer to in general terms. In the clinical notes above, the client was described as being "embarrassed, struck, or 'frozen'." The notes do not show how this came about. At the moment, one aim of CA studies, as I see it, is to identify the loci of affect (cf. Besnier, 1990) in therapeutic interaction, i.e., the recurrent sequences and means of expression that convey participants' affective states, and serve as a means for their interactional management.

The emergent CA research on affect and emotion (e.g. Goodwin & Goodwin, 2000; Peräkylä, 2004a; Peräkylä & Ruusuvuori, 2006; Ruusuvuori, 2005) has shown how the expression and management of affect involves lexical and syntactic choices as well as prosody, gesture, and facial expression. However, regarding affect in psychotherapy, there is no prior CA research to build upon (see Leudar *et al.*, Chapter 9, this volume). Therefore, we are very much at the exploratory stage. In her ongoing dissertation work, Voutilainen (in prep.) examines the cognitive therapist's responses to assessments made by the client. There is frequently an affective dimension in these assessments – for example, the client may be assessing negatively people close to her, or events that she has participated in. Voutilainen has identified two different responses to assessments by therapists: one is to confirm the assessment, and the other is to interpret the assessment. In confirmation, the therapist makes a second assessment, claiming that the assessable is intersubjectively available. Thereby, the therapist reactualizes and intensifies the client's affect involved in the assessment. When interpreting the assessment, on the other hand, the therapist treats the affect as something that is in the client's mind but not as such shared by the therapist. Rather than sharing the affect, the therapist suggests that the participants should examine it further. So, in her ongoing work, Voutilainen is in the process of uncovering one "locus of affect" in therapeutic discourse.

Dreams and affect

I would like to suggest that talk about dreams serves as one locus of affect in psychoanalysis. Traditionally in psychoanalysis, dream interpretation has been understood as an exploratory area. Dream is considered as the "royal road to the unconscious": by examining dreams, the client and the analyst can access unconscious, repressed contents of the client's mind. By examining sequences of dream talk in our tapes, I have come to think somewhat differently. It appears that dreams are used, in our tapes, not so much to find new contents from the client's mind, but to return to something that is already known, and to re-cognize, to become once again aware of, the possibly painful affect that is related to those states of affairs.

Let us examine in more detail one recurrent detail in talk about dreams. Frequently in our tapes, one party, or both parties, uses a figure originating in the client's dream – i.e., description of a scene or an element of the dream – as a resource in the description of the client's "out-of-the-dream" circumstances. The figure from the dream is inserted in the description of the everyday reality. Through this insertion, the affect related to this aspect of everyday reality is recognized and often also intensified. Extracts 4 and 5 are examples.

At the beginning of the session from which Extract 4 is taken, the client reported a dream where the analyst tells her that she is exhausted and will take three months' sick leave, then falls down and cries in the client's arms. When the client in the subsequent talk describes her worries concerning the analyst's recent illnesses, the analyst in response inserts the figure of "nursing the analyst," originating in the client's dream, into her sympathizing assessments.

Extract 4 (tape recording)
(Cl is talking about her (and her friend's) worries concerning the analyst's recent illnesses)

```
   Cl:  (.hh) we were quite @anx[ious@[2] ↑a]nd wọrried and,
   An:                           [ °mhmm°   ]
   Cl:  .hhhhhhhh >SO< REALLY however [>so<
   An:                                [↑ye:a,
   Cl:  >like< quite (0.4) #really worr[ied plus#] then
   An:                                 [↑ye:a,    ]
   Cl:  the, .hhhhh (°somehow°) such a (1.0) ↑child's (0.2)
        thought that ↑this ↓ground is cracking no[w(h).
   An:                                           [yeah:.
        (1.0)
   An:  .yeah (0.2) °yes,°.
        (1.0)
→  An:  °you have to° start ↓nursing me and that is
        ↑quite (1.2) quite like (.) too ↓hard.
   Cl:  and it is con- so >somehow it< is connected also
        to the fact tha- or I mean this feeling. . . .
        ((Cl continues by describing her recent feeling of
        depression))
```

In line 8, the client's narration has reached its climax and can be heard as completed. Through the metaphor of "cracking ground," and by shifting in present tense in line 8, she creates a strongly affective scene. The analyst responds first by three softly uttered yes/yeah tokens (variants of Finnish *joo*). Thereafter in lines 13–14, she adds, as an extension to the client's narration, a figure from the dream ("you have to start nursing me") and then produces an assessment of this figure. These lines constitute a strong complaint which the analyst does on the client's behalf and through which she affiliates with the client. The inserted figure serves in recognizing once more the client's painful affect.

In Extract 4 above, the analyst's extension of the client's narration, by employing a figure originating from a dream, constituted an action whereby the analyst affiliated with the affect that the client had expressed in her narration. In Extract 5 below, the insertion of the figure from a dream does different kind of work. Here, as in a previous example, the insertion serves as a recognition of the client's affect; but in this case affect that the client has not brought about in his narration. In Extract 5, the client's initial dream was about a cow grabbing him in the neck and shaking him. After the client told the dream, the participants agreed that "cow" is a pejorative symbol for a woman. In the subsequent talk, the client describes a workplace meeting, with tension between the female and

[2] Material between @ signs displays a marked change in prosody.

male staff members. The client points out that during that tension he felt that he was allied with the women.

Extract 5 (tape recording).
(Cl telling about a workplace meeting)

```
     Cl:  mt .hhhh and somehow I sort of think so that the<
          the .hhhhhhhhhh ehhhh the hhh woman in me was
          then as it #were# (0.4) #somehow allied# (0.5)
          completely with< (.) with these women.=and and< and
          I understood the situation from their ↓perspective
          then or felt °it°.
          (0.4)
→    An:  mt .hhhh but at the same time a cow grabbed you
→         in the neck and shoo- shook you.
     Cl:  yes.
          (9.2)
     Cl:  .hhhhhhnfff #so (it comes)# >could you< >think that
          if one< takes as point of departure (the fact that). . .
          ((Cl continues about the "female" and "male" side in
          himself))
```

After a point where the client's narration can be heard as complete, the analyst here, as in the preceding example, produces an extension in which he employs a figure originating in the dream (in this case, the grabbing cow). The extension accomplishes recognition of the negative affect between the client and the women in the meeting: the sensation of a cow grabbing and shaking one's neck is an unpleasant one, and the participants have also agreed that the cow refers to women in a pejorative way. However, unlike in the preceding example, here the extension is not in line with the thrust of the client's preceding narration. In his story, the client felt at one with the women; the extension points out an uneasy relation between them. The client merely acknowledges the extension (line 10) without taking up the perspective suggested in it. In the subsequent discussion (data not shown) the analyst pursues – but no more successfully – his point about the unease in the relation between the women and the client.

So, it seems to me that figures originating in the client's dream, when inserted into extensions of narratives about out-of-the-dream reality, can be used to recognize the client's affects related to the events that are narrated. Let's consider Extract 6 as a further, and somewhat more complex, example. In the talk some time before this extract, the client recounted a dream in which an acquaintance ("Hanna") insists on moving into Cl's house, against her will. After the dream telling and some discussion on it, the client and the analyst have discussed the client's recent bereavement after the death of her partner ("Jussi"). The client has also reported another dream. In the segment that we will see, the figure of somebody moving by force into Cl's house is inserted into the description of Cl's current life situation after the death of her partner ("Jussi"). The dream is "retold" so that "(Jussi's) death" takes the place of "Hanna".

Extract 6 (tape recording).

```
     An:  .mhhhh So I do think that both the dreams
          are dealing with (0.3) Jussi's death (0.6) and< of course
          its no wonder that they deal [with it.
     Cl:                               [Well how would that apply to the
          dream about Hanna then.
          (0.3)
     An:  It has (0.3) happened again to you that somebody has (.)
          .hhh taken something away from you (0.3) by force.
          (2.4)
     Cl:  er[m::
     An:    [H- Hanna had as it were once again entered into your
          li°fe°.
          (0.4)
     Cl:  In which wa[y.
  →  An:              [In the shape of death.
          (0.7)
  →  Cl:  So that she comes lives in my .hhh death comes to live
  →       in my home.
          (.)
     An:  Yes.
          (0.9)
     Cl:  Y[es.
  →  An:   [Jussi's death lives now in your ho°me°,
          (0.5)
     Cl:  Ye:ah it is<=
  →  An:  =Even though you wouldn't e- in any way want [°that°.
     Cl:                                                [tch Right.
          (2.0)
  →  Cl:  So that I fight (.) fiercely (0.5) against that.
          (0.7)
  →  An:  But nevertheless it comes.
          (2.0)
     Cl:  Yes.
          (0.3)
  →  An:  In a rude and arrogant [°way°.
     Cl:                         [.hhh Yeah,
          (2.2)
     Cl:  Maybe there is (something) °( )( )°
          (4.0)
     Cl:  Yes but how d- did you #connect as it were m- my#
          mother to that (2.0) so of course >I can say
          that<...((continues))
```

In lines 1–2, the analyst suggests that both dreams that the client has reported during the session are related to the recent death of her partner. In lines 4–5, the client challenges that interpretation regarding the dream about "Hanna" moving into her house. An exchange between Cl and An ensues (lines 7–15) which ends up with the analyst suggesting that Hanna has "once again entered" the client's life, "in the shape of death." The expression "in the shape of death" (line 15) invokes the strong negative affect associated to death. This interpretation of the dream is taken up by the client. In lines 17–18, she produces a formulation, or candidate understanding, of the analyst's suggestion, narrating anew the key content of the dream, through a self repair substituting "death" for "she" initially referring to Hanna. The final version of the utterance, "death comes to live in my home," emphasizes the negative affect by linking "death" and "home," i.e. the ultimately fearsome and the ultimately safe. After a cycle of confirmatory "yes" / (Finnish *nii*) tokens, the analyst in line 23 rephrases the core narrative. By substituting "lives now" for "comes to live," and by specifying "death" as "Jussi's death," the analyst may emphasize the actual presence of death in the client's life and thus upgrade the affect. In line 25 the client initiates a sentence that seems to be aiming at a further description or evaluation, but cuts off and aborts her utterance. The analyst then expands his earlier description in line 26 by characterizing the client's unwillingness to accept the situation; and this expansion is agreed on by the client in line 27. After a gap, the client in line 29 again produces a formulation, or candidate understanding, now regarding the analyst's characterization of her attitude in line 26. The candidate understanding upgrades the affect through the words "fiercefully" and "fight." The description is yet again expanded by the analyst in line 31, and after the client's agreement, still once again in line 35.

So, in Extract 6, there is a sequence where the participants collaboratively tell anew the core content of a dream reported earlier. The dream was about an acquaintance moving by force into the client's house. In the retelling, the participants substitute an object from the client's everyday life ("Jussi's death") for one element of the dream ("Hanna"). The participants do not orient to ideas about the client's bereavement as something previously unknown (they had, indeed, discussed the bereavement shortly before), while the connection of these ideas to this particular dream is presented as novel understanding. The dream was used as a resource of description that made it possible to return once again to this bereavement, to recognize once again the client's affects related to it. This recognition of affect was embodied particularly in the lexical choices of the collaboratively produced descriptions.

On the basis of the examination of sequences of dream discourse with linguistic features similar to those in Extracts 4–6, I would like to suggest that sequences where figures of dream are inserted to descriptions of everyday reality are indeed one locus of affect in psychoanalytic discourse. In other words, they are sequences that allow for recognition affect, involving moments of mutual understanding (for example, in the affiliative scene in Extract 4) as well as moments where understanding is not achieved (for example, in Extract 5). But this is but one specific locus of affect – there is much work to be done in explicating the others.

Intersubjectivity

During the past decade or two, the concept of intersubjectivity has entered into the vocabulary of a number of psychoanalysts. Ideas associated with this term involve a major shift in the conceptualization of the psychoanalytic process: while it has traditionally been considered to be a process taking place within the client's mind, intersubjectivists consider it to be a process that involves not only two minds but, perhaps more importantly, something that these two minds create together, a process that cannot be traced back to the individual minds (see Streeck, 2001; Chapter 10, this volume). Ogden (1994), who is one of the leading proponents of this thinking, has given the name "analytic third" to this emergent extra-individual dimension of the analytic situation.

Stern (2004) defines intersubjectivity as "mutual penetration of minds" (p. 75), that is, the ability to experience what the other is experiencing (cf. Aron, 1991; Benjamin, 1990). This capability is neurologically and developmentally anchored in us, and Stern argues – in line with classical social psychological theory – that our sense of a differentiated self arises from the intersubjective. Like the development of the child's mind, the therapeutic process also occurs "in an ongoing intersubjective matrix" (Stern, 2004, p. 78). Stern also talks about short-lived moments of special complementarity of actions and understandings beween the therapist and the client. Such "moments of meeting" are, according to Stern (2004) and his colleagues (Bruschweiler-Stern *et al.*, 2002; Stern *et al.*, 1998) of special importance in transforming the "implicit relational knowing" of the participants (see Streeck, Chapter 10 this volume).

Conversation analysis involves a particular, empirically grounded theory of intersubjectivity. According to Heritage (1984b) the sequential organization of talk is the key for the possibility of intersubjectivity: in each turn at talk, the speaker shows his or her understanding of the preceding speaker's actions and intentions (see also Lerner, 1991; Levinson, 2006; Schegloff, 1992).

Even though there is not a full match between the psychoanalytical and the conversation analytical concepts of intersubjectivity, we can use CA to learn something more about intersubjectivity in therapeutic interaction. From the perspective of both CA and intersubjectively oriented psychoanalysis (as I understand these two traditions), "mind as experienced," "mind as expressed," and "mind as understood" cannot be strictly separated. In conversation analysis, what we have access to is expressions of mind and the ways in which these expressions are received and understood by the co-participants; and it is to that multifaceted field that I refer to below, when talking about "mind."

In the final part of this chapter, I will look back at some of our examples, so as to examine once more the construction of intersubjective understandings in them. I will focus on the collaborative construction of description, i.e. segments of interaction in which the participants jointly, turn-by-turn, produce a description (cf. Ferrara, 1994; Vehviläinen, 2003a). In a way that I find intriguing, what might be called communion and divergence of minds seem to be quite tightly intertwined in these examples.

Let us first return to Extract 2. As we saw earlier, in lines 18–21, the analyst gives an interpretation linking the client's experiences in her current bereavement, and her childhood experiences. He expands the interpretation twice. In lines 27 and 29, the client elaborates the interpretation by saying "just to dance and to sing." Thereby, the client displays her understanding and acceptance of the analyst's preceding interpretation. I think this can be considered as a point where the client's and the analyst's minds – as expressed and as responded to – come together in describing collaboratively the client's childhood experience.

Segment of Extract 2 (tape recording).

An: .hhh I do think that it has (0.5) uh considerable
dimensions that thing so that it .hhh again I would
indeed connect it to your (0.4) childhood situations
to these (.) gre[at sorrows.
Cl: [Yeah:,
(0.3)
An: When >you have the kind of< feeling that they must just
(0.4) be left behind right °away°.
(0.5)
Cl: ye[:s (just<)
An: [One shouldn't be drawn in[to grie°ving°.
Cl: [To dance and to sing.
(.)
An: Yes,
Cl: So that others would be happy (.) and pleased with me.
(.)
An: Yes and you too would feel bet°ter°.
(2.3)
An: But there is the problem then that .hhh

how much of that grief then goes completely un°grieved°.
Cl: Yes well: now at this moment so far there's not any
.hhh .hhh ((coughs)) (0.4) ((coughs)) (0.4) mt .hhh
great danger yet that I #would get rid of it#.

In and through the unfolding of a collaborative description, the minds of the participants remain together for a short while. The final point of the collaboration is in line 34 where the analyst, in extending the client's prior turn, shifts the perspective from the expectations of "others" to the dynamics of the client's own mind. This shift of perspective is met by the client's silence, and the collaborative production of description is halted. By now, it seems that the communion of minds, as incorporated in the sequential relations of the adjacent turns, is dissolved. The further two turns at talk confirm this divergence: the analyst produces an assessment of the client's attitude (lines 36–37), and the client declines the relevance of that assessment (38–39).

So, in terms of the mutual penetration of minds that Stern talks about, there is in Extract 2 a short "moment of meeting" which is followed by divergence of the perspectives displayed in the participants' talk. There is no evidence about a dramatic change in the participants' ways of relating to each other (cf. Stern, 2004, pp. 165–176). Rather, there is a brief moment where their perspectives touch one another after which they move along their divergent paths.

Also in Extract 6 shown earlier, the participants were involved in collaborative description, in this case telling anew the client's dream, with the key figure ("Hanna") substituted by "death." The client takes an active part in this collaborative production through her utterances in lines 17–18 and 29. Communion and divergence of minds are here even more inextricably intertwined than in the previous example.

Segment of Extract 6 (CA materials).

An: H- Hanna had as it were once again entered into your
li°fe°.
(0.4)
Cl: In which wa [y.
An: [In the shape of death.
(0.7)
Cl: So that she comes lives in my .hhh death comes to live
in my home.
(.)
An: Yes.
(0.9)
Cl: Y[es.
An: [Jussi's death lives now in your ho°me°,
(0.5)
Cl: Ye:ah it is<=

```
An:  =Even though you wouldn't e- in any way want [°that°.
Cl:                                                [tch Right.
     (2.0)
Cl:  So that I fight (.) fiercely (0.5) against that.
     (0.7)
An:  But nevertheless it comes.
     (2.0)
Cl:  Yes.
     (0.3)
An:  In a rude and arrogant [°way°.
Cl:                         [.hhh Yeah,
     (2.2)
Cl:  Maybe there is (something) °(    )(    )°
```

The client takes part in the joint production of the affective description of her painful situation in an ambiguous way: partly designing the descriptions as ones that arise from her own experience, and partly designing them as her understandings of the analyst's talk. I will first explicate the latter aspect. The client uses turn initial *että* in both her utterances (lines 17 and 29). I have translated Finnish *että* as "so that." This turn beginning frames the ensuing utterances as the speaker's, i.e. the client's, understandings of what the other party was suggesting, not as her own suggestions. "So" alone – Finnish *siis* – would tie the utterance more closely to the speaker's perspective, as would, in the case of the second formulation, the use of "and" or no turn initial particle at all. So, as a whole, the segment of talk extending from line 17 to line 36 is hearable as an insert sequence (Schegloff, 2007) through which the client establishes what the analyst means by "in the shape of death" in line 15. After the insertion, the client in line 38 takes stance to the analyst's initial statement.

Yet, the client does not at all employ all available means for portraying her talk as (just) a candidate understanding of what the other party has said. She doesn't preface her candidate understandings with any question components, such as "do you mean that?" She uses indicative, not conditional form (she says "death comes" and "I fight" instead of, for example, "death would come" or "I would fight"). She also upgrades the affect in her candidate understanding in line 29. And she produces, after all, *nii*-agreements at some key points respective to the analyst's talk.

The analyst, in turn, does not frame his extensions of descriptions (see especially lines 23 and 31) as clarifications of the proposal that the client is striving to understand – which he could do for example by saying "I mean that" or "So," but rather, offers them as extensions to descriptions, the meaning or validity of which is not under question.

So, in a closer look, it appears that the client in Extract 6 is at the verge of fully subscribing to the affectively dense description of "death living in her house," but still withholds the final step. In other words, the claim of recognition of the client's affective experience conveyed by the analyst's utterances was not fully met by the client. Communion and divergence of minds were inextricably intertwined.

In Extracts 2 and 6, reexamined above, what at first sight appeared as an intersubjective moment of meeting turned out to be, on closer analysis, something where complementarity of actions and understandings between the client and the analyst is mingled with non-complementarity. I believe that these are not just odd, individual cases (for comparable patterns in clients' responses to interpretations, see Peräkylä, 2005).

Further explication of the interactional ways in which the matching and mismatching, complementarity and non-complementarity of the therapist's and the client's actions takes place, is probably one of the central tasks of conversation analysts investigating psychotherapy. I believe that our method is sensitive enough for that task – much more sensitive than, for example, the psychoanalytic case reports based on clinical notes can ever be.

Conclusion

Conversation analytic research does not entail any theory of psychotherapeutic process. However, the observations presented above can be discussed in the context of such theories, and they may raise questions to them. In the contemporary models which seek to show the parallels between psychoanalysis and early interaction, the early interaction is described as consisting of phases of regulated affective interaction and phases of dysregulation, that is, phases of match and phases of mismatch between the child's and the carer's actions. The dysregulation and mismatch can involve, for example, the carer trying to make an infant continue to smile and play in such a moment when the infant turns her gaze away, wanting to withdraw. The analyses presented above hint towards the possibility that psychoanalytic interaction is more saturated by moments of mismatch than we are used to thinking. If that's the case, then the task of psychoanalysis can be to work with these mismatches, again and again, so as to allow opportunities for the interactional, relational, cognitive, and affective patterns associated with them to be transformed. Occasionally, there may be genuine "moments of meeting," but more often, we may find the communion and divergence of minds intertwined, as in Extracts 2 and 6. Mismatch between the analyst's and the therapist's actions need not be something that should be overcome, but it can also be a trigger of the growth of the client. In any case, it appears to me that conversation analysis has the potential to elucidate interactions that can be at the very heart of the talking cure (see also Streeck, Chapter 10, this volume).

Through the data analyses presented in this chapter I have wanted to convey the notion that psychoanalysis needs conversation analysis to enhance its self-understanding. The turn towards affective interaction and intersubjectivity in psychoanalytic theory has created new opportunities for the meeting between psychoanalysis and interaction research. Right now, CA can offer new ways for dealing with questions that arise from psychoanalytic theory and practice.

7 Identifying and managing resistance in psychoanalytic interaction

Sanna Vehviläinen

In various institutional settings, professionals encounter moments where clients resist their actions and institutional agendas. In CA research on institutional interaction, such resistance has been mostly examined as overt client resistance to particular professionals' actions, especially as non-aligning responses to turns that present professionals' perspectives to their clients. The focus has mainly been on client resistance to professionals' recommendations in health care and counselling settings (Heritage & Sefi, 1992; Silverman, 1997; Stivers, 2005; Vehviläinen, 1999; Waring, 2005). Typically, professionals have the means of pre-empting such resistance (Heritage & Sefi, 1992; Maynard, 1991; Silverman, 1997). If they nevertheless do meet resistance, they typically pursue and elaborate the resisted action. Another strand of literature has shown how clients resist questions with embedded presuppositions, especially in media interviews (Berg, 2001; Clayman, 1993), but also in therapeutic settings (Halonen, Chapter 8, this volume; MacMartin, Chapter 5, this volume).

When examining psychotherapies that are based on a concept of the unconscious, the issue of resistance becomes more complex. Psychoanalysis, especially, is based on a multifaceted theory of the unconscious, as well as an elaborate technique of dealing with it. A central aim of psychoanalysis is to expand the area of consciousness, to include ideas and affects that have been repressed. This has various consequences for what resistance means for therapeutic practice, what counts as resistance, and how resistance is managed in the interaction.

For psychoanalysis, identifying resistance constitutes a starting point for exploration rather than an interactional failure (Frosh, 2002; Ikonen, 2000; Spacal, 1990, pp. 84–85). A central principle of psychoanalysis is to identify points where the client is resisting the analytic work. These moments represent, for the analyst, instances of the client blocking from the conscious mind something important but painful. Thus, from the psychoanalytic point of view, such situations are not only expected, but crucial to the analytic work. Furthermore, resistance for the analyst consists of more than overt interactional resistance to the analyst's suggestions. For instance, features that are treated as problems of spontaneous expression of thoughts (remaining silent, editing one's talk) or other "problems of participation" (arriving late, missing appointments or payment) are treated as indexing resistance. Psychoanalysis – like other therapies which include a concept of resistance – also has a notion of how clients must, at the proper time, be made to face their resistance and, gradually, learn about the "important but so far avoided" contents of their mind. Thus, various means of confronting the client become relevant: firstly, identifying potential indexes of resistance and secondly, showing the client what they mean and exploring them with the client (Vehviläinen, 2003a; compare Arminen & Leppo, 2001; Halonen, Chapter 8, this volume).

Psychoanalytic interaction: Working with "puzzles"

Conversation analysis begins with a data-driven analysis of what participants do and how they shape their turn-by-turn interaction. The findings may or may not resonate with the practitioners' theory of their practice (Peräkylä & Vehviläinen, 2003; Peräkylä, Ruusuvuori & Vehviläinen, 2005). Sometimes interactional practices do not fit very well to the practitioners' theories or ideals they are supposed to incarnate – this may be what the conversation analyst finds when exploring the relationship between empirical findings and theories of the practice (Vehviläinen, 1999). However, with psychoanalysis, interactional findings usually do find a match within psychoanalytic theory (see Peräkylä, Chapter 6, this volume). This is not to claim that the perspectives of CA and psychoanalysis on the interactional phenomena would be the same. It is more an observation that the "stock of interactional knowledge" (Peräkylä & Vehviläinen, 2003) of psychoanalysis is relatively refined: within psychoanalysis there is a detailed body of knowledge on interactional phenomena.

In a corpus of Finnish classical psychoanalysis collected by Anssi Peräkylä and myself, the interplay between the client's free associations (spontaneous talk about one's experience) and the analyst's interventions takes place through a stepwise movement we have called "the interpretative trajectory" (Vehviläinen, 2003a; Peräkylä, 2004a; 2005; Chapter 6, this volume). In listening to the client's spontaneous talk, the analyst attends to potential indications of underlying conflicts in her or his mind. At times, the analyst makes a so-called interpretative statement to show what he or she takes to be the analytic meaning of the client's talk.

The analyst does preparatory work to create the relevance, and an interactional "slot," for the interpretation, thereby co-constructing it with the client. Connections and contradictions in the associated materials, pointed by the analyst, provide puzzles: noteworthy, enigmatic issues calling for

Thus, noticings include a blaming element, making the client accountable. They also accomplish what my-side tellings generally do: indirectly invite talk from the owner of the experience (Pomerantz, 1980). Thus, noticings also have a "fishing" element. (Bergmann, 2001.) In these data, we find the analysts' noticings of the clients' prior action work in a similar way.

Prior to the following extract, the client (Cl) has narrated a three-part dream and, thereafter, has been asked to provide her associations (i.e. whatever comes to her mind regarding the dreams). She has had some trouble doing that but, prior to the extract, she provided associations on the first part of the dream, and now proceeds to the second part, which she refers to as the "flower thing":

Extract 1 [II/7/B21].
(Analysis performed on the original Finnish recordings.)

```
          (6.5)
     Cl:  #yes# well then the flower thing,
          (3.0)
     Cl:  if I rush ahead now from here >I don't know-<
          (1.0) ('cause it) feels like I'm
     An:  .h[hh
     Cl:    [not able [(to say),
     An:              [(>in other words< you feel that you
          are rushing now.
          (.)
     Cl:  well I: because you didn't (0.7) say that (1.2)
          mhe hr mt @l(h)et's move to the next sequence,@ 1
          (0.7)
 →   An:  mt.hh now you are putting the responsibility on me
 →        aga[in.    ]
     Cl:     [yes yes] because I sort of- (0.7) you manage this,
          (0.5)
     An:  (.hh) (0.5) and not you.
     Cl:  nii, ((=yes/that's right.))
          (1.0)
     Cl:  that's how it is .hhh.
          (.)
     An:  .hh why,=
     Cl:  =to my opinion,
          (.)
     Cl:  well I'm manageable,
          (1.2)
     Cl:  I imagine,
          (4.2)
     Cl:  mt .hhh oh well,
```

1 Material between @ signs is delivered with a marked shift in prosody.

```
31          (5.2)
32    Cl:   .hhh >in any case if< I return to it so I'll say. . .
            ((continues to describe a tendency to offer help to
            others too easily))
```

The client shifts from one "dream item" to another (lines 2–7). There is no uptake from the analyst and the client begins an account dealing with the shift (lines 4–5). Her account is designed as an increment, and it seems to be building towards an insertion, legitimizing her move. She refers to her topic shift as "rushing." While the reason for the accounting is never produced, it is observable that the client deals with some problem of talking (not being able to say more of the prior item, worry of forgetting the other items, etc.).

At this point, the analyst is no longer aligning as a recipient of the client's associations on her three-part dream. Instead of letting her finish her turn, the analyst comes in, in overlap (lines 6, 8–9), with a conclusive statement that places the focus on the client's current experience of rushing. This turn is shaped like a formulation: a resaying of what the client said (Antaki, Barnes & Leudar, 2005; Vehviläinen, 2003a; see also Antaki, Chapter 2, this volume; Bercelli, Rossano & Viaro, Chapter 3, this volume; Rae, Chapter 4, this volume). However, it is treated by the client as a turn making relevant an account (rather than a confirmation). In effect, this move constitutes a topic shift, and it makes the client accountable for her action (i.e. rushing). The analyst thereby prevents the client from proceeding with her task of associating about the dream and introduces a new focus for the talk.

The client immediately begins to account for her action, referring to her expectations on their shared "routine" and how their interaction normally proceeds (lines 11–12). Instead of accepting this account, or giving his views on the matter, the analyst, again, makes the client's prior action the focus of the talk by a "noticing" about the client's current action "now you are putting the responsibility on me again" (lines 14–15). The immediacy of the observation is emphasized by the use of present tense and the word "now."

The client's reference to the analyst's behaviour is now treated as noteworthy, even problematic. In addition to noticing what the client has just done, the analyst's turn has the format of a complaint. By stating that the client is putting the responsibility on the analyst, he implies that the responsibility should be on the client. The word "again" constructs this as a repeated activity of the client's. When the client again provides an account, referring to the analyst's role as the manager of the agenda of the encounter, the analyst begins a Socratic questioning (see Rae, Chapter 4, this volume), beginning to explore these views and thereby perhaps building a case for an interpretation. However, at this point the client returns to narrating her dream (32), unwilling to explore the meaning of her "rushing" or "being manageable."

In Extract 1, the analyst, in response to something the client has said and using a formulation and a noticing statement, topicalizes the client's action. Thereby, he shifts the focus of the talk and makes the client accountable for her action. He treats the client's immediately prior action as noteworthy, and creates a puzzle to explore. Fittingly, the client responds by accounting. The puzzle, invoked by the analyst's focusing on the client's action, may later lead to pointing out to the client that she is resisting – thus working as a case-building device in the interpretative trajectory. Why, then, is rushing a puzzle? According to the psychoanalytic theory, attempts to control or edit one's talk can be treated by the analyst as resisting the spontaneous flow of free association (Rycroft, 1995, pp. 13, 158).

The analyst may also use a *why*-question or a parallel structure to call joint attention to the client's action which has, in one way or another, already been brought to focus. As in formulations and noticings, the analyst's intervention introduces a topical shift, but instead of observing that a particular action has taken place, it more directly requests an explanation for it. In the following example, the client has arrived late to the analysis and apologizes. In the focus line, the analyst refocuses on the lateness.

Extract 2 [I/22/A18].

```
     An:  Come in please.
          (9.3)((noise))
     Cl:  I'm sorry I'm late.
     An:  °That's all right°. You're welcome.
          (7.0)
     Cl?: .hhhhh mhhhhhhhhhh
          (2.0)
     Cl:  ähhhhhhhhhh
          (5.9)
     Cl:  .hfff
          (13.0)
     Cl:  .hhh ahem hmmm
          (2.3)
     Cl:  .hhh .hhf (0.8) mhhhhh
          (7.0)
     Cl?: .hhff
          (3.6)
 →   An:  As you know (0.6) .mhhhhhhh hhhh (0.8) this is the
 →        kind of place where apology is not enough.
          (0.2)
     Cl:  ehh heh he [he he   ] .hfff mhhhh
     An:             [hhe heh]
          (12.0)
     Cl:  .mthhhhh Yes: °well° I don't know exactly. hmmmm (0.4)
```

```
      .hfff (0.3) mhhhhh why I'm late.= I don't (    ) (  )
      .hhhhh er:: I left in time but simply sat having
      coffee (   )(late)(and). (0.6) was reading a magazine
      (2.0) It just happened and I didn't notice.
      (0.2) (  )(  ).
      (5.0)
An:   .hhhhh (on the other hand) it was quite an
      interesting lateness
      (1.0)
Cl:   Yes (.) there was no reason to it (.) .hhh or
      I can't explain it. (.) .hff
      (0.6)
?:    .hhhhh
      (10.2)
An:   well what do you think.
      (4.0)
An:   Or what comes to your mind.
      (12.2)
Cl:   .mthhhhhhhhhh hhhmmmmmmm (1.2) mhhhhhh
      (11.2)
Cl:   .mthhh there is indeed- =something like. mhhhh
      .mthhhh (0.2) hhh
      (8.0)
Cl:   .hhhhh (How) I wonder how it will go actually
      'cause- .hffff (1.1) mhhhh because. hmmmm
      (10.0)
Cl:   .mthhhh kröhh (There was) this ((treatment plan)) (0.6)
      thing there in Turku. . .
      ((begins to talk about a work-related issue))
```

The analyst's statement in lines 18–19 is an indirect way of asking: "why were you late, really?" This question, designed as "reminder," states a rule that is presented as known to the recipient. This turn invokes in a marked manner the "detective" orientation of psychoanalysis: that client's actions have a hidden meaning. The design of the turn is confrontative: by stating a general, mutually known rule regarding proper conduct in the setting at hand, it shows that the action the client performed (the apology) is insufficient. It is also claimed that the client knows this – thus, the client's prior silence is treated as resistance-relevant. On the other hand, the formulation can be treated as a non-serious one: a playful reference to the kind of place the analytic encounter is, showing to the client that some psychoanalytic business is at hand. The analyst's voice is smiley, the client responds by laughter, and the analyst joins in laughing.

Thus, although a confrontative move, this is also a collaboration-oriented one. By the playfulness of "reciting of rules of psychoanalysis" and by referring to them as already known to the client, the analyst shows he expects the client to be willing to observe his mind within the psychoanalytic frame.

The client's response is, indeed, a cooperative one, although he claims not to know why he was late (24–29). This response seems to work as a passage from the "everyday frame" to the psychoanalytic one (Goffman, 1974). The claim of not knowing reinforces the puzzle invoked by the analyst. As the client does not – consciously – have a particular explanation for the lateness, the participants can begin to look for an explanation from the unconscious, turning to free association (39–41). ("*What comes to your mind*" is the prototypical way to elicit free association in these data.)

Here the focusing on the client's action involves what Goffman (1974) called a "keying": the analyst suggests that the lateness should be regarded as an object in a psychoanalytic frame rather than everyday frame. It is something to explore and a potential cue to some underlying issue in the client's mind. It seems relevant, however, that the analyst first treats the lateness in the everyday frame by routinely accepting the apology. Otherwise, the intervention would have risked appearing hostile.

Extract 3 is another case where the client's action is keyed psychoanalytically, this time using a *why*-question:

Extract 3 [I/12/B18].

```
     Cl:  although I now must say that (0.3) here sort of (.)
          (    )(say that) I feel that (even) my (0.4) poor dogs have
          lost their meaning along with everything else.
          (.)
     An:  Yes and that's no wonder either.
          (2.0)
     Cl:  So:: I of course take care of them but (0.7) [but.
     An:                                                [.hhhhhhh
          But with less feeling.
     Cl:  ye:s.
          (3.2)
     Cl:  Should we (1.0) stop now.
          (1.0)
  →  An:  Why must we stop r(h)ight n(h)ow. (.) You (of course)
  →       may stop at any moment you li[ke.
     Cl:                               [Yes I know I may.
          (0.5)
     Cl:  Aha it is that (thing) again five t- five to that.
          (0.4)
     An:  Yes,
          (0.2)
     Cl:  hh That=s quite interesting.
          (0.2)
  →  An:  mt .hh I wonder what would have come to your mind if
```

```
→        you hadn=t ha- hadn=t begun to stop.
         (2.0)
   Cl:   What would have come to my mind.
         (0.2)
   An:   Yes.
         (0.2)
   Cl:   Aa::: just a minute just a minute what did we just talk
         about. .hhhhhh Ah dogs right.
```

The action in focus is the client's suggestion that they stop the session (12). The topic – the client's sorrowful mood – has come to a close, with the analyst's extension (Peräkylä, Chapter 6, this volume; Vehviläinen, 2003a) that the client has accepted. Instead of aligning with the client's suggestion, the analyst questions its grounds, laughing through the end of his turn. The laughter seems to treat the client's suggestion as unexpected or misplaced (whether it is heard as ironical or conciliatory) – as does the upgrade from the client's verb "should" to "must" ("why must we stop right now"). The analyst, then, elaborates that the client is "of course" allowed to stop whenever she wishes. He now considers the suggestion, but treats it as a redundant one (line 15). The analyst has shown in many ways that the client's suggestion to stop is a noteworthy, even problematic issue.

The client's response (line 16) deals with the latter component of the analyst's turn. If the analyst's turn at lines 14–15 showed that the client did not need permission, the client's response "Yes I know I may" shows that was not why she asked. The client evades the analyst's *why*-question, thereby resisting the implication that her suggestion is "puzzling" or that the puzzle would be solved by exploring what is in her mind. Instead, she now attends to the issue through the everyday frame. Her next turn is a statement prefaced with a change-of-state token (Heritage, 1984a) "aha" (line 18). She realizes that there is a five-minute time difference between their watches (or her watch and a clock somewhere in the room). This has been an issue in the prior session, and the analyst confirms this observation (line 20).

The client then comments on her own error with an evaluation "that's quite interesting," thereby treating the issue as noteworthy. Now, instead of maintaining the everyday frame, she opens up a possibility of treating her action as a puzzle to explore. Thereupon, the analyst, indeed, shifts to the psychoanalytic frame with a question at lines 24–25. His turn is a request for free association, designed as a hypothetical question. Using this design, the analyst manages to engage the client in further talk in such a way that the puzzle he has created remains relevant (see Peräkylä, 1995, on hypotheticals as a means for talk elicitation). Thereby the analyst shows the client why he has problematized her action (i.e. because asking to stop is a sign of resistance and therefore analytically interesting). This psychoanalytic rule – that resistance marks something relevant surfacing in the mind of the client – is not stated in so many words, but it is alluded to.

In Extracts 2 and 3, the analyst uses a *why*-question or a parallel structure to focus on the client's prior action. A "noticing" would not be relevant here: the client's action is, in a sense, already in focus. In both extracts, the action in focus is a generic matter of routine and convention. Both lateness, and the suggestion of ending the session (and thereby hurrying it up) can be considered signs of resistance, and clients are likely to know this. At least, such knowledge is oriented to by the analyst in these cases.

Although the client's action is already in focus, the *why*-question results in a shift of focus. The analyst thereby misaligns with the action initiated by the client. In Extract 2, the analyst first accepts the routine apology but then presses for a differently framed explanation for the lateness. In Extract 3, the analyst avoids taking issue with the client's suggestion to end the session and, instead, focuses on the fact that she suggested it. And, as a result, the session does not end.

Compared to formulations or noticings, the *why*-question is more explicit in terms of asking for an explanation, and therefore might be heard as more confrontative. However, it is used here in situations where the psychoanalytic relevancies of the situation are more available to the client. Many features in Extracts 2 and 3 indicate that the analyst treats the noteworthiness of the problematized action as available to the client too: he expects the client to know that the mentioned action is canonically a puzzle to be attended to. In the two cases shown here, the client does cooperate and proceeds to free association, although this does not mean that the client would automatically align with the analyst's initiation to work on the puzzle.

In this section, we explored the way in which the client's prior action can be made the focus of the talk. The actions that are focused on are those that can be grouped under the rough psychoanalytic category of resistance such as not talking, editing (and thereby attempting to control) one's talk, arriving late (Rycroft, 1995, pp. 13, 158). By focusing on the client's actions in the here-and-now, the analyst can identify "puzzles" and, thereby, initiate interactional trajectories towards a psychoanalytic interpretation.

Characterization of the client's prior action presented as evidence

Another sequential position for the analyst's references to the client's immediate actions is in situations where it is offered as grounds for the analyst's interpretative statement. Usually such a suggestion concerns observations about the client's resistance to the analytic work: the analyst suggests or claims that the client is avoiding recognizing her or his real dispositions.

Extract 4 [I/8/A11].

```
          (37.0)
     Cl:  .hhhh hH #Hh#h hymm
     An:  °what are you thinking about now°
          (15.5)
     Cl:  mt .hhhhhh mhhhhh
          (1.2)
     Cl:  .hhhh I was just thinking about this sort of, mhhhh
          (3.2)
     Cl:  mhhhhhhhh
          (4.6)
     Cl:  mt .hh a need to withdraw (.) sort of away:.
          (1.6)
     Cl:  from other people.
          (1.8)
     Cl:  so is it some kind of.
          (2.2)
     Cl:  °some kind of, mhhh°
          (60.0) ((sighs and silence))
→    An:  I wonder what you are thinking about.
          (9.5)
→    An:  mt.hhhh (apparently-) (.) it may very well be that
→         (.) that there's so- something (0.8) a bit more
→         difficult here because (0.8) you have such long (.)
→         <pauses> °now°.
          (2.6)
→    An:  during which you must be thinking about
→         something crucial.
          (130.0) ((heavy sighing))
     Cl:  mt .hhhh nff (0.5) mt I don't know 'cause it somehow
          feels (.) (-) mm it just sort keeps going in circles
          that there's the thought that, (0.2) what does it
          really (0.4) mean then that (-) (.) .hhhhhh
          (0.4) that hiding.
```

At line 3, the analyst asks the client what he is thinking about. This question is not the typical request for free association (in our data, the formulaic question for this would be "what comes to your mind?"). The analyst's question rather deals with the silence prior to it. The client responds by nominating a topic (the reason for his tendency to withdraw from other people) but when beginning to elaborate, pauses for a long time and leaves his turn incomplete (7–17). A gap of about one minute ensues (line 18). The analyst again prompts the client to talk (line 21 onwards). The format "I wonder" treats the client's silence as problematic by displaying the unavailability of the other's mind, thus upgrading the initial prompt.

The client does not say anything for another 9.5 seconds, and the analyst goes on to suggest that the client has difficulty in saying what is in his mind (lines 21–24). The design of his turn ("apparently," "it may very well be that") again displays the unavailability of the other's mind. The analyst then supports this suggestion by referring to the client's silence: "you have such long pauses now" (lines 23–24). Although the word "resistance" is not uttered, it is alluded to, especially in the elaboration at lines 26–27.

Again, a very long silence ensues (line 28), before the client begins to explain (line 29 onwards) that his thoughts are going in circles around what "hiding" means to him, thus returning to the issue he raised in lines 7–17. This account attends to the issue of lengthy pauses, but does not admit to "avoiding a difficult issue." Some moments later, the analyst explicitly suggests that they should put this topic aside and, instead, focus on the massive pausing as an indication of resistance.

In Extract 4, the analyst suggested there are "difficulties" in saying what is in the mind. In Extract 5 below, the confrontation is stronger: the analyst suggests the client is expressing the opposite of her true disposition. He argues for his point by describing the way the client has talked. ("Hanski" is the client's late husband and "Markus" her son.)

Extract 5 [II/8/B21]

```
01  An:  .th well >it is< interesting that .hh that Hanski
02       and possibly Markus too were going (.hh) for a sailing
03       trip but >you hadn't been invited< along.
         ((25 lines omitted: PA explains she usually sailed
         if their son was there, although sometimes Hanski went
         with his mates))
29  An:  or they left er without Markus but in a group of guys.
30       (.)
31  Cl:  well such things did happen too,
32       (1.6)
33  Cl:  absolutely erm such things [happened and, .hh
34  An:                              [.hhh
35  Cl:  and I was often (1.2) I: was by no means #mm eh hm#
36       hurt I mean I thought (0.7) it had its certain advantages
37       that (0.5) first of all I was (.) as an understanding wife
38       I had the opinion that of course (1.0) mt one needs to get
39       out with the guys every now and then,
40       (1.5)
41  Cl:  (I mean like) who'd always want to hang around with old
42       ladies (0.5) mt as (I- had-) I had learned this then.
43       (.)
44  Cl:  .hhh and secondly then (.) I was (0.7) I had sort of
```

```
45             ( ) some peace of my own,
46       ?:    .nff hh
47             (1.2)
48  →    An:   .thh somehow one gets the impression that you would
49  →          assume that the issue is quite the opposite. .hh
50             (.)
51  →    An:   when >you explain< that it is by no means annoying to
52  →          you and .hh and that well who would always want to be
53  →          with old ladies anyway,
54             (.)
55       Cl:   HUH [.hh
56  →    An:       [you were an old lady.
57       Cl:   .hh yes well there was I referred to it because
58             m m Hanski had the habit (0.5) sometimes (.) m (.hh)
59             it maybe doesn't sound the same in Finnish but .hh
60             in Swedish (1.0) °he° he would use this,
61       An:   .hhh ((coughs)) (.) mt m
62       Cl:   #er::# word <tant>.
               ((Swedish tant = "aunt", "old lady"))
63             (1.0)
64       Cl:   "well y'know one can't talk with old ladies ( )"
65             ((=in Swedish))
66             (0.5)
67       An:   yes then you were one of the tan  [tar(-).]
68       Cl:                                     [ye:s   ] so I
69             was (.) so I was terribly offended . . .
```

The topic of the talk is the client's dream and the associations presented thereafter. The analyst suggests at lines 48–56 that the client is presenting in her talk the opposite version of her true dispositions, arguing for this by describing and animating her prior action (lines 51–53). The client initiates a repair (Schegloff, Jefferson & Sacks, 1977) with a surprised "huh" (line 55), and the analyst explicates his point by a statement: "you were an old lady." Thus, he indicates that the way client has categorized herself in the story, testifies for a different attitude than she overtly puts forward. The client's account that follows explains the use of the Swedish word "tant" (aunt, old lady), but does not attend to the claim that she has failed to present her real dispositions. In effect, her account works to undermine the implications of her lexical choice.

However, from line 69 on the client proceeds to a narrative (not shown in the data) about feeling offended because of having been denied a much-awaited sailing trip as Hanski had decided to go with the guys. For the analyst, this does not yet constitute "facing the issue." After a while, he begins to confront the client with the issue of Hanski having in fact treated her cruelly and been unfaithful to her. According to this interpretation, the client's being one of the 'tantar' constituted a much more serious blow than she was ready to admit.

In both Extracts 4 and 5, the characterization of the client's action is presented in tight connection with the analyst's claim to resistance to the analytic work. Furthermore, in both cases, it seems the client's account deals with some aspect of the accountable action (pausing, choosing the word *tant*) rather than the claimed "avoidance of the actual dispositions" or the difficult issue the analyst is after (cf. Peräkylä, 2005). In other words, the clients account for their actions, but without admitting to avoiding speaking of their "real dispositions."

Extract 6 differs from the two prior ones in that the environment for topicalizing the client's actions is that of overt, interactional resistance: the client disagrees with the analyst's assertions.

Extract 6 [II/2/B1:22–24].

```
01          (1.2)
02      An: I think this feature sticks with you quite tightly that
03          (0.6)
04          (  ) everything must be done for others.
05          (1.4)
06      Cl: yes,
07          (5.0)
08      Cl: yes,
09          (5.0)
10      Cl: yes
11          (.)
12      Cl: .mhhh HHHhhhh
13          (4.0)
14      ?:  mt
15      Cl: [But you know there are others
16      An: [(You<)
17      Cl: that are even worse than me.
18          (2.0)
19      Cl: Hhhh £(-[-)£
20      An:          [(he he ha)
21      An: £But are there ones that are even better.£
22      Cl: .mhh Even wor[se< ]
23      An:              [I   ] rather (.) think you are (0.2)
24          (-) good.
25          (2.0)
26      Cl: Wh[at (good),]
27  →   An:   [I mean    ] good in the sense that you >want to<
28  →       .hh want to do things for other people.
29          (1.2)
30  →   An: Then you call it being bad.
31          (1.0)
```

32 Cl: Yes yes but (.) you know there is this (point)
33 however that,
34 (1.0)
35 An: mhh >I think that< these (things) are also connected
36 in the sense that .hhh that – (1.2) >you< always have
37 the feeling that you are (0.2) bad and wrong.
38 (0.4)
39 Cl: y:e:s,
40 (.)
41 An: So that's why you must (0.6) no matter how much you
42 (0.4) do favours for others (1.0) you are always
43 the one who is the bad one and done something wrong.
44 (2.6)
45 Cl: Yes well I don't (0.2) completely (.) #a# #a# always (0.2)
46 think like this, hh so don't,
47 (0.4)
48 → An: This is not a reproach.
49 (1.6)
50 → An: But you ( )- (.) experience it as a (sort of a) reproach
51 ?: .mth
52 Cl: I mean [I know that I have this .hhh I have I have
53 An: [( )
54 Cl: a tendency for this, (1.6) a:nd I have I have (0.4)
55 a certain weakness, (0.2) here but (0.2) .hh (0.6)
56 But I mean >I'm not like< a sort of a (0.4) any (1.2)
57 How shall I put it now (0.4) >sort of< (1.8)
58 j- je <Jesus syndrome>, hh
59 An: £mmhh meh£
60 (0.4)
61 Cl: May I leave now to the< (1.4) ( ) ( ) ( )-
((mentions a hospital ward; PA's going to see a relative))
62 >I must<
63 (1.4)
64 → An: So< (0.3) yes isn't it interesting that, .hh even
65 → to that you need to have permission.
66 Cl: Yes,
67 → An: You are leaving to serve another person.
68 → hh Stop serving [me.]
69 Cl: [Yes we]ll this is a bit .hh (1.0)
70 mt difficult 'cause . . .

At lines 2–4, the analyst provides an interpretative statement: he asserts that the client has a strong tendency to do things for others, implying she thereby neglects herself. The client responds to this with repeated *nii*s (translated as "yes") *Nii* is the Finnish response particle that can be used to convey agreement with a point which is not news (Sorjonen, 2001). She then goes ahead to mitigate: "there are others that are even worse than me" (lines

15, 17), thereby treating the interpretation as an accusation, and resisting it by downgrading its relevance.

That the client chooses to do this, is what the analyst now treats as an accountable issue. We could say that the design of the analyst's interpretation has invited a defensive response, as it has many features of a complaint: the extreme-case formulation "everything" and "sticks with you tightly" implying that the feature is unwanted. However, the analyst treats this choice as one that reflects solely the client's mind and reactions. The analyst shows this in his next turns (lines 47–70), cleverly taking advantage of the design of the client's turn: there are some that are worse – but are there some that are better? Thus, he makes a point that doing things for others is "good," but when the client is shown that she does it, she defends herself and thus considers it "bad." "Then you call it being bad," now places the focus on the client's prior action. The client begins to respond, but the analyst proceeds to provide an interpretative statement where "doing things for others" and "feeling that one is bad" are linked together (lines 35–43). This interpretation builds upon the initial one and links the client's responses to it as its additional evidence.

The client's response is defensive, making the point that her tendency to serve others is not that strong (lines 45–46). The analyst, again, focuses on the client's prior action (of defending) by a reference to his own action: "this is not a reproach – but you experience it as a (sort of a) reproach" (lines 48, 50).[2] When the client responds (lines 52–58), her turn initial particle *et* (translated here as "I mean") connects it to her own prior turn (45–46), as its elaboration. Thus, she does not attend to the analyst's turn, but recycles her earlier point: she admits only to a slight tendency for serving others. She then asks for a permission to leave. Instead of responding to her request, the analyst, for the third time formulates the client's action as evidence for his interpretation: that she is constantly, also at this moment, serving others (lines 64–68).

We should signal that here the characterization of client's action is used as an argumentative resource. Each turn the client takes when reacting to the analyst's interpretation is treated as evidence that reinforces the interpretation. Our data contains several sequences such as this one. Characterizations of the client's action (or sometimes emotion, Vehviläinen, 2003b) appear in chains, the analyst persuasively arguing for his point.

[2] Sandlund (2004, p. 156) has observed a parallel professional's intervention in academic seminars, calling it an activity-type formulation. In her analysis, the professor uses it when downplaying students' expressions of frustration. According to Sandlund, it operates as a device for "exercising the institutional role-related right to stipulate and momentarily 'fix' the meaning of what is going on."

Discussion

These examples show how the analyst's central business at hand – identifying puzzles in the client's talk or behaviour – is prone to invite argument and defensive talk. Consider the following observations: (1) Turns that topicalize or otherwise characterize the client's action are challenging, sometimes even blaming, by format. They make the client accountable for her prior action and treat it as something to explore. (2) Focusing on the client's prior action enables the analyst to direct the focus back to the client herself (Bergmann, 2001) and, importantly, to maintain that any accounting or explaining of her actions should be done with reference to her own mind, not to the analyst's actions. This also enables the analyst to avoid aligning with the action the client has initiated in her first turn. (3) The practices of accounting used by the client often entail elements that are prone to be treated by the analyst as noticeable. They may contain references to the analyst's actions or analyst's agenda; or defensive elements such as accounts or mitigations. These elements, in turn, lead the analyst to focus again on the client's action. Thus, focusing on the client's action may lead to confrontative sequences where each client's move is focused on as evidence of the analyst's interpretation (see Extract 6). Indeed, this device often appears in chains: if one occurs, a set of them is bound to occur and an argumentative sequence ensues. If, however, the client collaborates and aligns with the analyst's invitation to treat her own action as a puzzle to explore, free association or self-reflection follows (see Extracts 2 and 3).

Why is focusing on the client's prior action such a compelling form of evidence to support the analyst's interpretative statements? This strategy draws upon actions that have taken place in the "public" space between the participants. This, indeed, is what the analyst takes such care to show. It is difficult for the client to deny that some action just took place, although it is, of course, possible to argue against a particular interpretation regarding that action (i.e. that such action means one is resisting the analytic work).

Confrontations and claims of resistance, such as the ones studied in this chapter, run the risk of being treated as hostile. They implicitly question the motives of the other speaker in that they implicate denial of "true dispositions." In psychoanalysis and some addiction therapies (Arminen & Leppo, 2001; Halonen, Chapter 8, this volume), such confrontational interventions are nevertheless systematically used. Based on the present analysis, it is possible to conclude that the defensive and resisting responses that the clients give to the professionals confrontative moves can be understood, not only as results of the mental states of the clients, but as products of the shared interaction. This is despite the fact that in the cases analysed here, only the clients become accountable for their actions.

In psychoanalytic interaction, the analyst may suggest to clients what their talk says about their dispositions – sometimes against their own (shown) conviction. This is in contrast with the idea of ownership of experience, the organizing principle of many phenomena of ordinary conversation as well as institutional interaction (see Rae, Chapter 4, this volume). It is part of our everyday life to treat each other as owners of our experience (Peräkylä & Silverman, 1991; Sacks, 1984). The conviction that the analyst can deal with the client's unconscious alters this orientation. The analyst is seen as able to interpret the meaning of the client's talk before and beyond the client's awareness of it, and eventually to help the client to reach a new awareness of her or his experience. This asymmetry has been a major reason for criticisms targeted at psychoanalysis. Analysing psychoanalysis as an institutional interaction provides an empirical handle on this asymmetry on the level of particular conversational practices. The device described here – focusing on the client's prior action – is one such practice, maintaining the asymmetry in a compelling way.

The identification and management of unconscious resistance – the key orientation of the analyst – is embedded in practices of confrontation and management of explicit client resistance. As stated, such resistance is not merely treated as an interactional problem, but, rather, as a starting point for exploration. Data-driven conversation analysis identifies particular ways of confronting clients and making them accountable for their own actions, and using their actions as evidence for what is happening in their minds. Psychoanalytic theory, for its part, provides concepts that are taken by the practitioners to be the institutional legitimation for such interventions. With conversation analysis, it is also possible to characterize the dynamics of this type of intervention and explicate its interactional consequences: namely, that topicalizing action tends to instigate argument, and that the defensiveness the client becomes accountable for is a result of the interaction between the two participants.

8 Person reference as a device for constructing experiences as typical in group therapy

Mia Halonen

Sharing one's experiences is a crucial activity in group therapies. In such therapies, groups can be either constituted around one problem or goal common to all the clients, or the group can work as a place in which clients can learn from one another and share experiences whether their individual problems are similar or not. Almost all (psycho)therapy types have a group application, and groups are assumed to be rather efficient in psychological progressing (see, e.g. Corey, 1986; Wootton, 1977).

In this article I will concentrate on one type of group therapy, namely the Minnesota model group therapy for addicts, and examine how the clients share experiences and, especially, how they construct their experiences as typical or identifiable. First, I will briefly introduce the ideology, therapeutic goal, and practices of Minnesota model group therapy. Then I will show that the dynamics of talking in a group seem to direct the participants to orient towards each others' stories as a template in which to fit their own experiences. The core of this article is a detailed analysis of how therapists use variation of person reference terms as a linguistic device to construct the experiences of the participants as typical of addicts.

The therapeutic goal of identifying with each other

The theory of Minnesota model therapy, also called 12-step treatment, is based on the ideology of Alcoholics Anonymous (see, e.g., Mäkelä *et al.*, 1996, pp. 194–196). The cornerstones of the theory are: (1) addiction is a disease from which one can recover only by choosing complete abstinence and joining AA, and (2) the disease has to be recognized and accepted by the clients themselves. (For the AA ideology, see Mäkelä *et al.*, 1996, pp. 117–132.) These two views are to be taught to the clients in four weeks, which is the time of clinical treatment. Unlike in AA, the clients in the clinic are usually not voluntary but are sent there, for instance, by their employer. Clients often resist the diagnosis of addiction, which is why confronting the clients with the facts of their lives and ways of speaking is seen as being crucial in this therapy (see, e.g., Johnson, 1973, pp. 24–31, 43–55;

Laundergan, 1982, pp. 32–33, 38–41; Vehviläinen, Chapter 7, this volume). A major device for both recognizing addiction and joining AA is identifying with each other, that is, other addicts. The treatment was developed for alcoholics but nowadays drug users are also treated together with alcoholics. The setting differs in many ways from more canonical (psycho)therapies. The therapists describe themselves as addicts (even after decades of abstinence). They do not normally have any kind of formal education for being therapists. All the clients have the same problem, and the treatment is relatively short.

The ideology of the therapy is clearly stated. Elsewhere I have deconstructed the ideal and the practice of the treatment (Halonen, 2002; 2006). Close analysis of the interaction can reveal practices that work towards the therapeutical ends without that being their purpose, and practices that do not work in a way they were supposed to. For instance, "talking in circles" (each participant taking an extended turn) is supposed to guarantee everyone space to talk about just their own feelings, but conversation analysis shows that it actually creates a series of stories all in some way related to the first turn. The dynamics of talking in circles does serve the ideal of clients identifying with each other but makes it difficult to talk about a whole new topic unrelated to the ones in the previous turns. Professional ideology and actual interaction might lie quite far from each other. (For a more detailed discussion of this kind of relationship, see Peräkylä & Vehviläinen, 2003.)

The dynamics of talking in a group

The data analysed in this chapter consist of nineteen hours of group therapy sessions from two therapists (referred to as Th1 and Th2) from an in-patient clinic in Southern Finland. The therapy is done in groups with a therapist and six to ten clients. The sessions are based on talking about own experiences. Every morning the group starts with the so-called morning or feeling circle during which each client talks about her or his present feelings. The clients also tell the story of their addiction once, the so-called "drunkalog," in which they tell others how their addiction developed. The clients' own stories can offer material for the therapists to confront clients with.

Sharing is exclusively an activity of talking in groups but what counts as sharing is a more complex issue (see Wootton, 1977). What is typical for talking in groups in Minnesota model group therapy is that participants talk mostly in circles, that is, taking a turn is expected of everyone, and refusal to talk is treated as an accountable issue. What the participants also have in common is the in-clinic environment where everyone has basically the same routines. Furthermore, addiction and experiences related to it are familiar to everyone. The first one to speak often creates a kind of first story (see Sacks, 1992b, pp. 249–263), and everybody rehearses their own, second, stories in their minds. Second stories are used as a therapeutical device also in AA-meetings where each participant in a group has a turn. Arminen (1998, pp. 179–80) has studied AA meetings and showed how telling stories is a means to give and gain mutual help: one's own experiences are fitted into others' stories. This does not mean that the experiences are similar but that the participants orient to show that their stories occasion from others' stories.

In everyday conversations people do collect different kinds of happenings, like "Remember this, so that you can tell about them to somebody else" (Sacks, 1992b, pp. 258–260). What psychotherapists have to learn is to listen to their clients without a second, interpretative story in their mind. Sacks refers to Fromm-Reichman's work (1967) *Principles of psychotherapy*, where she states that the most important ability of the therapist is to learn to listen without their own lives in mind. Second stories are not central and relevant means of interpretation or problem solving in psychotherapies, but in Minnesota model group therapy also they are one therapeutic device.

In Minnesota model group therapy, the most straightforward, and the most frequently used, way to indicate that a feeling or experience is similar, is for the speaker to explicitly assert the similarity. Direct reference to each other is also the way the participants in AA meetings share their experiences (Arminen, 1998, pp. 113–140). In the morning circles and after the clients' drunkalogs, clients refer to each other's turns; for instance, *niinkun Tarjaki sano* "just like Tarja said too" and then talk about their own experience, showing that the experience talked about is shared. Talking in circles particularly creates dynamics in which especially the first but also all the previous turns constitute a template for the forthcoming turns. The clients compare their feelings to each other's feelings and express their similarity or dissimilarity. The similarity or dissimilarity of the experiences is thus treated as a fundamental issue in the group.

It thus seems as if the participants are constantly constructing and orienting to mutuality through all of their devices. We will look briefly at two extracts that will show this. In the first one, Hanna, a female client (all names are fictitious), has just ended her drunkalog and at the beginning of the extract the therapist opens up a space for others to pose questions to Hanna (line 1). However, what happens first is not clients posing questions, but another female client, Tarja, relating her experience of the time of constructing their own house to Hanna's previous story (line 3). She even calls her action "saying," not questioning or asking.

Unlike in other chapters using non-English data in this book, in this one the original transcripts are also shown. This is because I will discuss the kind of linguistic devices that do not all belong to the repertoire of English. The extracts are, however, somewhat simplified in order to bring up the most significant devices used. The focus items in the extracts are in bold.

Extract 1 Similar situation [TN/PR2].

01 Th2: °oisko°, (1.2) halukkaita kysyjiä,
°are there°, (1.2) any questions,
02 (5.0)
03 Tarja: minä **sanon** vaikka heti että **aekalailla**,
*I'll **say** let's say right away that **pretty much**,*
04 (0.4) **samallaista** et niiku tuo rakennusvaihek**kii** et
*(0.4) **similar** to that constructing stage **too** like*
05 sit ku talo ol valamis ni
when the house was finished then

Tarja asserts the similarity of the experiences by saying her life has been *aekalailla samallaista* "pretty much the same" and using clitic particle *-kin*, in this context best paraphrased as "too" or "as well" (lines 3–4).

Extract 1 is an example of a client explicitly asserting that her experience is similar to that of another. The next case is an example of an orientation to comparing experiences and discussing them also when they differ from each other. Here, a morning circle has just ended. The first turn after the circle comes from Aija, a female client who starts by asking for permission to still add something. After getting permission she explains how she is different from the others in the sense that they are homesick but she is not (lines 3–7). In the extract there is a "0" mark (lines 1 and 6) which refers to so-called zero-person construction. We will get back to this construction later in this article; it is not relevant in the following analysis.

Extract 2 Not homesick [TN/PR1].

01 Aija: ↑saaks 0 viel #y-# #semmosen yhden asian sanoo#;
↑may 0 still #y:# #say something
02 Th2: ↑mm
03 Aija: .hhh että:< #e# et ku näistä< et teil on, (.)
like:,< #e# when these< like you have (.)
04 ↑nytkin on **kaikilla muilla** .hhh on nyt (.)
*even ↑now too **everybody else** .hhh has now (.)*
05 mielessäh, (.) kotiasiat tai ↑sillä lailla
in their in mind, (.) things at home or ↑like that
06 kun:< (.) 0 on yksinnään ↑niin ↑semmonen huoli on
when< (.) 0 is alone ↑then ↑that kind of worry is
07 kokonaan pois.
totally absent.

Aija had started the whole circle at this session and since her turn five more clients had spoken. Being the first one had put her in a situation where she had not heard about others before her own turn. The orientation to talk about same things seems to drive Aija to declare that she, unlike the others, is not homesick and she even asks for an "extra" turn to do so. Even though the purpose of the circle is that each client talks about their own feelings, the others' turns seem to create that strong a template that the others also report feelings they do not or did not have.

Here I have discussed two cases in which it was shown how the clients make their experiences and stories fit to each other's. Next, I will turn to analyse a device used by therapists to construct experiences as identifiable with or typical to addicts, namely person references.

Variation in person references as a device for constructing experiences as identifiable

Therapists in Minnesota model group therapy have many experiences similar to their clients since they are (former) addicts themselves. It may happen that therapists in other sorts of psychotherapy have experiences similar to their clients but this fact is not made manifest or known to the clients. In Minnesota model group therapy only people with the same kind of background are present.

The main aim of the therapist is to make clients see themselves as addicts and to accept that they need the help of AA. Some clients are very compliant, seemingly willing to admit their addiction and join AA. Some are far more resistant. The ideal of the therapy is then to confront these clients by making them see the patterns of addiction in their behaviour. A major device for doing this is to bring up experiences of other clients and the therapist and construct them as identifiable. Therapists can make clients relate a typical occasion in an addict's life by directing the story using questions. They can also make direct use of their own experiences by talking about them. Even though everybody in the therapy group shares something which is typical of addicts, clients are naturally otherwise different from each other, and facing the fact that they are addicts might be very difficult for some of them. The issue is delicate and even though in this therapeutic model confrontation is both accepted and encouraged, the therapists still orient to that delicacy by constructing many experiences as something they all presumably share. An important linguistic device for doing this is the person references the therapists use.

In Finnish, in addition to six person references, there are grammatical constructions that refer to an indefinite group of people, in which anyone can interpret themselves as included. (For the Finnish person reference system, see e.g. Hakulinen, 1987; Helasvuo & Laitinen, 2006.) One of these constructions is the so-called passive or indefinite person (Shore 1988), also called the "fourth" person (Hakulinen & Karlsson, 1979, p. 255; Tuomikoski, 1971,

p. 149). For example, the phrase *siellä juotiin* literally means "there was drunk" and more idiomatically something like "there were people who drank." What is missing in the Finnish construction is the subject or the agent – the "person" of the idiomatic translation. Still, this kind of construction always refers to some personal actor so that, in some contexts, hearers can perceive themselves as the agent. The passive form has also been grammaticalized into the verb form for the first-person *we*, but in these cases the personal pronoun is typically stated as well. Because of this, phrases without the personal pronoun might in certain contexts also convey a strong implication of the speaker including him- or herself as the referent. (For more about the Finnish passive, see Hakulinen *et al.*, 2004, pp. 1253–1281; Helasvuo, 2006.)

Another indefinite person reference type is the so-called zero-person construction. In this construction the verb form is the third-person singular *menee* "goes" but there is no stated subject or object, or agent. The missing part can be marked by "0" (zero) into a transription in order to make the construction more accessible and understandable, e.g., *jos 0 menee* "if 0 goes." The zero can also appear in positions other than subject or object but in therapy examples these are the most typical positions. (For zero-person construction see Hakulinen *et al.*, 2004, pp. 1283–1299; Laitinen, 2006.) Also the second-person forms and especially the second-person singular and plural pronouns *sä* or *sinä* or *te* "you" can also be used in the same generic way as singular and plural *you* in English (see Helasvuo & Laitinen, 2006; Laitinen, 2006; Seppänen, 2000). In the extracts we are going to examine, I have put in bold the zero-person constructions and inserted 0 in place of missing subject or object.

The variation of possible personal reference terms enables the therapists (and the clients) to create a very complex and dynamic picture of alcoholism and addiction. The richness of reference variation can function as a face-saving strategy by not explicating who belongs to the frame of reference, that is, the participants can talk about delicate addiction-related issues without taking full responsibility or showing who should take it. The dynamics enable talking about difficult issues without pointing a finger at anyone specific.

In the next extract the therapist has asked a question that makes it possible and even relevant for the client to admit that his behaviour has been addict-like for quite some time. He has not, however, explicitly admitted this. The therapist now starts to produce a story about the client's hangover relying strictly on what the client has already said. As we can see, the story starts with a zero-person construction *0 o juonu* "0 has drunk" (line 1) which leaves the reference open. This constuction here, in the story preface, frames the whole story as something that typifies addicts and thus is possible for anyone in the group the identify with. Immediately after the preface she changes to addressing the client, Juha, by changing to the second-person verb form *heräät* "you wake" and *lähdet* "you go" (lines 3 and 4). In the omitted part of the story she continues to describe the hypothetical day and confronts the client by asking if he has ever thought that there might be something wrong with his behaviour. The client does not concede this, justifying himself by claiming that he does not always start drinking before evening. Later (from line 17 on), however, he admits that he often drinks in the morning. This is where the therapist once again intervenes with a question that dramatizes the client's situation (lines 20–23).

Extract 3 Urge to drink [TN/PR10].

```
Th2:  no entäs aamulla ku:, sanotaa että 0 o
      well how about in the morning when let's say 0 has
      juonu enemmän illalla ja aamulla ku
      drunk more in the evening and in the morning when
      heräät nii, nii ku on kankkunen ja,
      you wake up so, like when there is a hangover and,
      ja tota lähdet
      like you go
((12 lines omitted. The therapist describes the patient buying
beer; the patient has himself talked about drinking beer as a
chaser. A little later, the therapist asks whether the patient
thought that there might be something wrong with his behaviour. He
admits this, but also starts to tell how he could wait until noon
or even evening despite having no specific reason for staying sober
that day.))
Cl:   mut useesti ku on aikaa ni kyl se,
      but often when there is time then really it,
      tai useammi, ni sillo, sit 0 tulee otettuu,
      or more often, so then, then 0 happens to have,
      joskus aamusta.
      have something, sometimes from morning on.
Th2:  no onks sul semmone tunne
      well do you have that kind of feeling then
      sit aamulla että, pakko
      in the morning that, there is an urge
      saada. mä e niinku, mä en selvii
      to get something. I won't like, I won't get
      täst päiväst jos en mä saa.
      through this day if I don't get something.
Juha: no se- se, se harvemmin kyl sillä tapaa
      well it- it, it's actually rarely that way
```

The therapist does the dramatizing by fictional reported speech using the first-person singular *mä* "I" (lines 22 and 23). It is obvious that in this context this "I" is a generic reference. It is thought important that the therapist chooses the first-person pronoun which is most often used to refer to a speaker exclusively. Knowing her background it is also possible that she is talking with her own experiences in mind and that she is highlighting this possible interpretation by the choice of the reference term. She could also have used some more "conventional" generic reference term, e.g. the zero-person construction, but did not. By choosing the first-person pronoun the therapist makes it possible to hear her question as one that also brings her own experiences up. By alluding that she is talking also about her own experience, the therapist may encourage the client to reciprocally see and admit his problems. In any case, it is clear that the therapist uses the generic first-person pronoun after trying for quite some time to get the client to admit to his addictive habits. As we can see from the beginning of the client's answer (line 24), this is not working since he claims not to recognize this pattern: *harvemmin kyl sillä tapaa* "actually rarely that way."

In line 18 also, the client uses the zero-person construction. The construction is thus also a device for a client to talk about his or her own delicate problem as something that others can also recognize and identify with, and not something specific to the speaker alone. Kurri and Wahlström (2007) have studied client's "agentless talk" in Finnish psychotherapy sessions. In their data the clients use the very same constructions of avoiding personal reference as in my data. It is of certain interest also that the problems of the client in Kurri's and Wahlström's study are strongly alcohol related.

Avoiding personal reference is of course not solely a Finnish phenomenon but in Finnish there are probably more linguistic devices to avoid talking directly about oneself than, for example, in English. In English-speaking data, clients seem to use generic *you* in therapy contexts when talking about delicate issues, e.g. in AIDS counselling when talking about a child living with an HIV-infected person (Peräkylä, 1995, see e.g. p. 132) or in motivational interviewing when talking about prostitution connected to drug abuse (Miller & Rollnick, 1991, pp. 286–287). *You* does not, however, seem to be frequent even when talking about topics as delicate as the ones mentioned.

The kind of dramatization with the first-person singular seen in Extract 3 also appears in Extract 4, in which the therapist has made direct use of his own experiences by talking about his life as both a therapist and an alcoholic. He has revealed that he got irritated with a client and could not figure out why until he began to think about his own drinking career: he had been a similar drinker to the client, and the irritation probably arose from that. In the extract he explains (line 1) that he told the story for therapeutic ends (lines 1–3). By explaining he also shows orientation to the norm that therapists do not usually talk about themselves – and not this extensively even in Minnesota model group therapy. At the very end of the story, he explains the general point that when irritated one should use the feeling to examine oneself. When making this point, the therapist changes to the generic zero-person construction *0 kannattaa kattoo* "it is worth 0 looking at" (line 4) and then dramatizes the "looking" by referring to it by the generic singular, the first-person pronoun (line 5).

Extract 4 Defence mechanisms [TM/PR16].

01 Th1: **mä puhun** tän vaan sen takia et et ku **te** tässä
*I **am saying** this just because when **you** [pl.] here*
02 näette miten **toiset**, **joku** potilas esimerkiks
*see how **others, some** patient for example*
03 aiheuttaa **teissä** ärsytyksiä
*causes irritation **in you** [pl.]*
04 ni yleensä **0 kannattaa kattoo** et mikähän kohta se
*then usually it is **worth 0 looking at** what the*
05 on=mitä se kertoo **musta**.
*point is=what it says **about me**.*

In this case the therapist is talking about himself but refers to himself in an intricate way. While the first first-person reference (line 1) refers exclusively to the therapist, the last reference *musta* "about me" (line 5) is a generic first-person reference term. The therapist has brought up a typical pattern through his own history but changed it into a more general picture by altering the reference terms first from the first-person singular to the indefinite reference terms *toiset* "others" and *joku* "some" to second-person plural (lines 1 and 3) and finally "back" to the first-person singular – now presenting a generic reference.

In the next case, the therapist has been trying to offer AA as a solution for a rather resistant client, Sari, for some time. Just before this extract, the therapist has made the clients describe a typical pattern of getting angry with someone without a reason by asking them questions. At the beginning of this extract, the therapist addresses Sari by asking her a question (lines 1–2) with second-person pronoun *sä* "you." Now, at this point Sari is involved, since she has answered and thus shown that she recognizes this imaginary situation.

Extract 5 What to do? [TM/PR2].

01 Th1: no mitä sitten ku **sä** oot pyytäny joltain
*and what then when **you** have*
02 anteeks ni minkä**s**lainen olo
*apologized to somebody then **what(+s)**[1] kind of a*
03 olo **sul** on tullu.
*feeling **have you** got.*

[1] "What(+s)" is a sign that, in Finnish grammar, implies the questioner knows the answer; see text for explanation.

04 Sari: no< ky:l tietysti< (.) helpottunu
well< really relieved of course
05 no mitäs sitte **on tehty**=ku on ollu hyvä olo.
well and ***what(+s)*** *have [we]* ***done*** *when the feeling has been good.*
06 Matti: **menty** huikal[le.
[we have] ***gone*** *for a drink.*
[((joint laughter))
07 Th1: [näin on. taas sopii huikka erinomasesti.
that's right. again a drink suits perfectly.
[(laughter))
08 sopii joko hirveen pahaan oloon ja hyvää
it suits either a terribly bad feeling or a good
09 oloon ja valitettavasti siltä
feeling and unfortunately all the feelings
10 väliltäkin oleviin.
in between, too.
11 okei. nyt **sä** oot pyytäny anteeksi tulee taas
okay. now ***you*** *have apologized for the need for a drink*
12 huikan tarve nin mitäs **0 sit vois tehdä**.
comes again so ***what(+s) could 0 do***.
13 Pasi: sillo **0 vois mennä** AAha.
then ***0 could go*** *to AA.*
14 Th1: niin sää keksit. se on ihan totta. täällä
yes you found it. that is absolutely true. in here
15 olis nyt se puhdas AA mitä **me tarvitaan** et
there would now be the pure AA which ***we need*** *like*
16 **menisin** AA:han ja **kertoisin** tämän kokemuksen.
I would go *to AA and* ***share*** *this experience.*

What the therapist does next is change the person reference in the next question into the passive form, the "fourth" person (line 5), which enables and furthermore invites anyone to identify with what is described and in that sense also become an addressee of the question. The passive form can here also be heard as referring to the first-person plural "we" which would include the questioner, that is, the therapist, himself. In addition to the generic forms the therapist uses he does not exclude others by gazing only at Sari. As we can also see, here Sari is not the one who answers, since another client, Matti (line 6), does, producing a grammatically fitting answer in the passive form. The therapist confirms that this is exactly the answer he was after.

After summing up the importance of alcohol for relieving feelings, the therapist again gets back to the imaginary story (line 11) and now the person reference is again singular the second-person *sä* "you." This could be again referring to Sari, trying to possibly draw her back into the conversation and make her the addressee. The therapist also gazes at her. In this context, however, after just having changed from the address term "you" to a "generic" passive form, the "you" here is quite possible to understand as a generic reference. Furthermore, the therapist again changes the person reference imposing a new question (line 12). Now it is a zero-person construction, again a deictic device that does not show who the description includes but can invite anyone to respond. Yet another client, this time Pasi, produces the answer (line 13) and, just as Matti did, he uses the zero, the same construction as the therapist. The therapist explains that it was exactly the answer he was after.

As we see, every question the therapist asks contains the marker *-s* (bold in the original and the translation) in the question word. The *-s* is a clitic particle which indicates that the questioner knows the answers, or, more precisely, that she or he is after a particular answer. Without the particle the questions could be heard as simply seeking information about specifically Sari's experiences. The particle adds an implication that the anticipated answer is common knowledge. It also has a patronizing tone; it is frequently used by teachers in Finnish elementary schools (Halonen, 2002, pp. 182–204).

Last, the therapist sums up the point of the whole story he has built with the clients, which is that attending AA meetings is the means of staying sober. In this summary, he once again changes the person reference, first to the first-person plural *me tarvitaan* "we need" (line 15) and again also to the generic first-person reference which we saw in the previous extracts: *menisin* "I would go" and *kertoisin* "I would say" (line 16). Here it is obvious that the reference is a generic one since it would be absurd if it referred only to him.

In this extract the therapist addresses the issue of joining AA as a solution for the future. The whole sequence building the picture of addictive behaviour arises from Sari's resistance to AA. The therapist draws Sari into the "the realm of reality" of the narrative by addressing a question only to her and then asking more generally, using the passive and zero-person constructions, about the patterns the clients choose or used to choose. The outcome is thus a jointly constructed story about a problem and a solution to it; and importantly, a story about the world to which Sari, too, belongs. In the summary, the therapist once again shows that this is a problem for all of them, including himself, in the group needing AA and uses the first-person reference to dramatize the solution.

The richness of the person system enables avoiding personal reference, constructing the experiences as shared, and inviting participants to identify with the "missing" person. When speakers use the passive and zero-person constructions, neither they nor their hearers can exclude themselves from the group of reference. The speaker leaves the group of reference open, thus inviting others to identify with the description, along with the speaker him- or herself. At least, the speaker shows that the issues described are not exclusively his or her experiences but are presumably more general.

Therapists can use almost all the singular variants of the Finnish person reference system in a generic way. They have the passive form – which can be described as somewhere between singular and plural (see Helasvuo & Laitinen 2006, p. 176) – as an option for making generic reference. They use zero-person construction to construct the experience as something that anyone can identify with. They can do exactly the same thing with the second-person singular forms and even with the first-person singular. The second-person singular *sinä* or more colloquial *sä* can also be used as a generic reference. In dramatizing the fictional but typical stories of addictive behaviour, they can use the first-person singular as a generic form. What is of importance is that the first-person singular is not a conventionally used generic reference term, but a term most often used to refer to the speaker exclusively. This conventional usage may convey an implication of a stronger self experience of the speaker than other generic reference terms. This device can thus imply that even the therapist has had similar experiences. Dramatizing with the first-person even when one has not "been there" is perfectly possible and "grammatical," but so far its use in other therapeutic contexts has not been reported.

Conclusions

In Minnesota model group therapy it is crucial to get the clients both to recognize and admit to being an addict and join others in the same situation (that is, by signing up to the AA) very quickly. This aim is itself quite abstract, and the question I posed was: what does it mean in practice, and how do the clients show that they are now spontaneously identifying with each other or that the therapist is pushing them to do so? In this chapter I have examined dynamic person reference devices used to construct experiences as shared or identifiable.

I have shown how the choice of the person reference can be used in constructing experiences as shared. I discussed how some features of the person reference system in Finnish, especially the passive and the zero-person constructions, enable clients not to talk exclusively about their experiences, but to construct them as something general, which anyone could identify with. Therapists use the same constructions to show that the pattern they are describing is typical and general to all addicts. The therapists also seem to use a great variety of the other person references available to construct experiences as shared. Using the second-person singular, which is the unmarked, normal term of address, they can both address a particular client or make a generic reference. With the first-person singular they can dramatize an event. It seems to be the case that the therapists choose this means of reference when the client has long been resistant to AA or to anything that suggests that she or he is an addict. A non-typical generic reference term may here serve as a device by which the therapists can highlight that they are included in the frame of reference. In this context, this device can at the same time remind clients about the fact that the therapists have similar experiences to their clients.

In the variation of person references that the therapist uses in Minnesota model group therapy in order to achieve the therapeutic goals, we can see the relation of grammar and interaction as Schegloff, Ochs and Thompson put it:

> Grammar is not only a resource for interaction and not only an outcome of interaction, it is part of the essence of interaction itself. . . . As an utterance proceeds, its lexical and grammatical structuring may open up, narrow down, or otherwise transform the roles of different participants to the interaction (1996, pp. 38–39).

We have seen that the work of constructing one's experiences as identifiable can be done through the dynamics of person reference. The therapists vary the person reference devices in order to invite, or push, the clients to recognize that they share many experiences. For a successful outcome, it is probably even more crucial for the client to identify with the others than merely to confess aloud to being an addict.

9 Conversation of emotions: On turning play into psychoanalytic psychotherapy

Ivan Leudar, Wes Sharrock, Shirley Truckle, Thomas Colombino, Jacqueline Hayes, and Kevin Booth

This chapter is a collaboration between academic researchers and psychoanalytic child psychotherapists working in an economically deprived part of a large city in England. We explore the ways in which the psychotherapists' training and experience – what we refer to as their "therapeutic orientation" – are made relevant and consequential in their therapeutic interactions. We argue that such therapeutic orientation needs to be taken on board by analysts of interaction if they are to grasp the relevant sense of therapeutic activities carried out in and through talk.

The chapter presents an ethnomethodological case study. We examine four consecutive group psychoanalytic psychotherapy sessions – how they unfold and how children come to use what the situations afford. Alongside the audiovisual recordings, we scrutinize the therapists' own write-ups of the sessions, which were produced after the event by the trainee sitting in on the sessions. These write-ups display the therapists' professional orientation to the activities in sessions and consequently enable understanding of the interactions in terms of the "schooled experience" of the therapists. Moreover, in preparing this chapter, the "first pass analyses" of the video recordings have been discussed with the authors who acted as therapists. These discussions pinpointed misunderstandings, omissions, and errors, and made it possible to correct and extend the initial analysis and highlight the real differences of opinion among the authors as to what may be happening. We use transcripts of these discussions below to detail the issues that arise in using theories in the analysis of concrete therapeutic interactions – this turns out to be by no means straightforward.

Our aim is to document psychotherapists' practices, but not simply to duplicate their understandings of the events in the therapeutic sessions – we take advantage of the sensitivity the talk and interaction of that ethnomethodology provides and this is where the psychotherapists profit from the cooperation.

Action under description and psychotherapy

Psychotherapy may be a "talking cure" but tell a psychotherapist that it is just talk! It is not difficult to imagine a piece of talk in therapy that can be described both as a "comment" and as an "interpretation," and another describable both as an "answer" and as a "defence." In general, the activities of the participants in psychotherapy can be described using the resources everyday language provides, such as verbs of communication, but also using terms such as "active listening," "unconditional positive regard," "defence," "projection," "transference," and so on. The former "stock of descriptions" is available to any competent speaker of English, but the latter are not available to the technically unprepared. Our list, moreover, indicates that we should not start by thinking about unified psychotherapy – there are very different schools and experienced practitioners within schools vary their practices[1] (Bongar & Beutler, 1995).

We start with a working assumption that each school of psychotherapy has an open-ended and mutable but (relatively) systematically organized and mutually dependent "stock of descriptions" (see Winch, 1972, pp. 95–97).[2] A stock of descriptions considered as a repository contains similar kinds of objects to Peräkylä and Vehviläinen's "professional stock of interactional knowledge" – theories, models, rules of thumb, concepts, etc. Peräkylä and Vehviläinen's strategy is to set up a dialogue between conversation analysis (CA) and the professional stock of interactional knowledge – in practice using CA to correct SIKs, describe them in detail, and to expand them. We are doing what Peräkylä and Vehviläinen left for another day – our aim is to study "the ways in which the practitioners' theories and concepts are actually referred to and made use of in the actual practice of their work" (Peräkylä & Vehviläinen, 2003, p. 729). The aims are complementary.

Any competent member of our society can understand a piece of psychotherapy as talk and most will no doubt also understand that it is psychotherapy. Only someone familiar with that variant of psychotherapy, however, could recognize innumerable instances of the therapeutic practice for what they are. An additional problem arises when one considers being in therapy as a client – can one participate simply as one does in everyday talk? That may be how a "novice" client starts, but is something more not required eventually? A preliminary: what is "going on therapeutically" often seems only asymmetrically recognizable – that is, not necessarily recognizable by either the client or the uninitiated investigator for that matter.

1 Only the last three terms would be used by our psychotherapists.

2 Winch stressed that the "stock of descriptions" is grammatically organized, and any new description can be added only if it fits into the conceptual grammar.

In part, this is a feature of the forms of therapy where the therapist is engaged in a kind of "unobtrusive leading" of the patient's activities.[3] The therapist's own participation is carried through actions which are readily identifiable under regular conversational descriptions – as questions, continuers, etc. – but which do not thereby reveal their form as therapeutic interventions (cf. Schegloff, 1963).[4] Working with two descriptive languages is then required to understand some asymmetries in therapy.

Labov and Fanshel (1977) distinguished "surface" speech acts from therapeutic actions and sought the coherence of therapy in the sequences of the therapeutic acts, requiring formal "translation rules" to map therapeutic actions onto surface speech acts (cf. Levinson, 1981). In our approach, no translation rules are required – the relationship between the "levels of description" is managed through broadening the contextual relations of an action in question (cf. Wittgenstein, 1958, §659). This approach to relating conversational and therapeutic practices is best explained by reference to Anscombe's notion of action as being identified "under a description," a conception which is very much akin to Ryle's idea of "thick description" or White's insistence that any one action can be of many different kinds (Anscombe, 1959; Ryle, 1949; A. R. White, 1979). Anscombe pointed out that any given action may be correctly identified in any one of an open-ended plurality of ways. The descriptions are not, however, rivals – in the way that, say, murder and accident would be – they differ in respect of the extent to which they provide only bare descriptions of the movements involved in an action or incorporate more or less extensive information about the context – in the way that, for example, shooting, fatally wounding, and killing can all be correct descriptions of the same actions. An identification of an action may include more or less extensive reference to the mechanics of the action's behaviour, reference to the intention with which the action is done, the consequences of the action, and the like.

There is no *a priori* limit to the range of circumstances that can be included in a description and in this sense talking about levels of description may be misleading. This notion of actions as identified "under a description" should dispel any impression that there must be some single description which provides the definitive identification of an action. There are potentially multiple correct descriptions, and a preference for one over the other is not dictated by correctness, but by the relevance of the

[3] In client-centred therapies, the therapist works within the client's frame of reference and uses their language. The degree of asymmetry between therapist and client may vary with different therapeutic schools.

[4] Schegloff describes the ways in which the psychoanalytic method equips therapists to build preparatory defences against the prospect that patients will – under transference – put words into their, the therapists', mouths.

information that the description provides. We are *not* proposing that the therapists' understandings provide *the* account of activities in therapy (though these are privileged with respect to formulating what the therapist is doing therapeutically). We are simply concerned with therapeutic activities "under a description" relative to the context of therapists' backgrounds, objectives, and tasks in hand. We are therefore concerned with the institutional character of therapeutic interactions. Our approach draws on the work of Hester and Francis (2000), who argued cogently that the distinct character of an institutional interaction is generated through the participants' orientation to the relevant institutional context and knowledge. A "stock of descriptions" must be prior to and independent of a concrete therapeutic engagement, even though when used descriptions are always realized in a specific and recipient-designed form.

The psychotherapists organizing the groups that we study have previously worked with individual children but, for practical reasons, now find themselves working with groups.[5] Their work is exploratory because they have had little previous experience of group work. They do not regard what they do as "group therapy," but rather as psychoanalytic psychotherapy delivered through working with groups. Working with groups is, however, not an altogether radical departure for them – both modes of engaging children are informed by their psychoanalytic background, stemming from frameworks provided by Klein (e.g. Klein, 1975; 1988a; 1988b) and Bion (e.g. Bion, 1984). Let us briefly consider what Melanie Klein had to say about starting school, when children are separated from their parents and have to interact with strangers in unfamiliar circumstances:

> In the life of a child school means that a new reality is encountered, which is often apprehended as very stern. The way in which he adapts himself to these demands is usually typical of his attitude towards the tasks of life in general (Klein, 1988b, p. 59).

So whilst the transition to school seems to her a source of distress for most children, different children cope in different and variably consequential ways. The children, however, do not express their anxieties in ways that are conventional, immediately obvious, or deliberate. According to Klein, children's actions are symbolic of their anxieties.

> At any given moment we are confronted with one dominant trend of anxieties, emotions, and object-relations, and the symbolic content of the patient's material has a precise and exact meaning in connection with this dominant theme (Klein, 1975, p. 12).

[5] Our psychotherapists work with groups of six children in four to five sessions of approximately twenty-five minutes duration. The interactions take place in a regular classroom that is set aside for these occasions. The participants sit round a low table and each session is video recorded using two cameras.

We can formulate three Kleinian therapeutic "background maxims" (i) "new environments and separation are sources of anxiety," (ii) "children express the anxieties symbolically but without necessarily knowing that they do so," and (iii) "all children are different in how they cope and what they have to cope with." The question is, though, can we really read the background therapeutic maxims of our experienced therapist colleagues from books, even those they accept as the classics? The answer, based on ethnography, is cautiously affirmative. For instance, one therapist, in discussing a first pass analysis, formulated the following maxim consistent with Klein.

Extract 1 FPAD09/09.

```
01  Th4:  I was just, I was thinking about what you were saying
02        about how conscious he is, of, I mean clearly it's
03        a terrifying thing for any kid to go into an
04        institution and work out how the institution works.
```

The next question is, though, when and how do the therapists use therapeutic maxims in concrete circumstances? As policies in politics, so these maxims cannot be applied dogmatically. It is very unlikely that our experienced psychotherapists would act as novices and follow therapeutic maxims like recipes (cf. Dreyfus & Dreyfus, 1985).

Their basic strategy is to be attentive to the ways in which the unconscious is expressed in the actions of individuals. Following Bion's formative *Experiences in groups*, however, it is clear that the psychotherapists also must treat the group as a unit, relate to it, and manage it. The practices of the therapists in this project are guided by understandings about working in groups that are meant to be both tentative and non-dogmatic – they are trying things out, seeing what, in their view, works, and what does not, with a wariness of making preconceptions about children into rigid expectations. This is their basic stance as they expressed it. Their participation in the group is intended to be responsive to what the children's behaviour reveals, rather than vigorously to pursue conceptions of what kinds of experience the children *must* be having. In their words, therapeutic maxims are somewhat like evolving maps of an unknown country (cf. Leudar & Costall, 1996, on acting with flexible plans).

A comment on method

Before embarking on the analysis of video recordings, we need to make clear the following guidelines. First, not every therapeutic maxim is likely to be relevant and consequential at any point in talk – as with other rules, its use in talk is occasioned and its "manifestation" is variable. Schegloff (1972) demonstrated that information external to a conversation affects how places (and persons) are formulated. He also introduced a "consequentiality" criterion for the use of contextual information in analysis, arguing that such information should inform analysis when it has demonstrable local consequences. These ensure the relevance of contextual information and that participants' and analysts' understandings do not diverge (see Schegloff, 1972; 1991). The consequences in question for Schegloff are sequential properties of talk-in-interaction. Our own focus is on how background information allows the analyst to grasp the sense of professional activities done in and through talk.

Second, children can avail themselves of the opportunities a situation affords but they do not have to, and when they do, each can do so in a very different way. The aim, therefore, has to be not just to analyse how the psychotherapists inscribe their therapeutic maxims into the interactive environment, but also how different children make diverse use of what the therapist presents them with.

Third, the therapists provide children with things to play with – small figurines, playdough, crayons, paper – in a setting which is "safe" and in which the children's imagination is taken seriously (cf. Klein, 1975). Children can express themselves through play, but the therapists try to convert the play into therapeutic interaction. Our concern is with how they do this – how their therapeutic orientation is made consequential, making the interactions recognizably psychoanalytically psychotherapeutic, for participants and observers. The practice under investigation has two components, which are differently organized as social engagements. One is a turn-taking element which is sequentially organized and locally managed, (see Sacks, Schegloff & Jefferson, 1974; Schegloff, Jefferson & Sacks, 1977), but with the proviso that the occasion is not wholly or straightforwardly a conversation, and that sometimes several conversations are taking place around the table and sometimes just one. The other is imaginative play – all the children are playing more or less continuously, but with an eye and ear on each other and on the psychotherapists. What one child does affects other children by, for instance, distracting or inspiring them. As we shall see these two components are not independent, partly because the children talk to each other, but mainly because the therapists recruit the play and its products into sequentially organized therapeutic transactions.

Fourth, the present investigation is a case study. We examine four consecutive sessions of psychotherapy, and in doing so we focus on how the interaction becomes recognizably a Kleinian psychoanalytic psychotherapy. We also concentrate on the "psychotherapeutic career" of one boy, "Abu". Our interest is in how the therapists find that he has responded to what the sessions afford him. Conversation analytic studies often draw on discourse from distinct therapy courses and from different types of therapy, and through combining and comparing these, CA can demonstrate which discursive strategies are generic to psychotherapy and which are specific to a particular school (e.g. Leudar, Antaki & Barnes, 2006). Ethnomethodology's research strategy is complementary to CA – through case studies we investigate the sequential unfolding of specific courses of psychotherapy. Case studies provide information on how participants' conduct and engagement change (cf. Davies, Thomas & Leudar, 1999). Judiciously chosen series of case studies are useful in assessing in appropriate terms the changes in and the effects of a psychotherapy and can provide an alternative to quantitative studies of outcome (see Leudar *et al.*, 2005). This does not mean that case studies cannot provide information about generic aspects of psychotherapy – as we shall see, our own study suggests some candidates for generic devices used in psychoanalytic psychotherapy carried out in groups.

Psychoanalytic psychotherapy for children starting school

The occasion is novel for the children and so the therapists have to find ways of explicating it to the children. This they do by contrasting the occasion with regular schooling, acknowledging its potential strangeness for the children, and giving assurances about its privacy from teachers and parents. Every first session started with an introduction in which the situation is framed by the two psychotherapists (Extract 2).

Extract 2 Group 4, session 1 (11.56).[6]

```
Th1:  Ye:s. and ↑you
      (0.5)
      Nora you were, weren't ↑you
      (0.6)
      But you are new. ((to Jack))
      (1.0)
      and that's hard and Ben is new and that's
      hard. And all the other kids know each other
      and you are in a new place
      (0.3)
      there's new teacher.
      (1.0)
      and you don't know all the other kids.
      (1.2)
      makes it really hard
      (1.0)
      °yes°
      ( 0.4)
Th2:  and you don't know us.
```

[6] In these extracts children are referred to by pseudonyms. Therapists are referred to as Th1 and Th2.

(1.0)
and you don't know what's happening here
(2.4)
it's very worrying.
(1.0)
What we want you to do
(0.7)
is we want you to te:- to tell us and teach us
(0.8)
by showing us, by using the playdough (0.3) and the (.)
drawing equipment - paper, pen, and pencils
(0.7)
what it's like to be
(0.7)
five year old
(0.4)
and in a reception class.
(2.4)

It is not difficult to read the three background maxims we started with into this introduction even though they are fitted to the circumstances. The problems for the children are

- being new in a novel situation with strangers (lines 1–19)
- not knowing the therapists or the purpose of the meetings (lines 19–23).

Th1 formulates a theme of anxiety about new situations (lines 3–23). She however does not attribute the anxiety to all children. In Extract 2 she divides the children into those who have been in the school for some time and those who are new. In specifying the problems of the latter individuals she displays to all the children her understanding and empathy. The second therapist, Th2, develops the theme by applying it to the therapeutic situation (lines 19–23). The school and the therapy session are thus unified in that both can engender the same problems for the children. In therapy, however, the problems can be made public and worked through (lines 25–36). The analogy between school and therapy could be thought of as a form of "transference." Discussing the sequence in Extract 2 the therapists, however, rejected that way of thinking, partly because the connection between the two domains of experience was explicit rather than unconscious.[7]

The play is specifically set up as the means of communication (lines 25–36), this being consistent with the use of toys in therapy by Klein (1975).

[7] Note, however, that in some aspects, the framing of the situation is not Kleinian – children are invited to "tell" and "teach" the therapists things about themselves (line 27) rather than expected to reveal themselves unconsciously. In this respect the interaction is framed more as an anthropological encounter than as psychotherapy.

Psychotherapists do not have to tell children what to do with the props they provide. Abu, like most of the other children, takes the ball of playdough out of the tub and starts banging it flat (Extract 3).

Extract 3 Group 4, session 1 (4.25).

Abu: *((loudly banging his clay with his fist))*
Th1: Abu has to be [ve::ry:: big and v:e:r:y: strong]
Tam: [*((bangs her clay loudly))*]
Th1: >and so has Tam<
(1.0)
so that they can feel in ↑cha:r:ge.
Abu: *((bang bang bang bang))*
((Tam and Abu giggling hysterically))
Th1: <and Col is watching ↑q:ui:e:tly: and saying>
I wonder what >this is gonna=be like<
(1.2)
I'm not sure I ↑like it.
Abu: *((bang bang bang bang))*
Th1: but Abu is still saying "I::'M: going to bang,
I:'m=going=to m::a:ke my m:ark
(0.5)
I:::'m going to MAKE this the way=I: want=it to=be
((Abu, Tam laugh))
Th1: I:'m not gonna=be sca::red.
(1.0)
yeah?

The therapist Th1 attributes a meaning to the banging in line with the anxiety theme – it is not an act of play alone, but Abu's way of coping with a scary situation (line 19) – he is asserting himself (line 6), taking control and changing the situation (lines 14–17).

Th1, moreover, does not deal with Abu's reaction in isolation. She generates a list of what different children are doing to cope – Abu is banging, another child, Col, is sitting and watching the proceedings (lines 9–12). In this list, children's doings are grouped together so that both similarities and differences between them are made manifest (lines 6 vs. 9). This is one important way our psychotherapists produce "focused interactions" – in producing "lists" they draw the children's attention to family resemblances between what they do and make, and in doing so make therapeutic maxims relevant to the situation at that point. In working with a group in this way, the therapist displays orientation to all three therapeutic maxims we started with – children's actions have determinate symbolic meaning, the children are finding the situation scary, and different children cope differently. We have in fact two candidates for generic devices whereby individual symbolic play is converted into psychoanalytical psychotherapy. One is providing the doings of group participants – in this case, the play activities of individual children – with meaning in accordance with developing therapeutic themes. The other is conjoining individual children's activities into a common or collective event through inclusion in a list.

None of these children have experienced therapy before and the question is how far they buy into this transformation of the play. Abu seems to bang notably more loudly following Th1's interpretations (lines 7, 13) and he and another child, Tam, seem to find the interpretations funny (line 18). The connection between interpretations and children's subsequent conduct is perhaps more obvious in what happens next. Abu not only bangs the play-dough, but starts roaring loudly (Extract 4, line 1), this with two consequences – two of the girls giggle (line 4) and Th1 proposes that he is now a big monster (line 6).

Extract 4 Group 4, session 1 (4.58).

```
01  Abu:  ar=rar=RARGH
02        (0.4)
03        Ar-RARgh:::
04        ((Tam and Amy continue to giggle))
05        (1.0)
06  Th1:  you're being a B::I:G:: monster now.
07        ((Abu bangs louder, and Tam and Sal join in))
08  Abu:  ArGH=H:::AR:GH::::=ha=ha ((holding plasticine up
09        to his face))
```

Abu fulfils the therapist's interpretation by putting the mask to his face – he is indeed a monster now. (See also line 9, Extract 5 where he confirms this in words: "Yeah: a monster".) Abu therefore plays along with the therapeutic maxim implicit in the therapists actions – "the play is meaningful." The specific meaning is of course not pre-determined – it develops through his contribution and in collaboration with the therapist.

Just playing imaginatively with others is only the first step though towards participating in psychoanalytic child psychotherapy. Th1 continues the transformation by endowing "being a monster" with a specific psychological meaning – she accepts that Abu is a monster but asserts that he is also a frightened little boy, who is using the monster to hide behind (Extract 5, lines 10–13, 15–16). Th1's interpretation turns the interaction into one that is recognizably psychoanalytic – it is tangibly resourced by the concept of "psychological defence."

Extract 5 Group 4, session 1 (5.08).

```
01  Th1:  Right between the eyes you've got a mask now
02        and I'm not allowed to see. (0.2)
03        d'you know what I think's hiding behind that mask?
04        (1.0)
```

05 ((Amy and Tam giggling and Abu banging))
06 Th1: Abu, you know what I think's=hiding behind
07 that B:::I::G:: fierce mask?
08 Abu: ((stops banging and looks at Th1))
09 Yeah, a monster::, ARo::GHH:
10 Tam: ((giggling))
11 Abu: ARoGHH::
12 Th1: A mon:::ster >Abu and behind that monster Abu<
13 °there's a small Abu who's=saying°,
14 (0.6)
15 [↑"Mon:ster Abu, keep me safe."]
16 Amy: [some people are coming down] stairs again
17 Th1: "keep me safe monster Abu cos I'm
18 [not sure I like=it here."]
19 Abu: [AERGHH] ((holds plasticine to his face))
20 I'M=AERGHH:: I'M >AN::GRY::< A:R::GH::
21 I:::'M
22 (1.2)
23 >↑ANGRY<
24 Th1: a hungry monster?
25 Th2: =angry monster
26 Th1: an an::gry: hun::gry:: mon::s:ter

Abu of course has no idea of what psychological defence is, but even so, does he accept that being a loud monster is a defence? Not obviously: going by the text, he *is* an "angry monster" (lines 18–21). About five minutes into the therapy, then, Abu accepts that play is meaningful in a way specified by the situation and so the therapists can in principle face him in public with different possible therapeutic meanings of his doings. This starts to indicate their therapeutic work.

Extract 6 shows Th1 trying to help Abu away from a "negative" way of coping with the situation, to enable a more personally constructive one. She puts it to him that he copes by trying to be big, strong, fierce, and wild (lines 11–13) and puts this into effect in being the monster. In fact, like the other children present, he is big enough, she says. She also works directly on his feeling of insecurity – through stressing the group solidarity *vis-à-vis* himself (lines 2–4), which the little girl Amy beautifully demonstrates by putting her hand on Abu's shoulder (line 5).

Extract 6 Group 4, session 1 (9.38).

01 Abu: R::ER::::gh::::
02 Th1: I think that this monster needs somebody
03 to >put=her hand on his shoulder and say<,
04 "It's alright (.) Abu,"
05 ((Amy puts her hand on Abu's shoulder.
06 He goes quiet but turns toward her with

07 *the mask still over his face.))*
08 Th1: °it's al::right.° You don't have to be a monster
09 here. You're safe.
10 (2.0)
11 It's=all=right you don't h::ave: to be big, you
12 don't have to be strong, you don't have to be
13 fierce, you don't have=to=be wi::l:d.
14 Abu: *((is almost cowering with his mask over his face))*
15 (1.0)
16 Th1: little boys are quite big=enough to be in this::=room
17 °with us.°
18 (1.0)
19 And little ↑GIRLs are quite big=enough,
20 (1.2)
21 because we like little boys and little girls h:::ere,
22 (0.2)
23 and we're not gonna=eat them up.
24 Amy: *((presents her plasticine and says))* ↑trou::sers.
25 Th1: trou::sers? (1.2) is that for a boy?
26 Amy: *((smiles and nods))*
27 Abu: >RIGH:T: I've broken=it<
28 (1.0)
29 the monster is bro:ked=.th:
30 *((Abu breaks up his clay and Amy takes her hand away))*
31 Th1: okay, so=are you going=to make something n:e::w::?
32 Abu: yep. ((*nods at Th1 slightly*))
((3 lines omitted))
33 Abu: WATch this:::, >I am gonna=make=a<
34 (0.2)
35 sq::uare.

Abu's reaction is significant – he goes along with Th1's explanation and Amy's hand on his shoulder and publicly breaks the mask (lines 27–30). But how do we know that he does this in response to what Th1 had said so far? It is indicated by the activities immediately prior to the breaking of the mask. Whilst Th1 comments that he does not have to be strong and cope by being a monster (lines 8–9) he freezes and "looks" at Th1 through the mask (but since it has no holes he is in effect hiding). Amy is meanwhile holding her hand on his shoulder. Subsequently, (lines 14–23) Abu continues to be oriented towards Th1 but he is now not simply hiding behind the mask as she generalizes her point. He slightly lowers his mask and looks at Th1 over its top – he does this twice creating the impression of tentativeness which is consistent with the idea that the mask provides him a defence. What he also does is to show the therapist the face behind the mask. Th1's talk and Abu's movements of the mask, are finely coordinated – the first peek comes during the one second pause in line 18, the second peek coincides with the word "he::re" and the pause in line 22. Then Abu lowers the mask altogether, during talk in lines 24–25, looking down at it. He tears the mask into pieces slowly in three jerky movements during 26; he is quiet but looking directly at Th1. Th1 also noted this as a significant moment and in discussing the first pass analysis commented that this was the first time she had any eye contact from the boy. Throughout this episode, the other children are quiet, all fiddling with playdough and listening, and some are looking. The episode is of some importance to the group.

What is Th1's reaction to the breaking of the mask? It is not to comment on his accomplishment, it is more constructive – the breaking the mask allows him to try something else. Going over the analysis with Th1 subsequently she commented as follows:

Extract 7: FPAD09/09.

Th1: I want these kids to have the freedom to have fun
in school. To enjoy it. Yeah?
IL: yeah
Th1: I want them to have the freedom of choice to sit down
and concentrate or to be little buggers. Abu, at the
point where he was being the monster, didn't
have freedom of choice
IL: right

What Th1 asserted was that Abu was terrified and acted under compulsion. She explained that she was not trying to stop Abu from *ever* acting as a monster (there may be in his life situations where this is appropriate) but her aim was to enable him to stop and think if being a monster is necessary. The concept of compulsion is then important in understanding what Th1 is doing *vis-à-vis* Abu; but that she is using it, and how she is using it, is situation and child specific.

Note that Th1 does not assume that Abu's problem that turns him into a monster is gone. The problem is not with adopting the monster character, but with doing so as a compulsive reaction when it is unnecessary in the situation and not a good way of coping with new situations in general. In other circumstances, the monster part might be a good way of coping sometimes – the therapist's aim is to alleviate the compulsive aspect. She is momentarily successful, but Abu the Monster returns later in therapy several times, though Abu also tries out other ways of coping that he observes in other children. Extract 8 from the second session documents this.

Extract 8 Group 4, session 2 (12.24).

Abu: ><u>look</u>=at=me<
(0.2)
<what <u>sha:pe</u> is <u>th:a:t</u>?>
(1.0)

>what shape is=it?<
Th1: I don't know what shape is it Abu?
Abu: >I don'=know<
Tam: ghe=Hehh=Hee::
Th1: it's a big pi::le it's=a
Abu: a rectangle with that
Th1: ah::: the same as- (.) that yes that's a rectangle
Th2: you made an impression,
Abu: y:ea::h=
Th2: =and=of:=course you've made an impress:ion
on u:s.
Abu: y:ea:h:.
Th1: you've=all made your mark (.) inside us,
in our memories, in our hearts
(0.5)
there are sha::pes that jus:t fit ea:ch
one=of=you::.
(0.2)
Yeah?

In this sequence, to begin with, Abu is not a monster. Inspired by another child, he makes a rectangle instead. A rectangle, made previously by another child was glossed by Th1 as a "safe place for everyone." Abu's rectangle, however, does not obtain the same meaning – what matters about it is that it is big (line 9), and the two therapists working jointly interpret it as designed to "make an impression" (lines 12–15 and 17–21 respectively). Note that Abu receives this interpretation with clear response tokens expressing his agreement. Note also that Th1 generalizes the meaning she accomplishes with Abu for all the children in the group. Making an impression is something emotionally positive – each child leaves an individual mark in the therapists' hearts (17–21). Note that Th1 does not generalize just for Abu – she generalizes in focusing the interaction, moving from addressing Abu separately to addressing all the children collectively, and even though this does not show in the transcript, the children listen. This then is another instance where Th1 moves between working with individual children and the group, transforming children's play into group psychotherapy.

Our argument, that therapists' practice is resourced by their therapeutic maxims, and familiarity with these is needed to understand the interactions, seems warranted. We have seen so far that Th1 and Th2 oriented interactions to therapeutic themes that are recognizably Kleinian and used concepts of "defence" and "compulsion" to understand children's activities. These activity descriptions were, however, not applied mechanically. It is not the case that therapeutic maxims dictate specific and fixed courses of action which the therapists follow like novice cooks follow recipes.

Applying maxims and concepts characteristic of a psychotherapeutic orientation (and ignoring them when need be) is open ended and non-deterministic, and requires skill, accumulated experience, and a cultivated sensibility. The implication for analysis of interaction is that noticing the parallels between what one sees in interactions and background theories and concepts is not enough – what matters is how a therapeutic orientation works itself into the particular circumstances. It is also important that therapeutic maxims are also regularly ignored. This is what we turn to next.

The therapists do not just see what fits in with their background therapeutic maxims. The question here is what did Th1 think Abu was so scared of to need to be a big loud monster? In Extract 9, Th1 provides children with her tentative understanding of their common problem (lines 1–6) that roughly parallels Klein's thinking on the matter – they, the children, are frightened because they are small with big strangers in a novel situation. Her body is turned towards Abu and in this way she makes him the target of her remark, but what she says concerns all the children ("everybody" has those feelings and "nobody" quite knows how to cope), and all the children are listening. She does not assume that every child feels like this, it is rather a possibility that her experience indicates – note her use of epistemic status indicator "think" in line 1.

Extract 9 Group 4, session 1 (7.35).

Th1: but you ↑kno:::w:::? (0.6) I think everybody
felt a little bit small and a little bit frightened.
(1.0)
and didn't want to feel like that. And didn't
↑qui::te=know how=to >stop=it< without
being=a monster
Abu: *((is looking down and banging his clay*
furiously))
Th2: <Abu is seeing everything throu::gh
mo:nster=eye::s: at the moment.>
Th1: °yes:°
(2.0)
Th2: everything is monste[rish.
Abu: [I'm=a] big
(ba::r::=of) stinky poo, ar:::GH::::
RAeR::gh::=RAeRR::GH::
Th2: >I think you're worried about us, what kind
of monsters are we?<
Th1: and whether we'll li::ke you,
(0.4)
or whether we'll think you::'r:e poo-ey.
Abu: *((from behind the mask))* AERRGH
Th1: and whether we'll see a b::eau::tiful boy

((Tam and Sal giggle loudly))
Th1: a b::eau::tiful b:rown b:oy beh:ind a b:l:u:e ma:sk.
Tam: *((bang bang bang bang))*

She does not formulate the problem as definitely Abu's or uniquely his, but possibly as one in common to the children in the group. So can we conclude that Th1 presumes that Abu's problem, against which he defends, is that he is small amongst big strangers and just that? Excerpt 9 disconfirms this. Abu does not acknowledge Th1's gloss, except perhaps negatively by drowning it in noise and he is keeping Th1 at a distance by separating himself from the group (line 6). The therapist Th2 picks up Abu's disengagement, and comments on his mode of defence (lines 9–10) endorsed by Th1. Th2 also provides a comment that possibly makes use of the psychoanalytic idea of projection – Abu does not only act as a monster but "everything is monsterish" for him (line 13). Abu connects to this immediately, interrupting Th2, revealing a very different anxiety and one specific to him – his problem is to do with his colour (line 25). (He is hiding a brown face behind the blue mask.) Th1 picks this up immediately and formulates Abu's dilemma for him. The way she does this is notable. Her formulation does not negate Th2's but instead is presented as an extension by being conjoined through the copula "and," thus speaking for both therapists (lines 19–21). The problem then is not just the therapists' size but their possible racism – "will they see me as I am?" or "will they only see me through my skin colour as a 'stinky pooh'?" The important thing is that Th1 formulates a positive alternative view of Abu – he is a beautiful brown boy – she later comments that this was said with the stress on "beautiful" and as her "present to him." Th1 then started from a Kleinian maxim, but did not impose it on children, and was instead attentive to whether her "guess" was borne out or not. She dispensed with the maxim when the engagement indicated otherwise. Moreover, there is no background maxim in the therapists' school that would draw their attention to skin colour. Yet the therapists are not only conscious of, but motivated by the fact that they are working in a socially disadvantaged neighbourhood, where class and ethnicity are live issues. Th1 revealed the following in the discussion of the first pass analysis:

Extract 10 FPAD09/09.

WS: no, you put it in, yeah? Is it for him to pick up?
For them all to pick up?
Th1: It was for him. That was my gift to him. Because
I have an Asian daughter, and know what an issue it was
for her at this age, I gave that to him quite
deliberately. And as I remember I got eye contact.
WS: yeah, no but I say it's not for them all to hear that
you think brown is beautiful, it's for him to hear.

So, the therapists may ignore background therapeutic maxims, and the problem for ethnomethodologists is that they might read these into interactions too readily, ignoring the sensitivity of therapists to the situation and the children. This is what has in fact happened in the first pass analysis of the above episode. The ethnomethodologists IL and WS had to discover in a discussion with Th1 that she was in fact guided by her personal experience and not by her therapeutic orientation. Joint analysis is thus needed in addition to general ethnography to ascertain how therapeutic maxims are used on specific occasions.

Conversation of emotions

In this section we make use of the notes written up by the trainee therapist Th3. She is present as an observer – she sits in a corner and her task is to write a report on each session from memory. Her notes exhibit the forms of accountability in terms of which, amongst therapists, events in group therapy are to be understood. The "recordings" help us to understand how our therapists understand the events in therapy. Extract 11 points to some features of Th3's orientation.

Extract 11 Group 2, session 1, Th3's record.

The playdough was taken out of the tubs and people began flattening it into pancakes, smacking it down with their palms. This soon became noisy banging with an anxious edge; Abu and Tam leading. Abu. held his flat piece of dough up to his face, covering his eyes, and made roaring noises. Carl looked at him with dismay and lowered his chin, as if he'd like to hide under the table. It became very difficult to hear people and difficult to think with Abu seeming to have lost control of his impulses to terrify his peers in a way which had a sadistic edge to it and which he seemed to be enjoying in rather an unhinged way. Th1 spoke about the monster on the outside but the small Abu underneath, and said he needed someone to put her hand on his shoulder and tell him it was alright. The moment this was said, Sal put her hand onto his shoulder, and he began to quieten, with Sal watching him kindly and I thought very bravely.

The text is pertinent to our own analysis of Abu's conduct. Th3 accords with Th1 in perception that Abu was not just banging – the behaviour was compulsive (rather than spontaneous). Now we, the academics, did not pick this up ourselves even though we are familiar with the concept of "compulsion," its history and general use (seen e.g. Leudar & Thomas, 2000, Ch. 4). This means again that knowing the therapists' background is not enough – ethnographic engagement with the therapists is required to ascertain when the concepts are used. The crucial point is, moreover, that the therapist's perception of certain of Abu's actions as compulsive is not superfluous – it is consequential to what happens subsequently in the therapeutic interaction. Certain of Th1's contributions to the interaction – calming Abu down and providing him with alternative means of coping – are predicated on Th1's perception that his behaviour was a compulsive result of an overwhelming fear. If Th1 had treated Abu's conduct as intentional, say as being badly behaved, the consequences would have been different.

Extract 11 in fact contains several technical *redescriptions*. Abu does not simply play at being a monster but he has lost "control of his impulses" (to terrify fellow children) and his behaviour has a "sadistic edge." Similarly, Abu and Tam's joint laughter is "hysterical." Some mundane terms acquire specialist meanings, as the word "containment" in "Sal made a tiny basket, which seemed a symbol of the *containment* given to the anxiety that was around." Most people will be familiar with these terms but not in their technical sense and with consequentialities used by the therapists. Moreover, the collective use of these terms locates the therapists in their field – cognitive behaviour therapists, for instance, would not use these terms.

Other recordings, e.g. of the children making playdough pancakes or Abu making the mask, are, however, straightforward behavioural descriptions and no technical background whatsoever is required to understand them. Or is it? Th3 does not record every movement of every child. We note that behaviours recorded are all psychologically annotated, done with certain emotions in them – e.g. "banging with an anxious edge" (line 3); done with "impulses to terrify." The psychotherapist, however, does not record all individual emotion-filled actions (Extracts 12 and 13).

Extract 12 Group 4, session 2, Th3's record.

Abu had trouble getting his dough out of the tub and began to panic, taking a lot of talking down by Th1, the panic rising out of him and spreading to those who weren't having any trouble themselves, putting people on edge.

Extract 13 Group 4, session 1, Th3's record.

Tam continually fuelled Abu's bubbling hysteria and joined in while it was rising, but then stopped when it got to its peak, leaving him to take the rap for it.

Both of these extracts indicate that the recorded activities are significant in terms of their consequences for the group (Extract 12, line 6; Extract 13, lines 1–2). One recorded consequence of being a big monster and roaring loudly is that it terrified another child and what he did had an "element of sadism" in it. Abu created an emotional effect and enjoyed it.

What the psychotherapist sees then is *emotional interaction* that we might call, borrowing from G.H. Mead, a "conversation of emotions" and particular behaviours are noted not just because they are significant in themselves, but in terms of their psychologically expressive significance in group interaction (see Peräkylä, chapter 6, this volume). It seems then that the psychotherapist does not pick up just activities, but *activities done with emotions that stir up emotions in others* (see comments on "doing things with feelings" in Wittgenstein, 1980).[8] The Extracts 14 and 15 contain more examples of such emotional interactions.

Extract 14 Group 4, session 1, Th3's record.

When he was asked what he was making he said "A castle"; his hands were working, but his eyes were on the events around him, he seemed ready to bolt if necessary. *Things calmed down considerably once the blue monster had gone.* People began drawing pictures of their families and talking about parents and siblings.

Extract 15 Group 4, session 2, Th3's record.

The convenors talked about the break next week and the two remaining sessions. They said it would then be the turn of other children to come to group. *The mood of the group sank.* Abu pressed a rubber into his dough to make an imprint,

Note that the activities described above are not locally circumscribed but cover longer stretches of interaction. In each description Th3 identifies a change in interaction that concerns the group and is distributed over, and emergent from, several local activities which are presumably both verbal and non-verbal. The question is again why the psychotherapist noted the happenings that she did and not others? The reply is that she identifies the global patterns in interaction in terms of their affective significance. So the focus on emotions we noted above applies to the descriptions of both group and individual activities and of global and local activities and is also an aspect of therapists' professional sensitivity.

Conclusion

We have documented the ways in which psychoanalytic psychotherapists convert children's play activities into psychotherapy. They did this by introducing therapeutic themes specific to their approach to frame the

[8] There is no reason to assume that CA, with its concerted focus on interaction, will not help psychotherapists to study emotional aspects of interactions. Some conversation analysts with anthropological backgrounds indeed study emotions in situated interaction (e.g. Goodwin & Goodwin, 1999).

interactions, and by topicalizing what a child's creations told them – in doing something a child was showing something else both to them and to the group. Through such comments, the play activities of each child were transformed into turns and shared in the group in therapeutically relevant ways. Moreover, individual children's ways of coping were joined by therapists in lists which highlighted both (i) family resemblances in children's experiences and (ii) differences in how they coped. Using these two devices – *topicalizing* and *joining up in lists* – the therapists were attempting to produce and sustain, using Goffman's term, "focused interactions" wherein therapists and children shared a single focus of attention (Goffman, 1963). The sessions were, however, not constantly or comprehensively focused or in a simple way organized through a turn-taking mechanism – many of the activities going on in the situation were done in parallel, all at the same time, but not by isolated individuals.

We have also documented, although not fully, one boy's recruitment into this unfolding therapeutic environment and its consequences. The recruitment converts the child's spontaneous play into a display of therapeutically relevant themes and gradually transformed play to allow reflections on how the boy coped with anxieties arising from certain situations. Psychoanalytic psychotherapists tried to free the boy from responding to these situations compulsively. They did this by mediating through foregrounding alternatives and they seem to have had some success in effecting change. Individual therapy with the boy would, of course, be longer and much more thorough. In this respect the chapter documents how working with cases allows ethnomethodologists to study change in psychotherapy.

We have also provided initial documentation of the fact that child psychoanalytic psychotherapy is sensitive and intricate work, and that a trained therapist's capacity to recognize actions and occurrences are therapeutically relevant matters. Moreover, to identify the form that these matters take under their therapeutic orientation requires considerable apprenticeship. The work of therapy is embodied in psychotherapeutic talk but not necessarily in the form someone other than the therapist can immediately recognize. We started this research thinking that our most important task was to document the language that allows psychoanalytic psychotherapists to redescribe mundane activities in therapeutically relevant terms, thus shifting and focusing their consequentiality. This aspect of therapeutic orientation is indeed important – the therapists used a stock of technical concepts and therapeutic maxims in just this way. We observed that the therapists framed the occasion in terms of their professional concerns, introducing themes and offering interpretations as a way of getting the occasion going and bringing developments in the group together in therapeutically useful ways. One important observation was, however, that the therapists used the stock of descriptions with care, strategically and flexibly and not as fixed recipes. Significantly, children's activities were professionally redescribed most often when they were carried out with therapeutically relevant emotions – then both were likely to be represented in language specific to the therapeutic orientation. Our conclusion is then that "stocks of activity descriptions" and the capacity to use them are embedded in a well-honed sensitivity to therapy-relevant emotions with which individual and collective actions are carried out.

Our emphasis on the specificity of "psychotherapies" must not be misunderstood as an insistence that each therapeutic school is utterly distinct from all others, or that the form of group practice pursued by our therapists is entirely unlike all other practices because their every move must be understood technically. Insistence on uniqueness of some aspects of a practice does not preclude recognition that in other respects their therapeutic work resembles, and has formal similarities to, practices in other schools of psychotherapy, as other chapters in this volume amply document.

10 A psychotherapist's view of conversation analysis

Ulrich Streeck

Psychotherapy is an ensemble of techniques the benefit of which is measured by their usefulness to cure or relieve mental disorders and diseases. Psychotherapeutic knowledge is predominantly knowledge of change. The aim of conversation analysis (CA) in psychotherapy is to analyse and document the means and strategies used by patients and therapists to produce talk in interaction happening in the treatment room. In explicating these means and strategies, CA is not primarily concerned whether the treatment is useful at that moment or not, with whether the therapist is acting competently or negligently, or with whether or not the participants perceive the present interaction as therapy at all. Instead, from a conversation analytic perspective the "How" of the present interaction and *the interactive production* of what is going on between patient and psychotherapist in every moment is in the foreground independent of the kind and quality of the actual events in the treatment room.

In psychotherapeutic theory there is some disagreement regarding the importance of interactive events between patient and therapist. From the very beginning of psychoanalysis, interaction between patient and psychoanalyst has been overshadowed by the suspicion of suggestion (Thomä & Kächele, 1994). For this reason, Freud wanted to create an arrangement that was meant to ensure that the psychoanalytic treatment is nothing else but an "exchange of words" (Freud, 1916/17). The words of the patient should reveal what is going on in him or her, and the words of the analyst should verbalize what he or she has understood of the unconscious mental processes of the patient. Nevertheless, the closest points of contact between conversation analysis and psychotherapy can be expected from those strands of psychotherapeutic theory that see psychotherapy as a thoroughly interactive endeavour as it is the case for example in modern psychodynamic psychotherapy and psychoanalysis.

The medical and the interactional model of psychotherapy

In the treatment of mental disorders and diseases, psychoanalytical (or rather psychodynamic) and cognitive-behavioural methods are most commonly used, as well as Rogerian psychotherapy and systemic approaches, which are of special importance in the counselling and treatment of families and couples. All therapeutic approaches emphasize the importance of the relationship between therapist and patient. Independent of the therapeutic approach a relationship which is experienced as helpful by the patient is considered as a general precondition for a successful treatment. Therefore the therapist should behave in a way that the relationship is experienced as helpful by the patient (Luborsky, Crits-Christoph, Mintz & Auerbach, 1988). Psychotherapeutic techniques use dialogue and communication to treat psychic disturbances and to improve the mental health of a patient. Most forms of psychotherapy use only spoken conversation; some also use various other forms of communication such as the written word, music, artwork, or bodily behaviour.

If one investigates how psychotherapists think about their field one may find at least two implicit models of psychotherapy: the first might be called a *medical model*, the other an *interactional model* of psychotherapy. In the medical model, psychotherapy in its fundamental principles is perceived as somewhat similar to the treatment of somatic diseases in other medical disciplines, namely as the treatment of mental disorders and diseases of patients, only with the difference that these diseases are not ascribed to somatic but to mental causes. Within this medical model psychiatrists and psychotherapists are regarded as experts in mental disorders and diseases in a similar way as somatically working physicians are experts in identifying and treating somatic diseases. And as medical competence proves itself by the ability to diagnose and treat somatic diseases, psychotherapeutic competence would prove itself by recognizing and eliminating inner psychic causes underlying the mental disorder.

The quality of the therapeutic relationship within this medical model of psychotherapy is seen as an important precondition for treatment, but it is only a marginal precondition for the actual therapeutic events, somewhat similar to somatic medicine where a good doctor–patient relationship is important for compliance. Interactions and interactive phenomena in the therapeutic process, like enactments or action dialogues, are seen as only transient events manifesting themselves as resistance (e.g. Schwaber, 1998), but they are not considered to be constitutive of the therapeutic events as such. Even if they might contribute to a deeper understanding, according to this viewpoint the therapy deviates from its ideal course during such phases. Therefore, the analyst's next step must be to try to withdraw from the interactive event in order to understand his or her counter-transference or acting out behaviour and to recover his or her position as a neutral, objective observer. Psychoanalysis here adheres to the notion that the psychic reality of the patient as such can be diagnosed and treated independently of the influence of the psychotherapist – comparable to the diagnosis and treatment of somatic illnesses.

The psychoanalyst Michael Balint criticized this still widespread, although mostly implicit, view or model quite some time ago, calling it one-body psychology and emphasizing that, in reality, the psychotherapist is not dealing with phenomena existing in the patient independently of his or her own influence, but with "interplays" between patient and psychotherapist (Balint & Balint, 1961). Following from Balint's view that "interplays" are always at work, what therapists "detect" in patients would not be independent of the *mutual* influence of patient and psychotherapist but rather based on their interaction. Moreover, in this view the role of the psychotherapist is not that of an expert using a therapeutic method for the treatment of a diagnosed pre-existing mental disease of his or her patient but a participant in an event developing between them, and where everything ascribed to the mental disorder of the patient is not only shaped by the patient but also by the therapist's own influence. Thus, in reality the psychotherapist would not diagnose a mental disease uniquely owned by the patient, but would always refer to something mutually created and designed. Unlike the medical model of psychotherapy one could call this view an intersubjective, or interactional, social model of psychotherapy.

Since the discovery of transference – the observance that early relationship experiences of the patient repeat themselves in the relationship with the therapist – the therapeutic relationship in psychoanalysis and in psychotherapeutic methods derived from psychoanalysis is not only an unspecific marginal condition of the therapeutic events but the most important vehicle for the understanding of the mental disease of the patient. Nevertheless, it is often held that it is possible to finally detect the unconscious psychic reality of the patient by analysing transference and counter-transference and to reconstruct how it is formed independently of the influence of the analyst, thus returning to the one-body model of psychotherapy. In the interactional model the behaviour of patient and psychotherapist, their interaction and the relationship they create is constitutive of psychotherapy itself. The interactive phenomena do not indicate, from this viewpoint, that the therapeutic process is deviating from its ideal course, but rather underline its constitutive, interactive character.

A two-body psychology and an interactional model of psychotherapy according to which all events in the treatment room are co-productions of patient and psychotherapist are only slowly coming to be accepted. The intersubjective, interactional model of psychotherapy has only recently gained influence – especially within psychoanalysis. The proponents of so-called relational psychoanalysis (e.g. Aron, 1996; J. Benjamin, 1998; Mitchell, 2000) consider everything that happens in the treatment as being influenced by both the patient and the therapist. They hold that all phenomena that psychoanalysis deals with – transference, counter-transference, resistance, defence and so on – are produced by both participants. One can never say clearly which part in the therapeutic process is the patient's and which is the therapist's. In other words, relational therapists consider the therapeutic process always as mutually created by patient and therapist, and they assume that the psychotherapist never gets to see or hear what was already present as such in the psyche of the patient, but only that experience of the patient which has been shaped by the therapist and his or her presence (Brodbeck, 1995; Hoffman, 1992; Levine & Friedman 2000; Mitchell, 1988; Rabin, 1995). Thus, interactive phenomena do not come to the fore as resistance once in a while to make way for the familiar events at the next moment, but everything happening in the treatment is an event interactively and commonly created by patient and therapist. In this regard relational psychoanalysis adheres to a two-body psychology in the spirit of Balint.

Relational psychoanalysis has much in common with interactionist sociology and especially with ethnomethodology and conversation analysis. From the perspective of a medical model of psychotherapy, conversation analytic studies of psychotherapy deal with more marginal phenomena; they consider the interaction of patient and psychotherapist as only extrinsic to the actual therapeutic events. Seen from the perspective of relationally understood psychotherapy, conversation analytic studies in contrast are clearly useful and in the centre of what psychotherapy is. Thus, conversation analysis can help to reconstruct the means and procedures by which patient and psychotherapist co-create the events in the psychotherapeutic treatment room.

The manifold meanings of psychotherapeutic concepts and the therapeutic "exchange of words"

When speaking about psychoanalysis and psychodynamic psychotherapy today one is moving on a very heterogeneous field comprising many opinions and positions, all conceptualized as "psychoanalysis." With behaviour therapy the situation is somewhat similar. The question, what is psychoanalysis and psychodynamic psychotherapy today, is therefore not easy to answer.

Within psychoanalysis there are the self-psychologists and object relation theorists, the drive theorists and the ego-psychologists, the traditionalists and the intersubjectivists, the Kleinians and Lacanians, the London middle group, the French school, the already mentioned relational psychoanalysts, and others. An even greater variety holds true concerning psychodynamic psychotherapy; here we deal with a multicoloured bunch of methodological orientations and therapeutic methods. The 1989 congress of the International Psychoanalytical Association in Rome on "the 'common ground' of psychoanalysis" tried to answer the question whether there is "one psychoanalysis or many" (Wallerstein, 1990) and which basic theoretical and clinical opinions are still shared by psychoanalysts if they act as psychoanalysts. This effort was not crowned with success; on the contrary it clearly revealed the heterogeneity of theoretical and conceptual differences within psychoanalysis. Even concerning such basic concepts and phenomena of psychoanalysis as defence, unconscious conflict, transference, or interpretation the psychoanalytic community was not able to agree on common opinions.

It is largely unknown whether the theoretical and conceptual variety within psychoanalysis is associated with a corresponding variety in therapeutic practice. The question concerning the relationship between psychoanalytic theory and psychoanalytic practice was originally raised by Ferenczi and Rank in their book *Development of psychoanalysis: The correlation of theory and practice* in 1924. It is also unclear if changes of therapeutic convictions among the psychotherapeutic experts are associated with changes in therapeutic practice or if both possibly develop largely independently from each other. Thus, for example, the so-called Kleinian concepts which have gained some importance in recent years are often formulated in very metaphorical language describing communicative processes of exchange as if they were really a transport, the containment and digestion of substances. But with few exceptions (see Leudar *et al.*, Chapter 9, this volume) it is not clear if this new metaphor is associated with a corresponding change in how these psychoanalysts communicate with their patients.

If psychotherapists and psychoanalysts speak about their clinical work they often refer to acknowledged concepts and technical recommendations, shared in their group of experts. That makes it possible to come to agreement on what happened in the treatment room. Concepts and technical recommendations on the other hand do not reveal in detail how psychotherapists handle the "exchange of words" (Freud, 1916/17) with their patients. They say for example that they recalled "a premature transference interpretation" and that "the interpretation was a source of strong turbulence; an alpha element was formed, an emotional pictograph" (Ferro 2002, p. 186), or they write that "the analyst and patient begin the treatment with a set of understandings about the 'frame' of analysis, although surely much of this remains in the background" (Goldberg, 2002, p. 875); in supervision therapists might inform the supervisor that they "confronted the patient with his defence," that they "interpreted the unconscious conflict," or that they made themselves "available as a container of unbearable emotions of the patient," etc. The concepts the therapists refer to in these examples do not tell in detail what was going on in the treatment, what exactly they said; the psychoanalytic concepts like transference, interpretation, defence, confrontation, or "being available as container" do not reveal what had happened in detail in the "exchange of words" in the treatment room and how exactly patients and therapists enacted their utterances.

The inexactness of psychoanalytic concepts has been described by Joseph Sandler (1983):

> In particular, concepts become stretched to encompass new insights and new ideas. Often such an expansion of the meaning of a conceptual term is not explicit, and one writer after another will attempt to define it in some specific way, or will reiterate the "standard", "official" or "public" formulation, taking it for granted that any respectable psychoanalytic concept will have one proper meaning only. The reality is, of course, that conceptual terms in psychoanalysis often have multiple meanings which vary according to the context in which the term is used. We have only to think of such notions as fantasy, trauma, identification, resistance, acting out . . . to become aware that each possesses elasticity, is pliable in its usage, having a whole spectrum of context-dependent meanings . . . Elastic concepts play a very important part in holding psychoanalytic theory together. As psychoanalysis is made up of formulations at varying levels of abstraction, and of part-theories which do not integrate well with one another, the existence of pliable, context-dependent concepts allows an overall framework of psychoanalytic theory to be assembled . . . The examination of the different dimensions of our major psychoanalytic concepts may then prove to be as profitable as the search for precise definitions – possibly even more profitable, for some of our most useful concepts are incapable of being pinned down by being defined, and today's precision may be tomorrow's rigidity (p. 35).

Experienced psychotherapists working successfully in clinical practice have "private theories" (Sandler, 1983) helping them to conduct therapeutic communication and to manage concrete situations in the encounter with their patients. These "private theories" are different from theories and concepts overtly discussed in the professional community; they consist of individual interactive knowledge enabling psychotherapists to adjust therapeutically to their particular patients and use their specific knowledge of change. Therefore, efforts to reconstruct psychotherapeutic concepts from a conversation analytic viewpoint – for example concerning the question of how the phenomena called defence are interactively produced, how interpretations are done, how patient and therapist co-produce transference – necessarily reach the limit of generalizability quickly. What is understood as defence in one patient–therapist relationship may be understood quite differently in another. As is the case with other concepts, defence is not a unique behaviour that can be identified, but it describes a function in therapeutic communication. For this reason, from a conversation analytic point of view it is more revealing to investigate specific psychotherapeutic dyads than to study the general meaning of "defence" or "transference" or "acting out" etc. in psychotherapy. This may lead to a variety of further themes – processes of mutual adaptation of patient and therapist, their "matching" (Kantrowitz, 1995), the dyad-specific development of a common language, the initiation of treatments, acting in the context of beginning and termination of sessions, changes of the patient, therapeutic effective and ineffective dyads, and so on. A conversation analytic explication of the interaction process can provide far-reaching insights on how patient and psychotherapist jointly create these phenomena.

Empirical psychotherapy research

Psychotherapy today must prove its effectiveness and efficiency, often in competition with psychopharmacology. Many findings of empirical research are important for political and economic purposes. In addition, psychotherapists engaged in empirical research sometimes express the hope that the heterogeneity of concepts and theoretical orientations within psychoanalysis and psychotherapy could be overcome by empirical research. They would like to find out which of the traditional basic assumptions of psychoanalysis and psychotherapy can be empirically verified, and to regain the lost common ground by taking these empirically verified assumptions as the new fundamental ground for psychoanalysis. Today some researchers place this hope especially on neurobiology which, from their point of view, can be regarded as a basic science for psychoanalysis and psychotherapy and as an ultimate instance for the verification of their concepts (e.g. Solms, 1995). These researchers consider assumptions as empirically verified in this context which correlate with detectable patterns of brain activity. There are even approaches to test the effect of psychotherapeutic interventions by means of brain imaging. The idea is that with the help of methods of neurobiological research, external criteria shall be obtained in order to determine the validity of psychotherapeutic interventions. From this reductionistic point of view, communicative behaviours of patient and therapist are seen only as epiphenomena. The neurobiological perspective, however, overlooks the reality-producing character of the communicative processes of psychotherapy. Conversation analysis, on the other hand, can show that the therapeutic endeavour cannot be accounted for as a manifestation of dispositions anchored in the biology of the actors, but is at each moment interactively produced.

When investigating therapeutic interactions and relationships, psychodynamic psychotherapy researchers with few exceptions rarely resort to conversation analysis (for example Peräkylä, 2004a; 2004b, Vehviläinen, 2003a). Instead they use methods which are far removed from basic ethnomethodological and conversation analytic assumptions. Peräkylä described differences by comparing the prerequisites of the interaction process analysis of Bales (1950) with those of conversation analysis. Similar differences exist between conversation analysis and empirical psychotherapy research. For example, the Core Conflictual Relationship Theme (CCRT) (Luborsky & Crits-Christoph, 1997) works on the assumption that the internalized relationship patterns are reflected in the verbal reports of relationship episodes that are delivered in therapy and that internalized relationship patterns determine behaviour in actual interpersonal relationships, including the therapeutical one. In fact, the CCRT does not examine interaction, it is rather a method for the examination of the verbal–dramaturgical formulation of narrations produced in a research context. The Structural Analysis of Social Behaviour (SASB) (L. S. Benjamin, 1996) uses self-report questionnaires and video taped sequences of assessment interactions. These are rated on dimensions of interactive behaviour reflecting categories defined in advance. The Inventory of Interpersonal Problems (IPP) (Horowitz, Rosenberg, Baer, Ureno & Villasenor, 1988), a screening instrument for self-assessment, assumes that the diversity of problems of patients concerning social behaviour and interpersonal interaction can be completely mapped within the dimensions provided in a circumplex model and with the categories defined in advance.

These methods of investigating the interactive process between patient and psychotherapist impose categories on what is taking place. The categories used by the patient and psychotherapist themselves to deal with their interaction and the various, often subtle means of speech in interaction are treated as at best a side issue. How exactly patient and psychotherapist adjust to each other so that the therapeutic dialogue can continue, how each behaves *in situ* and what subtle means are used is not the subject of these methods. In fact, from an ethnomethodological perspective the object of these research methods is not interaction but rather conceptualized individual experience of relationships.

Practising psychotherapists can rarely draw conclusions from these findings that would enable them to adjust better to their patients, develop more effective therapeutic strategies or to otherwise improve their therapeutic practice. Psychotherapy cannot be improved by bringing together different components that empirical research has found to be effective and neither can it be realized as an instrumental activity of the therapist in the face of an ill patient. It has to be conceived of as a dialogue in the course of which patient and psychotherapist mutually adjust to each other. Conversation analytic studies on the other hand do not inform psychotherapeutic practioners on how to conduct psychotherapy effectively. In contradiction to the medical model, they reveal that patient and therapist create psychotherapy together in the course of their "exchange of words" and they also reveal exactly *how* they did that. For psychotherapists those conversation analytic studies which might be most interesting refer to their knowledge of change and to practical topics, for example the self-categorizations of patients, the hidden interaction patterns between the patient and the therapist, or the patient's micro-reactions to the therapist's interventions.

Enactments and nonverbal behaviour

With respect to nonverbal aspects of utterances, the psychotherapeutic setting and the psychoanalytic setting in particular is a highly artificial one, compared with "natural," everyday situations. In everyday encounters, we communicate by interpreting our utterances reciprocally, in the light of foregoing remarks, and nonverbal behaviour plays a central role in this. If the "exchange of words" was not embedded in the context of nonverbal, body-gestural interaction, mutual understanding would be extremely difficult and require tremendous effort. Verbal behaviour on the one hand, and nonverbal, body-gestural behaviour on the other, are integral parts of expression that interpret each other reciprocally (Goodwin & Goodwin, 1992; Kendon, 1994). They do not convey different contents, but rather are both parts of communicative actions.

Even in the couch setting, nonverbal aspects of expression may not be put completely out of action, and the therapeutic process never evolves simply as an "exchange of words." Close scrutiny reveals that analysand and analyst interaction is mediated by subtle but effective nonverbal signals. Thus the therapeutic process unfolds not only as an "exchange of words," but also in an "enacted dimension" (Katz, 1998). Psychotherapists not only pay careful attention to the content of the statements and narratives of the patient, but also to how patients relate them and how they behave – their subtle fleeting gestures, their body postures, the peculiarities of how they speak and pause, and how they produce their speech (e.g. Boesky, 1982; Busch, 1995; Chasseguet-Smirgel, 1990; Katz, 1998; Roughton, 1994; Streeck, 2004). McLaughlin (1991) spoke of a "steady clamor of nonverbal communication between the pair" (p. 598), and Treurniet (1997) called these subtle, often unnoticed actions conveyed via fleeting verbal and physical–gestural means "micro-acting out." Thus Treurniet continues in the direction of Freud's "Remembering, Repeating, and Processing": patients express themselves through the manner in which they behave and how they perform what they say in the therapeutic situation.

Laplanche and Pontalis (1973) called this "actualization in transference." Referring to similar phenomena, and especially to counter-transference, Jacobs (1986) introduced into psychoanalysis the concept of "enactment." Enactments are supposed to express important experiences with former relationships, especially those which are not symbolically represented. Sandler (1976), for example, described a patient who had succeeded in inducing him to talk more than usual during the analytical sessions. The patient contrived this "by means of a slight alteration in his voice" (p. 302). He ended each sentence as if it were a question, but without really asking one. Sandler said that during the transference of roles a "complicated system of transmitting and receiving unconscious signals" (pp. 304–305) is at play. With the help of this system, the therapist is actually induced to play the role the patient had consigned to her or him. Subtle, nonverbal communicative processes that usually escape conscious notice seem to play a significant role in this "complicated system." Despite all subtlety however, these signals can have a profound influence on the other person and hence on the interpersonal encounter.

Similarly, Klüwer (1983) described how psychoanalysts are led imperceptibly by patients "acting out" to act out themselves and to co-act out. As a consequence, unnoticed interactions take place that are perhaps similar to what Leudar *et al.*, this volume refer to as "conversations of emotions." Klüwer refers to these as "action dialogues." These are similar to enactments; they are interactive phenomena too which come into existence through the participation of both analyst and analysand. Enactments are co-productions of the analyst and the analysand – visible and audible actions with the underlying aim of inducing reciprocal behaviour in the other. Enactments – as they are mostly understood in psychoanalysis – turn a desire or an idea into a performance. Each party experiences the event as the result of the behaviour of the other (McLaughlin, 1991); Jacobs (1986) speaks of "avantgarde messengers." They precede the verbal message by expressing something that cannot yet be conveyed via verbal–symbolic means. Counter-transference enactments evolve basically as part of the therapist's reaction to the projective identification of the patient. The patient attempts through projective identifications to induce the therapist to adopt a behaviour that corresponds to the object that he or she is presently transferring to the therapist. And the therapist, without noticing it, indeed behaves in just such a way and the patient sees his or her transference expectations confirmed. Thus through her or his behaviour, the analyst exhibits aspects of a representation, a position to which the patient has brought her or him through projective identification. In this connection, projective identification and counter-transference enactment are mutually related phenomena (Gabbard, 1995).

All these phenomena give evidence that subtle nonverbal and body-gestural behaviour is an effective part of the relationship between patient and therapist, and an important channel for the transference. For this reason, the analysis of enactments and action dialogues must play a central role in research on interaction in psychotherapy. It can help us to understand the ways in which dovetailed interactions develop. Many case reports demonstrate that such interactions are called forth through hardly perceived, often minimal and highly ordinary modes of speech and behaviour. These may involve a particular way a patient ends his sentences (Sandler, 1976), a certain way of pausing during a conversation, particular positions of the body, subtle gestures, modes of speech, and other apparently minimal verbal and gestular means – in other words, everyday, usually unnoticed, but highly effective methods of conducting social interactions. So in many cases, understanding in psychotherapy requires careful attention to the nonverbal interaction between the patient and therapist in the context of their speech (and vice versa). The detailed conversation analytic reconstruction of what is going on verbally and nonverbally between patient and psychotherapist can reveal significant elements of unconscious communication between patient and psychotherapist. There is no equally accurate empirical research method besides conversation analysis for the investigation of interactions in this respect and thus for the study of patient–therapist interaction.

The effects of psychotherapy

There is an ongoing debate on how the therapeutic effect of psychotherapy and psychoanalysis should be conceived. Clinically working psychotherapists and psychoanalysts are predominantly interested in knowing how to assess change. The traditional view that psychoanalytic treatments in particular are effective because hidden childhood memories become conscious with the help of interpretations is not sustainable any more. The fact that repressed memories become conscious and can be told rather seem to be epiphenomena independent of the therapeutic effectiveness of psychoanalysis (Fonagy, 1999). Changes are probably, or at least predominantly, not reached by narrations and their interpretation or by changes in the autobiographic memory, but by modifications of the implicit relational knowledge of the patient and new experiences of being with others that are gained in the course of therapeutic interaction (Bruschweiler-Stern *et al.*, 2002). Thus the effectiveness of psychoanalysis and psychodynamic psychotherapy is not only, and probably not primarily, explicable by reference to the interpretive activities of the therapist; instead "something more than interpretation" is in play (Stern *et al.*, 1998). Changes have to be ascribed mainly to the therapeutic relationship and to new ways of relating in the therapeutic situation. Under special circumstances, so-called "now-moments" (Stern, 2004), the relationship between patient and therapist is lifted onto a new level and the interaction is regulated on this new level henceforth. The effectiveness of psychotherapy is thus connected here with circumstances concerning the microregulation of interaction. This also should make it easy to bind together more closely clinical and conversation analytic approaches in this field (see Peräkylä, Chapter 7, this volume). It is not clear to what extent this might also be true for other psychotherapeutic methods.

Another important question in the current expert discussion concerns psychotherapists' self-disclosure. Psychotherapists who assume that therapists cannot avoid disclosing their own attitudes and opinions by just *how* they participate in the therapeutic process, argue for a more open expression of their own experience toward the patient and for making it explicit instead of trying to keep up anonymity and neutrality. Relational psychoanalysts especially support this opinion. These important questions concerning therapists' transparency are often discussed without reference to clinical data. Studying psychotherapeutic styles of interaction from a conversation analytic point of view might add important empirical findings to this discussion (e.g. Leudar *et al.*, 2005). It might be expected that conversation analysis can describe different styles of participation in the therapeutic communication and thus different qualitites of therapeutic relationships which might be more or less helpful.

Conversation analysts primarily reconstruct the *local* production of what is going on in social interaction. In order to be able to reconstruct the therapeutic process as interaction of patient and therapist in a manner useful for psychotherapists in clinical practice, conversation analysis should also examine greater passages of the therapeutic communication exceeding the turn-by-turn orientation as psychoanalysts often refer with their interventions to comments and events which occurred quite long ago, and patients know that this is so. With his interpretation the analyst often simultaneously refers to the patient's utterances from different periods of the analytic hour, for example what the patient said when he or she entered the consulting room, what he or she remembered half an hour later, some associations to what he or she did yesterday, and all these different events are reflected in the interpretation. At other times patient and therapist again and again refer to a specific event or memory or dream that they already have talked about several times before.

A somewhat different problem for conversation analytic investigations of psychotherapy may rise from the question, how does the therapist know how the patient understood what he or she, the therapist, said to him? In this respect, therapeutic communication seems to function in similar ways to everyday communication: what patients do, and how they do it, makes audible and visible what the preceding behaviour of the therapist means to them. What the therapist says and does in the next step places the therapist in relation to what the patient said and did before. From a conversation analyst's perspective this seems obvious. Nevertheless, in psychoanalysis this can be a tricky matter. Freud (1937) warned that a "yes" of the patient following an interpretation does not nessesarily mean that the interpretation was correct, and that a "no" does not always mean a rejection. Therefore it can be difficult to understand what is going on in their interaction if the conversation analysis only refers to the local situation.

Conversation analysis for psychotherapy research?

The aim of conversation analysis in psychotherapy is to examine and reconstruct the means and practices by which patient and therapist produce their therapeutic reality. In the conversation analytic approach utterances and nonverbal behaviour of patient and therapist are of interest primarily from the viewpoint of what is done with them – in other words, what their nature is as social actions. This involves the question of how patient and psychotherapist mould and maintain their relationship and their interpersonal reality with each other in specific therapeutic situations.

Conversation analytic studies of psychotherapy can reveal micro-interactions in the treatment room, as they hit upon subtle, communicative phenomena and methods. In many empirical studies beyond psychotherapy, conversation analysis has shown that these details play a significant role in the regulation of interactions and hence the shaping of relationships. One must regard it as likely that this is not fundamentally different in the therapeutic dialogue. Here, conversation analysis is especially concerned with therapeutic processes connected with means and practices that patient and therapist use to regulate their being in contact with one another, thus creating their own "local culture," their own types of interaction patterns (Kantrowitz, 1995). Normally the subtle means and strategies of interaction that conversation analysis deals with are phenomena which psychotherapists do not notice in therapeutic discourse or else regard them as meaningless peripheral or random details. Furthermore, they usually take verbal and bodily behaviour as indicators for psychic dispositions of their patients. In contrast, conversation analytic studies point to their function in interaction, making it clear that both participants, patient and therapist, use these means not only to indicate how they feel about what is happening at each moment but to produce what is happening. Only seldom can it be predicted what purpose these signals have. This is only recognizable from the particular behaviour that follows. The meaning of this behaviour is "agreed upon" cooperatively by the conversation participants. Verbal communication between patient and therapist is integrated with their nonverbal interaction and both are welded together. One cannot observe behaviour and then immediately say what it means. This can only be determined in retrospect because the meaning only becomes manifest through the interactive course of events. G.H. Mead (1934) said that the meaning of a gesture is in the subsequent action of the other person. Because gestural behaviour is only rarely a symbol, it first needs to become experience. Patients and psychotherapists cannot escape this unconscious communication or unconscious regulation of interaction. For the therapist, the primary question is therefore not whether this occurs, but how it contributes to each moment of what takes place in the therapeutic situation, and how, through the therapist's behaviour, he or she shows and has shown the patient how he or she views events.

Thus, from a clinical point of view conversation analysis might make important contributions to questions raised in clinical discussions. Not least, conversation analytic studies might contribute – among other things – to gaining more precise insights into what psychotherapists call unconscious communication. Under a magnifying glass that renders the details of the therapeutic dialogue between patient and psychotherapist visible, these micro-signals are revealed as a means of unconscious communication. Furthermore, in investigating micro-interaction, conversation analysis might help to reveal the mechanisms of interaction that are responsible for some of the often severe difficulties that patients with psychological problems have in their relationships with other people.

In addition conversation analysis can be used for purposes other than research. We have learned from experiences with conversation analytic data sessions how important it is to watch and listen several times to short sequences and even details of what is going on in interaction to identify finer points of social practices. In the course of our longstanding experiences with studies of micro-interaction in psychotherapy using video taped therapeutic dialogues we found it equally important to watch and listen several times to the details of therapeutic interaction to be able to detect the subtle means of unconscious communication of the therapeutic pair. That led us to the conviction that this minute verbal and nonverbal behavior has to do with the "occult phenomena" (Deutsch, 1926) that patient and therapist use to a considerable extent to produce and to regulate their therapeutic relationship. Conversation analytic studies of the details of therapeutic interaction are not least a good practice for accurate listening and looking.

Investigating details of utterances of patient and therapist puts a stop to the tendency in psychodynamic therapy to look away from what can be seen and heard in favour of leaning on fantasies about what lies behind, that is to solipsist cognitivism (see Leudar & Costall, 2004). If one resists the temptation to look for what cannot be seen, one can realize that patient and therapist communicate unconsciously with subtle verbal and nonverbal means much more than usually expected. Conversation analysis informs how this can be done. Thus, unlike any other empirical approach, conversation analysis promises a detailed insight into the "how" of interactive cooperative production and regulation of psychotherapy. Although there already are several conversation analytic studies concerning different aspects of psychotherapy, neither psychotherapy nor conversation analysis has as yet made full use of the opportunities inherent in their joining together.

11 A review of conversational practices in psychotherapy

Sanna Vehviläinen, Anssi Peräkylä, Charles Antaki, and Ivan Leudar

The aim of this chapter is to present a systematic overview of some of the research results presented in this book. An overview like this cannot cover all that was important in the preceding chapters, but it will bring out something from each. We present the key results in Table 11.1. We then unpack the contents of the table, and, by setting them against earlier conversation analytic research on psychotherapy, set the contributions of this book in context.

In order to summarize the research findings in a meaningful way, we have had to choose one analytic dimension from which to consider them. We have chosen one that is the cornerstone of all conversation analytic research: sequence organization (see Schegloff, 2007). We have chosen, from the wealth of material in each chapter, to emphasize what we learn about the ways in which the utterances of one participant are linked to utterances of the other(s) in the interaction. The apparently simple conjunction of one person's utterance with another's is a site at which many therapy-relevant phenomena happen.

There are two distinctions that we have made in organizing the research results of the book on the basis of the conjunction of utterances. One is the distinction between *initiatory* and *responsive* actions. An initiatory action is one that calls for, or makes relevant, a response from the co-participants. Responsive action is, of course, such a response. As Schegloff (2007) amply demonstrates, the organization of talk-in-interaction is not exhausted by initiations and responses but is far more complex. Many actions that have been analysed in the chapters of this book are, in fact, *both* initiatory and responsive: they occupy the initiatory position with regard to one thing and are in a responsive position with regard to something else. However, for the purposes of this summary, we will stick to the basic differentiation between initiation and response.

The other distinction that has helped us to organize the material in the preceding chapters involves what therapy is about more directly, i.e.

therapy as a particular kind of institutional interaction. It is a distinction between *action*, *local consequence*, and *therapeutic function*. Our basic unit of observation is action. Action is an initiative or responsive component of a sequence; or to put it in another (somewhat simplistic) way, it is an utterance that does (and is designed to do) some interactional work in relation to other utterances. "Questions" and "Answers" are paradigmatic examples of actions. Apart from such actions *per se*, however, the chapters of this book also describe what is accomplished in and through the actions. By *local consequence*, we refer to what a particular action brings about in its immediate environment: what the action does in this particular encounter, and how it changes the momentarily unfolding relation of the participants. Finally, by *therapeutic function*, we refer to the ways in which a particular action may contribute to, or resist, the overall objectives of a particular kind of psychotherapy; these objectives stretch throughout a therapeutic encounter and the entire therapy process. In sum: what we mean by action can be conceived as moving a piece in a chess game, while local consequence can be conceived as the move's contribution to the tactic, and therapeutic function as the move's contribution to the overall strategy.

A survey of research findings

The entries in Table 11.1 are generated from the work reported in this volume. The overall effect is bound to be somewhat miscellaneous and there are, clearly, significant gaps. Some of the gaps could be filled by referring to earlier CA work on psychotherapy (which is what we do later in this chapter) while many others are such that they require further research. CA work on therapy is still in its comparative infancy, and there is a great deal yet to be discovered.

A caveat: the entries in Table 11.1 ought not to be read as if they proceed, from left to right, i.e. from action through local consequences to therapeutic function, as automatic consequences which will be true in all cases. The local consequences of any action are contingent on what is going on in the environment that surrounds it. Thus, for example, Halonen's (Chapter 8) identification of questions employing zero-person and passive usage is only associated with the therapeutic function of "making clients admit they own a problem" in the specific circumstances of the usage she examines. Table 11.1, then, should best be seen as a listing of what features of talk have been studied (the left-hand column) and some cases of their local consequences *in situ* and their possible interpretations as a therapeutic function.

Table 11.1 *Summary of the Research Results*

1. Therapist's recipient actions

Action	Some local consequences	Possible therapeutic function
LEXICAL SUBSTITUTION (Ch. 4 Rae)	– intensifying emotion of description – showing attentiveness	– encouraging the client to talk more explicitly about feelings
EXTENSION (Ch. 6 Peräkylä)	– shaping client's talk according to therapeutic agenda – showing the therapist's access to what the patient is describing	– interpreting the unconscious – momentary meeting of the participants' minds
FORMULATION (Ch. 2 Antaki, Ch. 3 Bercelli *et al.*, Ch. 4 Rae, Ch. 6 Peräkylä, Ch. 7 Vehviläinen)	– "building a case" for interpretation – establishing facts – guiding descriptions towards the psychological – managing the progress of the therapy session	– interpreting the unconscious – giving new perspectives to client's life
REINTERPRETATIVE STATEMENT (Ch. 3 Bercelli *et al.*, Ch. 6 Peräkylä, Ch. 7 Vehviläinen, Ch. 9 Leudar *et al.*)	– presenting the therapist's understandings of the patient's talk and action – topicalizing action; confrontation	– interpreting the unconscious – explicating the symbolic meaning of the patient's action – identifying and managing unconscious resistance

2. Therapist's initiating actions

Action	Local consequence	Therapeutic function
OPTIMISTIC QUESTIONS (Ch. 5 MacMartin)	– presupposing optimistic attributes to the therapy client	– enhancing the client's agency
FOLLOW-UP QUESTION USING ZERO-PERSON (Ch. 8 Halonen)	– regulating the applicability of the narrative that is being told	– making clients admit their problem – making the identity of addict constantly relevant to clients

Table 11.1 (*cont.*)

3. Client's responding activities

Action	Local consequence	Therapeutic function
ANSWERS THAT RESIST THE QUESTION PRESUPPOSITIONS (Ch. 5 MacMartin)	– client resistance	– disavowing agency
DEFENSIVE RESPONSES TO TOPICALIZATIONS OF PRIOR ACTION (Ch. 7 Vehviläinen)	– client resistance	– resisting treating one's own actions as a psychoanalytical puzzle
ELABORATIONS (Ch. 6 Peräkylä); **EXTENDED AGREEMENTS** (Ch. 3 Bercelli *et al.*)	– response to (re)interpretation that shows strongest uptake	– showing one's perspectives according to the (re)interpretation – becoming aware of something previously "unconscious"

Therapists' recipient actions

As Table 11.1 indicates, the studies reported in this book examine actions, the way particular actions are used in the interaction, and the role they play in carrying out particular therapeutic policies. Moreover, we can see that the majority of these actions are the therapist's recipient activities in which the client's talk is in some particular way dealt with by the therapist. It is no coincidence that this has been the first focal point for comparison and accumulation of empirical knowledge in the CA study of therapeutic interaction. For one thing, at a general level, it has long been the case that CA studies of institutional talk have tended to focus on the talk of the institutional agent – be they doctor, teacher, emergency call-taker, news interviewer, or any other representative of an institution which brings off its work though repeated cycles of talk-based action. So the focus on the therapist, rather than the client, is in line with a general focus on the participant with identifiable service goals achieved by repeated routine conversational practices. As for the emphasis, within the therapists' practices, on how they deal with what their clients say, that is understandable as a reflection of psychotherapeutic expertise centring on the art of listening to, and interpreting, clients' talk. Another relevant feature of psychotherapeutic expertise which has to do with emotion – understanding, responding to, and in some particular way transforming the patient's emotion – is also prominently available for interactional examination in the recipient activities of therapists.

Lexical substitution

This is the first recipient action in Table 11.1. In lexical substitution, the therapist offers alternative words for a just-prior expression produced by the client. Lexical substitution is a specific way of doing what in CA is called *repair* (dealing with problems of speaking, hearing, or understanding). There is an extensive literature of repair in ordinary conversation (e.g. Jefferson, 1987; Schegloff, Jefferson & Sacks, 1977) and in some institutional environments (see e.g. Button, 1991; Moore & Maynard, 2002), but Chapter 4 in this volume by Rae is the first contribution to the uses of repair in psychotherapeutic encounters. Rae suggests that this particular type of repair is used to serve specific purposes in psychotherapy: to encourage clients to show more explicitly their emotional involvement in what they are talking about .

Extension

This is the second type of recipient action in Table 11.1. In an extension, a speaker (the therapist) produces an utterance that is designed as a syntactical continuation of the first speaker's talk. In earlier CA research, a particular type of extension (collaborative completion where one speaker completes a syntactical construction that the other has not (yet) completed) has been the subject of a number of studies (e.g. Sacks 1992b, 57–60; Lerner 1991). In therapeutic encounters, extension has been discussed by Ferrara (1994) and studied in more detail by Vehviläinen (2003a). The contributions to this book, alongside earlier research, show how therapists, by producing extensions, claim the availability of the topic for themselves, and through that also show that they have some access to the other speaker's experience. In her earlier study, Vehviläinen (2003a) showed how extensions are used in psychoanalysis to prepare the ground for an interpretation by shaping the clients' talk in such a way that brings to the fore a "puzzle" (which is later on solved by interpretation). In this book, Peräkylä (Chapter 6) discusses cases where analyst extensions bring about moments when the participants' minds, as expressed in their talk, merge.

There is one important feature that is common to the use of extensions and repairs in psychotherapy. In the cases of the chapters in this book, the therapists are shown to claim knowledge of, and access to, their clients' experiences through their repairs and extensions, thereby stretching the boundaries of ownership of knowledge. In many other situations, speakers take care to orient to other speakers' experiences by indicating their limited access to that (Pomerantz, 1984; Peräkylä & Silverman, 1991). In psychotherapies, we find moments when the therapist claims greater availability of the client's experience, for example through repairs and extensions. This kind of use of extensions and repairs may perform two quite different functions: confronting the client (i.e. showing or suggesting to the client that he or she does not fully recognize what is in his or her experience) or understanding the client (i.e. recognizing and validating the client's emotional experience).

Formulation

This is the next item in our table of therapists' recipient actions. Formulation has a rather long history as the target of CA studies on psychotherapeutic interaction (see e.g. Antaki, this volume; Antaki, Barnes & Leudar, 2005; Davis, 1986; Hak & de Boer, 1996). In the light of the earlier studies, formulation might appear as the "royal road into the practices of psychotherapy" (Antaki, Barnes & Leudar, 2005, pp. 269–70): it has been considered to be the general category for the interpretive work that the therapist does with the client's talk. Certainly, in this book, formulation is prominently present, but the picture portrayed by the studies is more detailed and focused. The research presented in this book has specified the role of formulations in at least two ways. The sequential properties of formulations were specified by Antaki in Chapter 2 and by Bercelli *et al.* in Chapter 3, by pointing out that rather than being any general descriptions of some aspect of the ongoing interaction, formulations in a specific way claim that they are saying what the other speaker said in his or her prior talk, and call for confirmation/disconfirmation of that understanding. At the same time, formulations involve selection and reshaping of the prior turn – and that is where therapeutic orientations come into the picture in a particular way. Besides their sequential properties, the local consequences of formulations were also specified in this book. Antaki (Chapter 2) outlined three kinds of work that formulations can do: they may (a) highlight some psychological state of affairs in the client's preceding talk and thus prepare for its further examination; (b) they may help the therapist to temporarily focus away from something and thereby to guide the progress of the interaction; or (c) they may serve as means for specifying diagnostically relevant facts.

Reinterpretative statements

We are also beginning to have a grasp of another type of therapist's turns, namely statement-designed turns that are constructed to explicitly exhibit the therapist's viewpoint. In Chapter 3, Bercelli, Rossano and Viaro discuss reinterpretative statements in cognitive and relational-systemic therapies.

In such statements, the therapist reacts to the material provided by the client. But unlike formulations, which are designed to show that the speaker is resaying what the client said, reinterpretations are designed to present the therapist's own understandings concerning the client's experience. As pointed out by Bercelli *et al.*, such reinterpretative statements are much like the interpretative statements found in psychoanalysis (Peräkylä, 2004a; 2005; Chapter 6 in this volume; Vehviläinen, 2003a) – in general, they are used to deliver to the client the results of the therapist's reasoning. In a similar vein, Leudar *et al* show in Chapter 9 how the therapists in Kleinian group therapy for children explicate in statement-formatted utterances what they take as the symbolic meaning of the children's play. Such statements in different types of therapies convey the therapist's view of the client's narration, mind, or action – the latter shown by Vehviläinen in Chapter 7 in the analyst's focus on the patient's prior action – and serve the therapeutic goal of challenging the patient's current understandings of his or her mind or action, and of offering new ones. As Vehviläinen shows, in psychoanalysis such challenges may function as prefaces to psychoanalytic interpretations, but also as an argumentative resource in the management of patient resistance and in pursuing interpretations. What is believed to be the significance of the new understanding that is proposed through statements varies according to the "school" of psychotherapy. In psychodynamic therapies, for example, these new understandings are thought to involve the expansion of the patient's conscious (as opposed to unconscious) experience, whereas in cognitive therapies, they might be thought of as involving more reality-oriented and functional ways of thinking.

Therapists' initiating actions

Questioning

Questioning is perhaps the most common type of initiating action in most institutional encounters (see e.g. Drew & Heritage, 1992). In many settings (though not in all), questions are a vehicle for the professional's (rather than the client's) conduct. Earlier research on counselling interaction has explicated a number of sequential and turn design properties in question–answer sequences that serve the therapeutic goals of family systems therapy (Peräkylä, 1995; Peräkylä & Silverman, 1991). In this collection, therapists' questions figure especially in three chapters. In Chapter 3 Bercelli *et al.*, while not focusing their study on questions *per se*, nevertheless point out the importance of questions in cognitive and relational-systemic therapies. Therapists' questions are one of the recurrent turn types in such therapies; question–answer sequences produce materials which may be later on "reinterpreted" through the therapists' statements and the clients' responses to them.

Two specific kinds of questions are examined in more detail in this book. Interestingly, both question types seem to work towards ascribing the hearers' specifically therapeutic relevant identities. In Chapter 5, MacMartin analyses questions with optimistic presuppositions in constructive psychotherapy. In particular, she focuses on *wh*-questions with presuppositions that affirm the client's "agency, competence, resilience, abilities, achievements, or some combination thereof" (p. 82). As she points out, the local consequence of these questions is to ascribe positive features to the client, and thereby, they serve the therapeutic goal of enhancing the client's agency. In Chapter 8 Halonen, on the other hand, analyses the choice of person reference in Minnesota model group therapy for addicts, focusing especially on the uses, in Finnish, of the so-called zero-person construction and the passive mood. Her materials show examples of various actions among which questions are one. She shows how the zero- and passive-formatted questions allow the participants to talk in such a way that the experiences that are referred to get treated as general, something that anyone present can identify with. Thereby, these questions serve the therapeutic goal of helping the clients to accept the identity of an addict.

Clients' responding actions

Perhaps unusually in CA-inspired work on institutional interaction, but certainly not uniquely, we devote time in this book to the practices of the person on the other side of the service encounter: the client. The clients' responding actions are analysed in four chapters. Two of them (Chapter 3 by Bercelli *et al.* and Chapter 6 by Peräkylä) focus predominantly on responses that align with the therapist's initiatory action, whereas the other two (Chapter 5 by MacMartin and Chapter 7 by Vehviläinen) analyse misaligned responses. Bercelli *et al.* discuss three types of client responses to what they call therapists' reinterpretations (see above) in cognitive and relational–systemic therapies : acknowledgment tokens, mere agreements, and extended agreements. In an extended agreement, the client not only claims his or her agreement, but also accounts for that agreement through descriptions or narrations that corroborate the therapist's previous reinterpretation. An extended agreement in cognitive and relational–systemic therapies comes very close to what Peräkylä in Chapter 6 (and in 2005) calls patient's elaboration in response to the analyst's interpretation in psychoanalysis: in them, the patients take up some part of the interpretation and continue it, in the patient's own terms, and thereby *show* their acceptance and understanding of the interpretation. The parallel between cognitive and systemic therapies on the one hand, and psychoanalysis on the other, is most interesting here and calls for further comparative research. In both kinds of therapies, these patient utterances seem to document the kind of uptake that the therapist is aiming at with his or her statement, which is formulated by Bercelli *et al.* as showing that the patients "display a change in perspective of their own events and experiences" (page 60).

Rather different patient responses were analysed by MacMartin and Vehviläinen. MacMartin (Chapter 5) shows some of the ways in which the patients can resist the presuppositions of the therapists' optimistic questions in constructive psychotherapy. Such responses can involve, for example, downgrading the optimistic content of the question, focusing away from such contents, or joking about them. Also Vehviläinen, in Chapter 7, analyses patient resistance. She deals with actions that are taken by analysts as indications of patients' unconscious resistance, as well as the defensive responses to the analysts' confrontative focusings to the patients' prior actions.

Clients' initiating actions

This book offers accounts of different actions and related sequential patterns in psychotherapy, summarized in table 11.1. However, the table involves one very significant "blank spot". "Clients' initiations" are missing from it. Most psychotherapies are based on the client's narratives – extended turns of talk on one's own experience. All the analyses of the therapist's recipient activities lean on the observations of the client's producing talk: either second-position responses to elicitations (Chapter 3 by Bercelli *et al.*) or first-position (spontaneous) tellings without the professional's opening initiation (as happens in psychoanalysis with so-called free association). It is perhaps symptomatic of the programme of the CA research on institutional interaction that, as we noted above, research first tends to turn towards the key activities of the professionals. However, the analysis of clients' initiative actions – narratives or other types of systematic action – is a topic that we expect to see more research on in the future.

One psychotherapy or many psychotherapies?

Table 11.1 presents a number of actions and suggests what interactional local consequences these actions might serve, and what kind of therapeutic practices they might be part of. As pointed out in Chapter 1, conversation analytic research on psychotherapy is lagging far behind the level of systematic description that has been recently reached in CA research on medical consultations. Table 11.1 on pages 190–191 is an effort towards systematization of the conversation analytical explication of psychotherapy. The research that the table seeks to encapsulate has identified and explicated a number of key actions. Further explication of these key psychotherapeutic actions (as well as the identification of others) is the task of future research.

However, one more question needs to be taken up. Unlike medical consultations which have rather uniform structure throughout the (Western) world, psychotherapy is divided into numerous approaches. Therefore, we need to ask to what degree the actions, local consequences and therapeutic functions summarized in Table 11.1 pertain to psychotherapy as a whole, and to what degree they are related to specific kinds of therapy.

At the moment, no definite answer can be given. With the exception of Chapter 2 by Antaki, each chapter presents data that comes from a particular type of psychotherapy. In that sense, the results are, in most cases, specifically related to those therapy types. In some cases, the fact that the actions described are therapy-type specific is apparent also because those actions are closely related to the "stock of interactional knowledge" related to a specific type of therapy – for example, the optimistic questions analysed in Chapter 5 (MacMartin) arise from the theoretical ideas of constructivist therapies and might not be found in this form in other types of therapy.

On the other hand, there are some striking parallels between explications of different types of therapies: the ways in which *formulations*, *therapist's statements* and *clients' responses to therapists' statements* are organized in different types of therapies have much in common. For example, Bercelli *et al.* (Chapter 3) and Peräkylä (Chapter 6) describe clients' responses to therapists' (re)interpretative statements in quite complementary ways, even though their data come from two different therapeutic approaches (cognitive and relational–systemic therapies vs. psychoanalysis). Not much more, at the moment, can be said about the generalizability of the research results across different psychotherapeutic approaches. Future studies comparing different types of psychotherapies will tell us more. For the moment, however, the accumulating evidence from a variety of CA researchers around the world suggests that the application of CA methodology and theoretical insights will continue to find useful things to say about the practices of psychotherapists and their clients, and round out the sociological picture of one of the main institutions of mental-health culture in the West.

Transcription Symbols

Contributors use notation based on the system established in conversation analysis and ultimately derived from the work of Gail Jefferson. This is the basic set. Other, infrequently used, symbols are explained in footnotes when they appear. For a full account, see Atkinson and Heritage, 1984, pp. ix–xvi, and Jefferson (2004).

(.)	Just noticeable pause
(.3), (2.6)	Examples of timed pauses
word [word [word	Square brackets aligned across adjacent lines denote the start of overlapping talk
.hh hh	In-breath (note the preceding fullstop) and out-breath respectively
wo(h)rd	(h) shows that the word has breathiness (or perhaps "laughter" or "crying") bubbling within it
wor-	A dash shows a sharp cut-off
wo:rd	Colons show that the speaker has stretched the preceding sound
(word)	A guess at what might have been said
( )	Very unclear talk
A: word= B: =word	The equals sign shows that there is no discernible pause between two speakers' turns. If put between two sounds within a single speaker's turn, shows that they run together
word WORD	Underlined sounds are louder, capitals louder still
°word°	Material between "degree signs" is quiet
>word word< <word word>	Inwards arrows show faster speech, outward slower
↑word	Upward arrow shows upward intonation
↓word	Downward arrow shows downward intonation
#word#	Material between hash marks is delivered in a "croaky" voice
£word£	Material delivered in a "smile" voice

, . ?	Punctuation marks are not used grammatically. The comma sign denotes a falling intonation, the period a terminal intonation, and the interrogation mark a rising intonation
→	Analyst's signal of a significant line
((*sniffs*))	Attempt at representing something hard, or impossible, to write phonetically

References

Anscombe, G. E. M. (1959). *Intention*. Oxford: Blackwell.

Antaki, C. (2004). Reading minds or dealing with interactional implications? *Theory and Psychology*, 14, 667–683.

Antaki, C., Barnes, R. & Leudar, I. (2004). Trouble in agreeing on a client's problem in a cognitive behavioural therapy session. *Rivista di Psicolinguistica Aplicata: Studying Social Interaction: The Contribution of Conversation Analysis*, 4, 129–140.

(2005). Diagnostic formulations in psychotherapy. *Discourse Studies*, 7, 627–647.

(2007). Members' and analysts' interests: "formulations" and "interpretations" in psychotherapy. In A. Hepburn & S. Wiggins (eds.), *Discursive research in practice: New approaches to psychology and interaction* (pp. 166–181). Cambridge: Cambridge University Press.

Arminen, I. (1998). *Therapeutic interaction. A study of mutual help in the meeting of Alcoholics Anonymous*. The Finnish Foundation for Alcohol Studies (Vol. 45). Helsinki.

(2004). Second stories: the salience of interpersonal communication for mutual help in Alcoholics Anonymous. *Journal of Pragmatics*, 36, 319–347.

(2005). *Institutional interaction. Studies of talk at work*. Aldershot: Ashgate.

Arminen, I. & Leppo, A. (2001). The dilemma of two cultures in the 12-step treatment. The professional responses for clients who act against their best interests. In M. Seltzer, C. Kullberg, S. P. Olesen & I. Rostila (eds.), *Listening to the welfare state* (pp. 183–212). Aldershot: Ashgate.

Aron, L. (1991). The patient's experience of the analyst's subjectivity. *Psychoanalytic Dialogues*, 1 (1), 29–51.

(1996). *A meeting of minds: Mutuality in psychoanalysis*. Hillsdale: Analytic Press.

Atkinson, J. M. & Heritage, J. (1984). Transcript notation. In J. M. Atkinson & J. Heritage (eds.), *Structures of social action: Studies in conversation analysis* (pp. ix–xvi). Cambridge: Cambridge University Press.

Avis, J. M. (2006). Escaping narratives of domination: Ideas for clinical practice with women oppressed by relationship violence. In R. Alaggia & C. Vine (eds.), *Cruel but not unusual: Violence in Canadian families: A sourcebook for educators and practitioners* (pp. 397–421). Waterloo, Ontario Canada: Wilfred Laurier University Press.

Bales, R. F. (1950). *Interaction process analysis: A method for the study of small groups*. Reading, MA: Addison-Wesley.

Balint, M. & Balint, E. (1961). *Psychotherapeutic techniques in medicine*. London: Tavistock.

Beach, W. A. (1995). Preserving and constraining options: "Okays" and official priorities in medical interviews. In G. H. Morris & R. J. Chenial (eds.), *The talk of the clinic* (pp. 259–290). Hillsdale, NJ: LEA.

Beach, W. A. & Dixson, C. N. (2001). Revealing moments: formulating understandings of adverse experiences in a health appraisal interview. *Social Science and Medicine*, 52, 25–44.

Beck, A. T., Rush, A. R., Shaw, B. R. & Emery, G. (1979). *Cognitive therapy of depression*. New York: Guilford Press.

Benjamin, J. (1990). Recognition and destruction: an outline of intersubjectivity. *Psychoanalytic Psychology*, 7 (suppl.), 33–47.

(1998). *Shadow of the other*. New York: Routledge.

Benjamin, L. S. (1996). Introduction to the special section on Structural Analysis of Social Behavior (SASB). *Journal of Consulting and Clinical Psychology*, 64, 1203–1212.

Bercelli, F., Rossano, F. & Viaro, M. (forthcoming). Clients' personal narratives in psychotherapy: The interactional accomplishment of different tasks in two different sequential placements. In A. De Fina & A. Georgakopoulou (eds.), *Text & talk, special issue on narratives*.

Bercelli, F., Viaro, M. & Rossano, F. (2004). Attività in alcuni generi di psicoterapia. *Rivista di Psicolinguistica Aplicata*, 4 (2–3), 111–127.

Berg, M. (2001). *Syytöksiä ja epäilyksiä. Toimittajan ja poliitikon vuorovaikutuksesta televisiokeskustelussa*. [Accusations and suspicions. On interaction between journalists and politicians in televised conversation.] Helsinki: Finnish Literature Society.

Bergmann, J. (1992). Veiled morality: notes on discretion in psychiatry. In P. Drew & J. Heritage (eds.), *Talk at work. Interaction in institutional settings* (pp. 137–163). Cambridge: Cambridge University Press.

(2001). *Refocusing other on the other's self*. A paper presentation in "Psychoanalytic and psychotherapeutic ," Workshop in Helsinki, Finland, 9–11 August 2001.

Besnier, N. (1990). Language and affect. *Annual Review of Anthropology*, 19, 419–451.

Bion, W. R. (1961). *Experiences in Groups*. New York: Basic Books.

(1984). *Elements of psychoanalysis*. London: Carnac books.

Boden, D. & Zimmerman, D. H. (1991). *Talk and social structure*. Cambridge: Polity.

Boesky, D. (1982). Acting out: a reconsideration of the concept. *International Journal of Psychoanalysis*, 63, 39–55.

Bongar, B. & Beutler, L. E. (1995). *Comprehensive textbook of psychotherapy theory and practice*. Oxford/New York: Oxford University Press.

Brodbeck, H. (1995). The psychoanalyst as participant and observer in the psychoanalytic process: Some thoughts on countertransference from a constructivist perspective. *Psychoanalysis and Contemporary Thought*, 18, 531–558.

Bruschweiler-Stern, N., Harrison, A. M., Lyons-Ruth, K., Morgan, A. C., Nahum, J. P., Sander, L. W. *et al.* (Boston Change Process Study Group, CPSG) (2002). Explicating the implicit: the local level and the microprocess of change in the analytic situation. *International Journal of Psychoanalysis*, 83, 1051–1062.

Bucci, W. (1995). The power of narrative. A multiple code account. In J. Pennebaker (ed.), *Emotion, disclosure and health* (pp. 93–103). Washington, DC: American Psychological Association.

Busch, F. (1995). Do actions speak louder than words? A query into an enigma in analytic theory and technique. *Journal of the American Psychoanalytic Association*, 43, 61–82.

Buttny, R. (1996). Clients' and therapist's joint construction of the clients' problems. *Research on Language and Social Interaction*, 29 (2), 125–153.

Button, G. (1991). Conversation-in-a-series. In D. Boden & D. H. Zimmerman (eds.), *Talk and social structure* (pp. 217–231). Cambridge: Polity.

Byrne, P. S. & Long, B. E. L. (1976). *Doctors talking to patients: A study of the verbal behaviours of doctors in the consultation*. London: HMSO.

Chasseguet-Smirgel, J. (1990). On acting out. *International Journal of Psychoanalysis*, 71, 77–86.

Clayman, S. (1993). Reformulating the question: A device for answering/not answering questions in news interviews and press conferences. *Text*, 13 (2), 159–188.

Clayman, S. & Heritage, J. (2002). *The news interview: Journalists and public figures on the air*. Cambridge: Cambridge University Press.

Corey, G. (1986). Theory and practice of counselling and psychotherapy (3rd edn). Monterey: Brooks/Cole Publishing Company.

Davies, P., Thomas, P. & Leudar, I. (1999). The dialogical engagement with voices. *British Journal of Medical Psychology*, 72, 179–187.

Davis, K. (1986). The process of problem (re)formulation in psychotherapy. *Sociology of Health & Illness*, 8, 44–74.

Denton, E. (2006). Negotiating anger and agency, responsibility, and change: Discourse-analysis of narrative therapy for men who have abused their intimate partners. Unpublished masters thesis. Guelph, Ontario, Canada: University of Guelph.

Dersley, I. & Wootton, A. (2000). Complaint sequences within antagonistic argument. *Research on Language and Social Interaction*, 33, 375–406.

Descartes, R. (1911). *Meditations on first philosophy. The philosophical works of Descartes*. (E. S. Haldane & G. R. T. Ross, trans.). Cambridge: Cambridge University Press. (Original work published 1641.)

de Shazer, S. & Berg, I. K. (1985). A part is not apart: Working with only one of the partners present. In A. S. Gurman (ed.), *Casebook of marital therapy* (pp. 97–110). New York: Guilford Press.

Deutsch, H. (1926). Okkulte Vorgänge während der Psychoanalyse. *Imago*, 12, 418–433.

Drew, P. (1992). Contested evidence in courtroom cross-examination: The case of a trial for rape. In P. Drew & J. Heritage (eds.), *Talk at work: Interaction in institutional settings* (pp. 470–520). Cambridge: Cambridge University Press.

(1998). Complaints about transgressions and misconduct. *Research on Language and Social Interaction*, 31, 295–325.

(2003). Comparative analysis of talk-in-interaction in different institutional settings: A sketch. In P. J. Glenn, C. D. LeBaron & J. Mandelbaum (eds.), *Studies in language and social interaction: In honor of Robert Hopper*, 293–308. Mahwah, NJ: Erlbaum.

Drew, P. & Heritage, J. (1992). Analyzing talk at work: An introduction. In P. Drew & J. Heritage (eds.), *Talk at work: interaction in institutional settings* (pp. 66–100). Cambridge: Cambridge University Press.

Dreyfus, H. & Dreyfus, S. (1985). *Mind over machine: The power of human intuition and expertise in the era of the computer*. New York: Free Press.

Dryden, W. (ed.) (2007). *Dryden's handbook of individual therapy*. London: Sage.

Edwards, D. (1994). Script formulations: An analysis of event descriptions in conversation. *Journal of Language and Social Psychology*, 13, 211–247.

(1995). Two to tango: Formulations, dispositions, and rhetorical symmetry in relationship troubles talk. *Research on Language and Social Interaction*, 28 (4), 319–350.

(2005). Moaning, whinging and laughing: The subjective side of complaints. *Discourse Studies*, 7, 5–29.

Ehrlich, S. & Sidnell, J. (2006). "I think that's not an assumption you ought to make": Challenging presuppositions in inquiry testimony. *Language in Society*, 35, 655–676.

Ellis, A. (1962). *Reason and emotion in psychotherapy*. New York: Lyle Stuart.

Ferenczi, S. & Rank, O. (1924). *Entwicklungsziele der Psychoanalyse. Zur wechselbeziehung von Theorie und Praxis*. Wien: Internationaler psychoanalytischer Verlag.

Ferrara, K. W. (1994). *Therapeutic ways with words*. Oxford: Oxford University Press.

Ferro, A. (2002). Narrative derivatives of alpha elements. *International Forum of Psychoanalysis*, 11, 184–187.

Fonagy, P. (1999). Memory and therapeutic action. *International Journal of Psychoanalysis*, 80, 215–221.

Forrester, M. & Reason, D. (2006). Conversation analysis and psychoanalytic psychotherapy research: questions, issues, problems and challenges. *Psychoanalytic Psychotherapy*, 20 (1), 40–64.

Foucault, M. (1967). *Madness and civilization. A history of insanity in the age of reason*. London: Tavistock.

(1977). *Discipline and punish*. London: Allen Lane.

Freedman, J. & Combs, G. (1996). *Narrative therapy: The social construction of preferred realities*. New York: Norton.

Freud, S. (1905). Fragment of an analysis of a case of hysteria. In *Standard edition of the complete psychological works of Sigmund Freud* (Vol. 7, pp. 7–122). London: Hogarth Press.

(1909). Two case histories "Little Hans" and the "Rat Man." In *Standard edition of the complete psychological works of Sigmund Freud* (Vol. 10). London: Hogarth Press.

(1916/17). Vorlesungen zur Einführung in die Psychoanalyse. *GW* (Vol. 11, p. 10). Frankfurt: Fischer.

(1937): Constructions in analysis. In *Standard edition of the complete psychological works of Sigmund Freud* (Vol. 23, pp. 255–269). London: Hogarth Press.

Freud, S. and Breuer, J. (1991). Fräulein Anna O. In S. Freud, *Studies on hysteria* (pp. 73–102). London: Penguin (Original work published 1985).

Fromm-Reichman, F. (1967). *Principles of intensive psychotherapy*. Chicago: Chicago University Press.

Frosh, S. (2002). *Key concepts in psychoanalysis.* New York: New York University Press.

Gabbard, G. O. (1995). Countertransference: The emerging common ground. *International Journal of Psychoanalysis*, 76, 475–485.

Gale, J. (1991). *Conversation analysis of therapeutic discourse: Pursuit of a therapeutic agenda.* Norwood, NJ: Ablex.

Garcia, A. (1991). Dispute resolution without disputing: How the interactional organization of mediation hearings minimizes argument. *American Sociological Review*, 56, 818–835.

Garfinkel, H. (1967). *Studies in ethnomethodology.* Englewood Cliffs, NJ: Prentice-Hall.

Garfinkel, H. & Sacks, H. (1970). On formal structures of practical actions. In J. C. McKinney & E. A. Tiryakian (eds.), *Theoretical Sociology* (pp. 337–366). New York: Appleton-Century-Crofts.

Goffman, E. (1963). *Behaviour in public places.* Glencoe: The Free Press.

(1974). *Frame analysis. An essay on the organization of experience.* Boston: Northeastern University Press.

Goldberg, A. (2002). Enactment as understanding and as a misunderstanding. *Journal of the American Psychoanalytic Association*, 50, 869–883.

Goodwin, C. & Goodwin, M. H. (1992). Context, activity and participation. In P. Auer & A. di Luzio (eds.), *The contextualization of language* (pp. 79–99). Amsterdam, Philadelphia: John Benjamins.

Goodwin, M. H. & Goodwin, C. (1999). Emotion within situated activity. In N. Budwig, I. C. Uzgiris & J. V. Wertsch (eds.), *Communication: An arena of development* (pp. 33–54). Stamford, CT: Ablex.

Green, G. (1996). *Pragmatics and natural language understanding* (2nd edn.). Mahwah, NJ: Erlbaum.

Greenson, R. R. (1967). *The technique and practice of psychoanalysis.* Madison, CT: International Universities Press.

Guidano, V. (1987). *The complexity of the self.* New York: Guilford Press.

(1991). *The self in process. Toward a post-rationalist cognitive theory.* New York: Guilford Press.

Hak, T. & de Boer, F. (1996). Formulations in first encounters. *Journal of Pragmatics*, 25, 83–99.

Hakulinen, A. (1987). Avoiding personal reference in Finnish. In J. Verschueren & M. Bertucelli-Papi (eds.), *The pragmatic perspective*, 141–153. Amsterdam: John Benjamins.

Hakulinen, A. & Karlsson, F. (1979). *Nykysuomen lauseoppi.* [The syntax of Finnish.] Helsinki: Finnish Literature Society.

Hakulinen, A., Vilkuna, M., Korhonen, R., Koivisto, V., Heinonen, T. & Alho, I. (2004). *Iso suomen kielioppi.* [Comprehensive grammar of Finnish.] Helsinki: Finnish Literature Society.

Haley, J. (1963). *Strategies of psychotherapy.* New York: Grune & Stratton.

Halonen, M. (2002). *Kertominen terapian välineenä. Tutkimus vuorovaikutuksestamyllyhoidon ryhmäterapiassa.* [Telling as a therapeutic device. A study of interaction in Minnesota model group therapy.] Helsinki: Finnish Literature Society.

(2006). Life stories used as evidence for the diagnosis of addiction in group therapy. *Discourse & Society*, 17, 283–298.

Helasvuo, M. (2006). Passive: Personal or impersonal? A Finnish perspective. In M. Helasvuo & L. Campbell (eds.), *Grammar from the human perspective: Case, space and person in Finnish* (pp. 233–255). Amsterdam: John Benjamins.

Helasvuo, M. & Laitinen, L. (2006). Person in Finnish: Paradigmatic and syntagmatic relations in interaction. In M. Helasvuo & L. Campbell (eds.), *Grammar from the human perspective: Case, space and person in Finnish* (pp. 173– 207). Amsterdam: John Benjamins.

Heritage, J. (1984a). A change-of-state token and aspects of its sequential placement. In J. M. Atkinson & J. Heritage (eds.), *Structures of social action. Studies in conversation analysis* (pp. 299–345). Cambridge: Cambridge University Press.

(1984b). *Garfinkel and ethnomethodology*. Cambridge: Polity.

(1985). Analyzing news interviews: Aspects of the production of talk for an overhearing audience. In T. A. Van Dijk (ed.), *Handbook of discourse analysis* (Vol. 3, pp. 95–117). London: Academic Press.

Heritage, J. & Atkinson, J. M. (1984). Introduction. In J. M. Atkinson & J. Heritage (eds.), *Structures of Social Action. Studies in Conversation Analysis* (pp. 1–16). Cambridge: Cambridge University Press.

Heritage, J. & Lindström, A. (1998). Motherhood, medicine, and morality: Scenes from a medical encounter. *Research on Language and Social Interaction*, 31, 397–438.

Heritage, J. & Maynard, D. W. (eds.) (2006). *Communication in medical care*. Cambridge: Cambridge University Press.

Heritage, J. & Raymond, G. (2005). The terms of agreement: Indexing epistemic authority and subordination in talk-in-interaction. *Social Psychology Quarterly*, 68, 15–38.

Heritage, J. & Sefi, S. (1992). Dilemmas of advice: Aspects of the delivery and reception of advice in interactions between health visitors and first-time mothers. In P. Drew & J. Heritage (eds.), *Talk at work: Interaction in institutional settings* (pp. 359–417). Cambridge: Cambridge University Press.

Heritage J. & Sorjonen M-L. (1994). Constituting and maintaining activities across sequences: And-prefacing as a feature of question design. *Language in Society*, 23, 1–29.

Heritage, J. & Watson, R. (1979). Formulations as conversational objects. In G. Psathas (ed.), *Everyday Language* (pp. 123–162). New York: Irvington Press.

(1980). Aspects of the properties of formulations. *Semiotica*, 30 (3/4), 245–262.

Hester, S. & Francis, D. (2000). Ethnomethodology, conversation analysis and "institutional talk." *Text*, 20, 391–413.

Hoffman, I. Z. (1992). Some practical implications of a social-constructivist view of the psychoanalytic situation. *Psychoanalytic Dialogues*, 2, 287–304.

Holloway, E. L., Freund, R. D., Gardner, S. L., Lee Nelson, M. & Walker, B. R. (1989). Relation of power and involvement to theoretical orientation in supervision: An analysis of discourse. *Journal of Counseling Psychology*, 36, 88–102.

Horowitz, L., Rosenberg, S. E., Baer, B. A., Ureno, G. & Villasenor, V. S. (1988). Inventory of interpersonal problems: Psychometric properties and clinical applications. *Journal of Consulting and Clinical Psychology*, 56, 885–892.

Hoyt, M. F. (ed.) (1994). *Constructive therapies*. New York: Guilford Press.
Hoyt, M. F. (2002). Solution-focused couple therapy. In A. S. Gurman & N. S. Jacobson (eds.), Clinical handbook of couple therapy (3rd edn., pp. 335–369). New York: Guilford Press.
Hutchby, I. (1992). *Confrontation talk: Arguments, asymmetries and power on talk radio*. Hillsdale, NJ: Erlbaum.
(1995). Aspects of recipient design in expert advice-giving on call-in radio. *Discourse Processes*, 19, 219–238.
(2002). Resisting the incitement to talk in child counselling: Aspects of the utterance "I don't know." *Discourse Studies*, 4, 147–168.
(2005). "Active listening": Formulations and the elicitation of feeling-talk in child counselling. *Research on Language and Social Interaction*, 38 (3), 303–329.
(2007). *The Discourse of Child Counselling*. Amsterdam: John Benjamins.
Ikonen, P. (2000). *Psykoanalyyttisia tutkielmia*. [Psychoanalytic studies.] Helsinki: Nuorisopsykoterapia-säätiö.
Jacobs, T. (1986). On countertransference enactments. *Journal of the American Psychoanalytic Association*, 34, 289–307.
Jefferson, G. (1987). On exposed and embedded correction in conversation. In G. Button & J. R. E. Lee (eds.), *Talk and social organisation* (pp. 86–100). Clevedon, Avon: Multilingual Matters.
(1988). On the sequential organization of troubles talk in ordinary conversation. *Social Problems*, 35, 418–441.
(2004). Glossary of transcript symbols with an introduction. In G. Lerner (ed.), *Conversation Analysis: Studies from the first generation* (pp. 14–31). Amsterdam / Philadelphia: John Benjamins.
Jefferson, G. & Lee, J. (1992). The rejection of advice: Managing the problematic convergence of a "troubles-telling" and a "service encounter." In P. Drew & J. Heritage (eds.), *Talk at work: Interaction in institutional settings* (pp. 521–548). Cambridge: Cambridge University Press.
Johnson, V. E. (1973). *I'll quit tomorrow*. New York: Harper & Row.
Jones, C. M. & Beach, W. A. (1995). Therapists' techniques for responding to unsolicited contributions by family members. In G. H. Morris & R. J. Chenail (eds.), *The talk of the clinic: Explorations in the analysis of medical and therapeutic discourse* (pp. 49–70). Hillsdale, NJ: Erlbaum.
Jones, E. E. (1997). Models of therapeutic action. *International Journal of Psychoanalysis*, 78, 1135–1150.
Kantrowitz, J. L. (1995). The beneficial aspects of the patient–analyst match. *International Journal of Psychoanalysis*, 76, 299–313.
Katz, G. A. (1998). Where the action is: The enacted dimension of analytic process. *Journal of the American Psychoanalytic Association*, 46, 1129–1167.
Kendon, A. (1990). *Conducting interaction. Patterns of behavior in focused encounters*. Cambridge: Cambridge University Press.
(1994). Do gestures communicate?: A review. *Research on Language and Social Interaction*, 27, 175–200.
Kinnell, A-M-K. & Maynard, D. (1996). The delivery and receipt of safer sex advice in pretest counselling sessions for HIV and AIDS. *Journal of Contemporary Ethnography*, 24 (4), 405–437.

Klein, M. (1975). *Narrative of a child analysis: The conduct of the psycho-analysis of children as seen in the treatment of a ten-year-old boy*. London: Hogarth Press.

(1998a). *Envy and gratitude and other works*. London: Virago.

(1998b). *Love, guilt and reparation*. London: Virago.

Klüwer, R. (1983). Agieren und Mitagieren. *Psyche*, 37, 828–840.

Kurhila, S. (2001). Correction in talk between native and non-native speaker. *Journal of Pragmatics*, 33, 1083–1110.

(2004). Different Orientations to Grammatical Correctness. In K. Richards & P. Seedhouse (eds.), *Applying Conversation Analysis* (pp. 143–158). Basingstoke: Palgrave Macmillan.

Kurri, K. & Wahlström, J. (2007). Reformulations of agentless talk in psychotherapy. *Text & Talk*, 27 (4), 315–338.

Labov, W. & Fanshel, D. (1977). *Therapeutic discourse: Psychotherapy as conversation*. Orlando: Academic Press.

Laitinen, L. (2006). Zero person in Finnish construction. In M. Helasvuo & L. Campbell (eds.), *Grammar from the human perspective: Case, space and person in Finnish* (pp. 233–258). Amsterdam: John Benjamins.

Laplanche, J. & Pontalis, J. B. (1973). The language of psycho-analysis. *The International Psychoanalytical Library*, 94, 1–497.

Laundergan, J. C. (1982). *Easy does it*. USA: Hazelden Foundation.

Lea, S. & Auburn, T. (2001). The social construction of rape in the talk of a convicted rapist. *Feminism and Psychology*, 11, 11–33.

Leiman, M. & Stiles, W. B. (2001). Dialogical sequence analysis and the zone of proximal development as conceptual enhancements to the assimilation model: The case of Jan revisited. *Psychotherapy Research*, 11, 311–330.

Leiman, M. & Stiles, W. B. (2002). Integration of theory: Methodological issues. In I. Säfvestad-Nolan & P. Nolan (eds.), *Object relations and integrative psychotherapy: Tradition and innovation in theory and practice* (pp. 68–79). London: Whurr Publishers.

Lerner, G. (1991). On the syntax of sentences in progress. *Language in Society*, 20, 441–458.

Leudar, I. Antaki, C. & Barnes, R. (2006). When psychotherapists disclose personal information about themselves to clients. *Communication and Medicine*, 3, 27–41.

Leudar, I. & Costall, A. (1996). Situating action IV: Planning as situated action. *Ecological Psychology*, 8, 153–170.

(2004). On the persistence of the "problem of other minds" in psychology: Chomsky, Grice and "theory of mind." *Theory and Psychology*, 14, 601–621.

Leudar, I., Sharrock, W., Colombino, T., Truckle, S., Hope, K. & Simon, S. (2005). How does it work? – Don't count, look! *The Bulletin of the Association of Child Psychotherapists*, 152, 12–15.

Leudar, I. & Thomas, P. (2000). *Voices of reason, voices of insanity. Studies of verbal hallucinations*. London: Routledge.

Levine, H. B., Friedman, R. J. (2000). Intersubjectivity and interaction in the analytic relationship: A mainstream review. *Psychoanalytic Quarterly*, 69, 63–92.

Levinson, S. C. (1981). The essential inadequacies of speech act models of dialogue. In H. Parret, M. Sbisa & J. Verschueren (eds.), *Possibilities and limitations of pragmatics* (pp. 473–492). Amsterdam: John Benjamins.

(1983). *Pragmatics*. Cambridge: Cambridge University Press.

Levinson, S. C. (2006). On the human "interactional engine." In N. J. Enfield & S. C. Levinson (eds.), *Roots of human sociality: Culture, cognition and human interaction* (pp. 39–69). Oxford: Berg.

Lipchik, E. (2002). *Beyond technique in solution-focused therapy: Working with the emotions and the therapeutic relationship*. New York: Guilford Press.

Luborsky, L. & Crits-Christoph, P. (1997). *Understanding transference: The core conflictural relationship theme method*. Washington: American Psychological Association Press.

Luborsky, L., Crits-Christoph, P., Mintz, J. & Auerbach, A. (1988). *Who will benefit from psychotherapy? Predicting therapeutic outcomes*. New York: Basic Books.

Luborsky, L. & Luborsky, E. (1995). The era of measures of the transference – The CCRT and other measures. In T. Shapiro & R. Emde (eds.), *Research in psychoanalysis. Process, development, outcome* (pp. 329–351). Madison, CT: International Universities Press.

Madill, A., Widdicombe, S. & Barkham, M. (2001). The potential of conversation analysis for psychotherapy research. *Counselling Psychologist*, 29, 413–434.

Mäkelä, K., Arminen, I., Bloomfield, K., Eisenbach-Stangl, I., Hermansson Bergmark, K., Kurube, N. *et al.* (1996). *Alcoholics Anonymous as a mutual-help movement. A study in eight societies*. Madison, WI: University of Wisconsin Press.

Maynard, D. (1991). The Perspective-Display Series and the delivery and receipt of diagnostic news. In D. Boden & D. H. Zimmerman (eds.), *Talk and social structure. Studies in ethnomethodology and conversation analysis* (pp. 164–192). Cambridge: Polity.

Maynard, D.W. and Frankel, R. (2006). On diagnostic rationality: Bad news, good news, and the symptom residue. In J. Heritage & D. Maynard (eds.), *Communication in medical care. Interaction between primary care physicians and patients* (pp. 248–278). Cambridge: Cambridge University Press.

Maynard, D. and Heritage, J. (2005). Conversation analysis, doctor–patient interaction and medical communication. *Medical Education*, 39, 428–435.

McGee, D., Del Vento, A. & Bavelas, J. B. (2005). An interactional model of questions as therapeutic interventions. *Journal of Marital and Family Therapy*, 31, 371–384.

McLaughlin, J. T. (1991). Clinical and theoretical aspects of enactment. *Journal of the American Psychoanalytic Association*, 39, 595–614.

Mead, G. H. (1934). *Mind, self and society*. Chicago: University of Chicago Press.

Miller, G. & Silverman, D. (1995). Troubles talk and counseling discourse: A comparative study. *Sociological Quarterly*, 36, 725–747.

Miller, W. R. & Rollnick, S. (1991). *Motivational interviewing. Preparing people to change addictional behavior*. New York: Guilford Press.

Mitchell, S. A. (1988). *Relational concepts in psychoanalysis*. Cambridge: Harvard University Press.

(2000). *Relationality. From attachment to intersubjectivity*. Hillsdale, NJ: Analytic Press.

Moore, R. J. & Maynard, D. W. (2002). Achieving understanding in the Standardized Survey Interview: Repair sequences. In H. Houtkoop-Steenstra, N. Cate Schaeffer & J. van der Zouwen (eds.), *Standardization and tacit knowledge: Interaction and practice in the survey interview* (D. W. Maynard, ed., pp. 281–311). New York: Wiley.

Nevin, B. (1994). Quandary/abusive questions. *The Linguist Discussion List*, 5, 754.

Nicholson, S. (1995). The narrative dance: A practice map for White's therapy. *Australian/New Zealand Journal of Family Therapy*, 16, 23–28.

Ogden, T. H. (1994). The analytic third: Working with intersubjective clinical facts. *International Journal of Psychoanalysis*, 75, 3–19.

(1997). Reverie and interpretation. *Psychoanalytic Quarterly*, 56, 567–595.

O'Hanlon, W. H. (1993). Possibility therapy: From iatrogenic injury to iatrogenic healing. In S. Gillian & R. Price (eds.), *Therapeutic conversations* (pp. 3–21). New York: Norton.

Peräkylä, A. (1995). *AIDS counselling: Institutional interaction and clinical practice.* Cambridge: Cambridge University Press.

(2004a). Making links in psychoanalytic interpretations: a conversation analytic view. *Psychotherapy Research*, 14, 289–307.

(2004b). Two traditions of interaction research. *British Journal of Social Psychology*, 43, 1–20.

(2005). Patients' responses to interpretations: A dialogue between conversation analysis and psychoanalytic theory. *Communication & Medicine*, 2 (2), 163–176.

Peräkylä, A. & Ruusuvuori, J. (2006). Facial expression in an assessment. In H. J. Knoblauch, J. Raab, G-H. Soeffner, B. Schnettler (eds.), *Video analysis: Methodology and methods. Qualitative audiovisual data analysis in sociology* (pp. 127–142). Frankfurt: Peter Lang.

Peräkylä, A., Ruusuvuori, J. & Lindfors, P. (2007). What is patient participation: reflections arising from the study of general practice, homeopathy and psychoanalysis. In S. Collins, N. Britten, J. Ruusuvuori & A. Thompson (eds.), *Patient Participation in Health Care Consultations* (pp. 121–142). Buckingham: Open University Press.

Peräkylä, A., Ruusuvuori, J. & Vehviläinen, S. (2005). Introduction: Professional theories and institutional interaction. *Communication & Medicine*, 2, 105–109.

Peräkylä, A. & Silverman, D. (1991). Owning experience: Describing the experience of other persons. *Text*, 11, 441–480.

Peräkylä, A. & Vehviläinen, S. (2003). Conversation analysis and the professional stocks of interactional knowledge. *Discourse & Society*, 14, 727–750.

Pittenger, R. E., Hockett, C. F. & Danehy, J. J. (1961). *The first five minutes. A sample of microscopic interview analysis.* Ithaca, NY: Paul Martineau.

Pomerantz, A. (1978). Compliment responses: Notes on the co-operation of multiple constraints. In J. Schenkein (ed.), *Studies in the organization of conversational interaction* (pp. 79–112). New York: Academic Press.

(1980). Telling my side: "Limited access" as a "fishing" device. *Sociological Inquiry*, 50, 186–198.

(1984). Agreeing and disagreeing with assessments: some features of preferred/dispreferred turn shapes. In J. M. Atkinson & J. Heritage (eds.), *Structures of Social Actions* (pp. 57–101). Cambridge: Cambridge University Press.

(1986). Extreme case formulations: A way of legitimizing claims. *Human Studies*, 9, 219–229.

Potter, J. (1996). *Representing Reality*. London: Sage.

(1998). Beyond cognitivism. *Research on Language and Social Interaction*, 32, 119–128.

Rabin, H. M. (1995). The liberating effect on the analyst of the paradigm shift in psychoanalysis. *Psychoanalytic Psychology*, 12, 467–481.

Rae, J. (2005). *Achieving a therapeutic stance: Some resources for responding selectively to a client's talk*. International Pragmatics Association Conference, Riva del Garda, Italy.

Rawls A. W. (2002). Editor's introduction. In H. Garfinkel, *Ethnomethodology's program. Working out Durkheim's aphorism* (A. W. Rawls ed., pp. 1–64). Lanham: Rowman & Littlefield.

Raymond, G. (2003). Grammar and social organization: Yes/no interrogatives and the structure of responding. *American Sociological Review*, 68, 939–967.

Robinson, J. D. (2001). Closing medical encounters: two physician practices and their implications for the expression of patients' unstated concerns. *Social Science and Medicine*, 53, 639–656.

(2006). Soliciting patients' presenting concerns. In J. Heritage & D. Maynard (eds.), *Communication in medical care. Interaction between primary care physicians and patients* (pp. 22–47). Cambridge: Cambridge University Press.

Rogers, C. (1951). *Client-centered therapy. Its current practice, implications, and theory*. Boston: Houghton Mifflin.

Rose, N. (1996). *Inventing our selves. Psychology, power and personhood*. Cambridge: Cambridge Univeristy Press.

Roughton, R. E. (1994). Repetition and interaction in the analytic process: Enactment, acting out, and collusion. *The Annual of Psychoanalysis*, 22, 271–286.

Ruusuvuori, J. (2005). "Empathy" and "sympathy" in action: Attending to patients' troubles in Finnish homeopathic and general practice consultations. *Social Psychology Quarterly*, 68, 204–222.

Rycroft, C. (1995). *A critical dictionary of psychoanalysis* (2nd edn.). London: Penguin.

Ryle, G. (1949). *The concept of mind*. London: Hutchinson.

Sacks, H. (1972). On the analyzability of stories by children. In J. J. Gumperz & D. Hymes (eds.), *Directions of sociolinguistics* (pp. 325–345). New York: Holt, Rinehart and Winston.

(1974). An analysis of the course of a joke's telling in conversation. In R. Bauman & J. Sherzer (eds.), *Explorations in the ethnography of speaking* (pp. 337–353). Cambridge: Cambridge University Press.

(1984). On doing "being ordinary." In J. M. Atkinson & J. Heritage (eds.), *Structures of social action: Studies in conversation analysis* (pp. 413–429). Cambridge: Cambridge University Press.

(1987). On the preferences for agreement and contiguity in sequences in conversation. In G. Button & J. R. E. Lee (eds.), *Talk and Social Organisation* (pp. 54–69). Clevedon, Avon: Multilingual Matters.

(1992a). *Lectures on conversation* (Vol. 1, G. Jefferson, ed.). Oxford: Blackwell.

(1992b). *Lectures on conversation* (Vol. 2, G. Jefferson, ed.). Oxford: Blackwell.

Sacks, H., Schegloff, E. A. & Jefferson, G. (1974). A simplest systematics for the organization of turn-taking for conversation. *Language*, 50, 696–735.

Sandler, J. (1976). Countertransference and role-responsiveness. *International Review of Psychoanalysis*, 3, 43–47.

(1983). Reflections on some relations between psychoanalytic concepts and psychoanalytic practice. *International Journal of Psychoanalysis*, 64, 35–45.

Sandler, J., Dare, C. & Holder, A. (1992). *The patient and the analyst. The basis of the psychoanalytic process*. London: Karnac.

Sandlund, E. (2004). *Feeling by doing. The social organization of everyday emotions in academic talk-in-interaction*. Karlstad: Karlstad University Studies 2004, 36.

Scheflen, A. (1973). *Communicational structure. Analysis of a psychotherapy transaction*. Bloomington: Indiana University Press.

Schegloff, E. A. (1963). Towards a reading of psychiatric theory. *Berkeley Journal of Sociology*, 8, 61–91.

(1972). Notes on a conversational practice: formulating place. In D. Sudnow (ed.), *Studies in Social Interaction* (pp. 75–119). New York: Free Press.

(1984). On some questions and ambiguities in conversation. In J. M. Atkinson & J. Heritage (eds.), *Structures of social action: Studies in conversation analysis* (pp. 28–52). Cambridge: Cambridge University Press.

(1991). Reflections on talk and social structure. In D. Boden & D. H. Zimmerman (eds.), *Talk and social structure* (pp. 44–709). Cambridge: Polity.

(1992). Repair after next turn: The last structurally provided defense of intersubjectivity in conversation. *The American Journal of Sociology*, 97, 1295–1345.

(1996a). Confirming allusions: Toward an empirical account of action. *American Journal of Sociology*, 102, 161–216.

(1996b). Turn-organization: One intersection of grammar and interaction. In E. Ochs, E. A. Schegloff & S. A. Thompson (eds.), *Interaction and Grammar* (pp. 52–133). Cambridge: Cambridge University Press.

(2007). *Sequence organization in interaction: A primer in conversation analysis*. Cambridge: Cambridge University Press.

Schegloff, E. A., Jefferson, G. & Sacks, H. (1977). The preference for self-correction in the organization of repair in conversation. *Language*, 53, 361–382.

Schegloff, E. A., Ochs, E. & Thompson, S. (1996). Introduction. In E. Ochs, E. A. Schegloff & S. A. Thompson (eds.), *Interaction and grammar* (pp. 1–51). Cambridge: Cambridge University Press.

Schegloff, E. A. & Sacks, H. (1973). Opening up closings. *Semiotica*, 7, 289–327.

Schiffrin, D. (1987). *Discourse markers*. New York: Cambridge University Press.

Schwaber, E. A. (1998). The non-verbal dimension in psychoanalysis: "State" and its clinical vicissitudes. *International Journal of Psychoanalysis*, 79, 667–678.

Seedhouse, P. (2004). *The interactional architecture of the language classroom: a conversation analysis perspective*. Oxford: Blackwell.

Seppänen, E. (2000). Sinä ja suomalaiset: Yksikön toisen persoonanyleistävästä käytöstä. [You and the Finns. About the generic use of the second person.] *Kielikello*, 3, 16–18.

Shore, S. (1988). On the so-called Finnish passive. *Word*, 39, 151–176.

Silverman, D. (1997). *Discourses of counselling. HIV counselling as social interaction*. London: Sage.

Solms, M. (1995). Is the brain more real than the mind? *Psychoanalytic Psychotherapy*, 9, 107–120.

Sorjonen, M-L. (2001). *Responding in conversation: A study of response particles in Finnish*. Amsterdam: John Benjamins.

Spacal, S. (1990). Free association as a method of self-observation in relation to other methodological principles of psychoanalysis. *Psychoanalytic Quarterly*, 59, 1990.

Stern, D. (2004). *The present moment in psychotherapy and everyday life*. New York: Norton.

Stern, D. N., Sander, L. W., Nahum, J. P., Harrison, A. M., Lyons-Ruth, K., Morgan, A. C. *et al.* (1998). Non interpretive mechanisms in psychoanalytic therapy. The "something more" than interpretation. *International Journal of Psychoanalysis*, 79, 903–921.

Stiles, W. B. (1992). *Describing talk. A taxonomy of verbal response modes*. Newbury Park, CA: Sage.

(1999). Signs and voices in psychotherapy. *Psychotherapy Research*, 9, 1–21.

(2002). Assimilation of problematic experiences. In J. C. Norcross (ed.), *Psychotherapy relationships that work: Therapist contributions and responsiveness to patients* (pp. 357–365). New York: Oxford University Press.

Stiles, W. B., Elliott, R., Llewelyn, S. P., Firth-Cozens, J. A., Margison, F. R., Shapiro, D. A. *et al.* (1990). Assimilation of problematic experiences by clients in psychotherapy. *Psychotherapy*, 27, 411–420.

Stiles, W. B. & Shapiro, D. A. (1994). Disabuse of the drug metaphor: psychotherapy process-outcome correlations. *Journal of Consulting and Clinical Psychology*, 62, 942–948.

Stiles W. B., Shapiro, D. A. & Firth-Cozens, J. A. (1988). Verbal response mode use in contrasting psychotherapies: a within-subjects comparison. *Journal of Consulting and Clinical Psychology*, 56, 727–733.

Stivers, T. (2005). Parent resistance to physicians' treatment recommendations: One resource for initiating a negotiation of the treatment decision. *Health Communication*, 181 (1), 41–74.

Streeck, U. (2001). "Ja, genau, genau." Bestätigungen als Versuche des Patienten, die Kompetenz des Psychotherapeuten als eigene zu deklarieren. Eine gesprächsanalytische Untersuchung. *Psychotherapie und Sozialwissenschaft*, 2, 74–94.

(2004). *Auf den ersten Blick. Psychotherapeutische Beziehungen unter dem Mikroskop*. Stuttgart: Klett-Cotta.

Tausk, V. (1933). On the origin of the "influencing machine" in schizophrenia. *Psychoanalytic Quarterly*, 2, 519–556.

Thomä, H. & Kächele, H. (1994). *Psychoanalytic practice I: Principles*. Northvale: Jason Aronson.

Treurniet, N. (1997). On an ethic of psychoanalytic technique. *Psychoanalytic Quarterly*, 66, 596–627.

Tronick, E. Z., Bruschweiler-Stern, N., Harrison, A. M., Lyons-Ruth, K., Morgan, A. C., Nahum, J. P. *et al.* (1998). Dyadically expanded states of consciousness and the process of therapeutic change. *Infant Mental Health Journal*, 19, 290–299.

Tuomikoski, R. (1971). Persoona, tekijä ja henkilö. [Person, agent and individual.] *Virittäjä*, 75, 146–152.

Vehviläinen, S. (1999). *Structures of counselling interaction. A conversation analytic study of counselling encounters in career guidance training*. Helsinki: University of Helsinki, Department of Education.

(2003a). Preparing and delivering interpretations in psychoanalytic interaction. *Text*, 23, 573–606.

(2003b). *Topicalizing the patient's emotion in psychoanalytic interaction*. Paper presented at the Communication, Medicine & Ethics (COMET) conference, University of Cardiff, 26–28 June 2003.

Viaro, M., Leonardi, P. (1983). Getting and giving information: Analysis of a family interview strategy. *Family Process*, 22, 27–42.

Voutilainen, L. (in preparation) Conversation analysis of cognitive-constructivist psychotherapy. PhD thesis in preparation, Department of Sociology, University of Helsinki.

Wallerstein, R. S. (1990). The common ground. *International Journal of Psychoanalysis*, 71, 3–20.

Waring, H. Z. (2005). Peer tutoring in a graduate writing centre: Identity, expertise and advice resisting. *Applied Linguistics*, 26, 141–168.

Wessely S. (2001). Randomised controlled trials, the gold standard? In C. Mace, S. Moorey & B. Roberts (eds.), *Evidence in the psychological therapies* (pp. 46–60). London: Brunner-Routledge.

West, C. (2006). Coordinating closings of primary care visits: producing continuity of care. In J. Heritage & D. Maynard (eds.), *Communication in medical care. Interaction between primary care physicians and patients* (pp. 313–339). Cambridge: Cambridge University Press.

White, A. R. (1979). Shooting, killing and fatally wounding. *Proceedings of the Aristotelian Society, new series 80* (pp. 1–16).

White, D. (1993). Deconstruction and therapy. In S. Gillian & R. Price (eds.), *Therapeutic conversations* (pp. 22–61). New York: Norton.

Winch, P. (1972). Understanding a primitive society. In P. Winch, *Ethics and Action* (pp. 78–111). London: RKP.

Wittgenstein, L. (1958). *Philosophical investigations*. Oxford: Blackwell.

(1980). *Remarks on the Philosophy of Psychology* (Vols. 1 & 2). Oxford: Basil Blackwell.

Wong, J. (2005). Sidestepping grammar. In K. Richards & P. Seedhouse (eds.), *Applying Conversation Analysis* (pp. 159–173). Basingstoke: Palgrave Macmillan.

Wooffitt, R. (1992). *Telling tales of the unexpected. The organization of factual discourse*. Hemel Hempstead: Harvester Wheatsheaf.

Wootton, A. (1977). Some notes on the organization of talk in a therapeutic community. *Sociology*, 11 (2), 333–350.

Zimmerman, D. (1992). The interactional organisation of calls for emergency assistance, in P. Drew & J. Heritage (eds.), *Talk at work: Interaction in institutional settings* (pp. 418–469). Cambridge: Cambridge University Press.

Author index

Subject index

For EU product safety concerns, contact us at Calle de José Abascal, 56–1°, 28003 Madrid, Spain or eugpsr@cambridge.org.

www.ingramcontent.com/pod-product-compliance
Lightning Source LLC
LaVergne TN
LVHW101501200926
848483LV00001B/192